Carrie Chapman

Dec 188-

THE PARTINGTON FAMILY

MRS. PARTINGTON'S

KNITTING-WORK;

AND

WHAT WAS DONE BY HER PLAGUY BOY IKE.

A WEB OF MANY TEXTURES,

AS WROUGHT BY THE OLD LADY HERSELF.

(BY P. SHILLABER.)

With Characteristic Illustrations by Hoppin.

"Various, that the mind of desultory man, studious of change, and pleased with novelty, may be indulged.'

PHILADELPHIA:
JOHN E. POTTER AND COMPANY.
617 SANSOM STREET.

PREFACE.

THE author of the present volume, while preparing it for publication, has been impressed with a due regard of its destined benefit to the world — and to himself — and, while thus obtruding himself, like a fist, into the public eye, * * * * * * * * * * * * * * * * * *

To the Publishers.

GENTLEMEN: It has suddenly occurred to me that a preface is altogether unnecessary, and, therefore, I positively decline writing one, inasmuch as I have commenced five already, and been compelled to abandon them all, from sheer inability to complete them. Prefaces have always seemed to me like drummers for a show, calling upon people to "come up and see the elephant," with a slight exaggeration of the merit of the animal to be exhibited; and though, in the present case, such enlargement of the fact would not be necessary, still those disposed to be captious might read our promises with incredulity. Mrs. Partington, no less than the Roman dame, should be above suspicion; therefore, this heralding should be avoided, and her name left with only its olden reputation resting about it, like the halo of cobweb and dust about an ancient vintage of port. Her coädjutors, Dr. Spooner, Old Roger, and Wideswarth, representing the profound, the jolly, and the sentimental, need no endorsement among the enlightened many who will buy this book; and we can safely leave them, as lawyers sometimes do their cases when they have nothing to say, without argument. Again, all will see for themselves the acid and sugar, and spirit and water, comprised in the contents of the volume, — forming the components of a sort of intellectual punch, of which they can partake to any extent, without headache or heartache, as the sedate therein forms a judicious corrective of the eccentric and gay which might intoxicate. The illustrations, by Hoppin, tell their own story, and need no further commendation than their great excellence. The local meaning of many of the sayings and doings of the book will, of course, be readily understood, without explanation or apology; and the new matter will be distinguished from the old, by the quality of novelty that generally attaches to that with which we are not familiar. I thought somewhat of giving the name beneath each individual represented in our frontispiece; but the idea was dispelled in a moment, by the reflection that Mrs. Partington — the central sun of our social system — could not be misinterpreted; while Dr. Spooner, Prof. Wideswarth, Old Roger, and Ike, were equally well defined; and the skill of the artist in depicting them needed no aid. Therefore, all things considered, I think we had better let the book slip from its dock quietly, and drift out into the tide of publication, to be borne by this or that eddy of feeling to such success as it may deserve, without the formality of prefatory bottle-breaking. I leave the matter, then, as a settled thing, that we will not have a preface.

Resolutely yours,

The Author.

Note by the Publishers. — There is an axiom which says that one needs must submit when a certain character drives; and hence we acquiesce, deeming that if a preface cannot be had, we will do without it.

CONTENTS.

THE GUARDIAN FOR IKE.

When Mrs. Partington first moved from Beanville, and the young scion of the Partington stock was exposed to the temptations of city life and city associations, it was thought advisable to appoint a "guardeen" over him. Ike was not a bad boy, in the wicked sense of the word bad; but he had a constant proclivity for tormenting every one that he came in contact with; a resistless tendency for having a hand in everything that was going on; a mischievous bent, that led him into continual trouble, that brought on him reproaches from all sides, and secured for him a reputation that made him answerable for everything of a wrong character that was done in the neighborhood. A barber's pole could not be removed from the barber's door and placed beside the broker's, but it must be imputed to "that plaguy Ike;" all clandestine pulls at door-bells in the evenings were done by "that plaguy Ike;" if a ball or an arrow made a mistake and dashed through a window, the ball or the arrow belonged to "that plaguy Ike;" if on April Fool's day a piece of paper were found pasted on a door-step, putting grave housekeepers to the trouble and mortification of trying to pick up an imagined letter, the blame was laid to "that plaguy Ike;" and if a voice was heard from round the corner crying "April Fool!" or "sold," those who heard it said, at once, it was "that plaguy Ike's." Many a thing he had thus to answer for that he did n't do, as well as many that he did, until Mrs. Partington became convinced of the necessity of securing some one to look after him besides herself.

In her exigency she bethought her of an old friend named Roger, who, because he was a single man, and had got along beyond the meridian of life, was called "Old Roger" by every one. He had lived in the city for many years and knew all its ways, and was just the one for the proposed station. He was "well off," as the world understands it, and was a very genial man, though rather hasty in temper, at times. She sent for him as she had proposed, and appointed a day for his calling upon her. On the afternoon that she had named for the visit, she and Ike were together in the little sitting-room, with the antique buffet in one corner, and the old chairs and tables arranged around, the walls hung with pictures of Joseph and his Brethren, and the Prodigal Son, and David and Goliath, — which last Ike admired the most, because he always fancied himself to be David, and Goliath a big butcher down street who had once set a dog at him, on whom he wished to avenge himself, and thought he could if there was n't a a law against "slinging stones." The profile of Paul Partington, Corporal of the Bloody 'Leventh, was conspicuous over the mantelpiece, while above it, supported by two nails, rested and rusted the Corporal's artillery sword, that had flashed so oft, in the olden time, over the ensanguined muster-field. She was engaged with her knitting, while the object of her solicitude was busy in a corner engaged in painting a sky-blue horse on the bottom of the old lady's best japanned waiter As she mused, in harmony with her clicking needles, her thoughts took form in words.

"How the world has turned about, to be sure!" said she; "'t is nothing but change, change. Only yesterday, as it were, I was in the country, smelling the odious flowers; — to-day I am in Boston, my oil-factories breathing the impure execrations of coal-smoke, that are so dilatory to health. Instead of the singing of birds, the blunderbusses almost deprive me of conscientiousness. Dear me! Well, I hope I shall be restrained through it all. They say that the moral turpentine of this place is frightful, but it is n't any use to anticipate trouble beforehand; he may escape all harmonious influences that would have a tenderness to hurt him, and, as the minister of our parish said, with judicial training he may become a useful membrane of society; though training is bad generally, and is apt to make the young run to feathers, like cropple-crowned hens. But he has genius," — looking at him; — "it comes natural to him, like the measles, and every day it is enveloping itself more and more. What are you doing, dear?" she said, rising and going towards him.

"I 'm drawing a horse," replied he, turning it round so that she could see it.

"Why, so it is! and what caricature and spirit there is in it, to be sure! I should have known it was a horse, if you had n't said a word about it. But have n't you given him too thick a head of hair on his tail, and a leg too many?"

"That 's his mane that you call his tail," said Ike, with some show of being offended; "and, suppose he has got five legs! — anybody can paint one with four; five shows what Miss Brush, my teacher, calls the creative power of genius."

"Well I must digest my spectacles," replied she, smiling upon him, "before I speak another time. But now

I want you to go down to the door and watch for a gentleman that I suspect, who may ask you to tell him where we live. He is to be your guardeen, that I told you about."

"Yes 'm," said Ike, dutifully, and passed out, whistling Villikins and his Dinah.

Mrs. Partington being a stranger in the neighborhood, it was not wonderful that the neighbors, of which there are many in almost every place, should call upon her; and among them Professor Wideswarth, who had long been familiar with her name, presented his card at an early period, as did Mr. Blifkins, and Mr. Slow, and many others, who, by a strange coïncidence, lived in the immediate vicinity. Mrs. Partington had deemed that the visit of Old Roger to her domicile would be an excellent occasion on which to invite her new acquaintances, and had accordingly asked their presence at that time. Among others with whom she had got acquainted was Miss Dorothea Chatterton, a good-looking spinster of some thirty summers, who had written for the papers, and was accounted a prodigy of refinement by the editors. As the dame sat at her work, after despatching Ike upon his mission, her door-bell rang, and, hastening to open it, Miss Chatterton burst upon her in the full flower of fashion and smiles.

"Good-afternoon, Mrs. P.," said she, shaking the dame enthusiastically by the hand. "I feared you might be lonesome, and so I have come to keep you company, if you will let me."

"Certainly," was the pleasant response, "I will, with the greatest reluctance."

"For my part," continued Miss Chatterton, "I love to be sociable. I can't bear those people who stand so much upon ceremony, and never get acquainted. I

He upon the curbstone sat looking for his future adviser up and down the street, amusing himself by occasionally throwing pebbles at a passing dog. P. 13

don't know what I should do, if I could n't talk. If an injunction was put upon my tongue, and my head depended upon keeping that member still, I believe I should forfeit it, and talk on to the last gasp. Some say I have remained a spinster because I would n't stop talking long enough to allow any one to pop the question. A mistake, I assure you."

"So you are a spinster, then?" said Mrs. Partington, as her visitor paused for breath. "Do you use a large or a small wheel?"

"I mean by spinster," replied she, blushing, "that I am a single woman, and, like many other *young* women, am acquainted only with spinning street-yarn, the only wheel used being that where I wheel round the corners."

"I 'm rejoiced that you have come," said Mrs. Partington, "for, my dear Miss Chatterbox, I am going to have a fine old unmarried bachelor here to tea, that I want you to get acquainted with. You will be perfectly vaccinated by him."

"Indeed! but is he a *very* old bachelor?"

"O, dear, no; he is n't more than sixty — just in the priming of life, so to speak. *I* never call a man old till he gets to be an octagon or a centurion, and can't lift a peck of wheat-bran."

The ladies sat down to their talk, while Ike upon the curbstone sat looking for his future adviser up and down the street, amusing himself by occasionally throwing pebbles at a passing dog, kicking his heels into the gravel, or throwing his cap in the air that it might drop upon his head.

"I wonder," said he, "what sort of an old chap this Roger is, that is going to look after me! I s'pose folks 'll tell him what a bad fellow I am. He 'll find that out soon enough, for I guess they don't like me pretty well round here. They don't want a fellow to have any fun at all, and I should like to know what fun was made for, anyhow. I don't believe I am half as bad as they make it out. Hello! here he comes, I guess. Big man — broad hat — red face — cane; — yes, this must be him."

"Can you tell me, my lad," said Old Roger, — for it was he, — "where a Mrs. Partington lives, somewhere about here?"

"I know where Mrs. *Partington* lives," replied Ike. "I don't know of any other Mrs. Partington in the world."

"Right, my lad, and that is she; there *is*, indeed, but one Mrs. Partington in the world. And her nephew Ike — do you know him? I hear strange tales about him, and little that 's good. What sort of a boy is he?"

"He 's a prime, tip-top fellow, sir; one of the tip-topest fellows you ever see."

"What sort of a looking boy is he?"

"O, he 's about my size, with blue hair and red eyes, —I mean he has red eyes and blue hair, — no, red hair and blue eyes. He is dark-complected, and has got a pugnacious nose. He is n't a very good-looking boy; but a boy should n't be despised because he is n't handsome, should he? You 're not remarkably handsome yourself, sir."

"Be civil, my young friend. Is this Ike an intelligent lad?"

"He is n't anything else. He came pretty nigh getting the medal once, for the master said he was the most medalsome boy in school."

"He must be a rare sprig of humanity, according to all accounts, and might be benefited by a little trimming."

"Sho!"

"What did you say?"

"I'll show you the way, sir, to Mrs. Partington's. You must go as far as you can see, yonder, then turn round the corner to the right, then take the first right-hand corner, then, after you turn the next corner to the right, two doors further along is Mrs. Partington's."

"Thank ye, my lad, and here 's a dime for you."

The intended guardian hobbled on his course, while Ike, with a mischievous twinkle in his eye and the dime in his hand, stood looking after him until he turned the first corner, when he darted into the house, telling Mrs. Partington that the expected guest was on his way, and would arrive in about a quarter of an hour, and then dashed out again and down the street.

After making the circuit of an entire square, "Old Roger" found himself on the precise spot from whence he had started, and looked around for the young scamp who had directed him. He recognized the trick at a glance, and, with a half chagrin, said to himself,

"I'll wager that Ike was the little villain that sent me on this circuit. The young jackanapes! if he were here, I'd put more cane on him than would make a fashionable lady's dress. Yet there's method in him, and it is far more satisfactory to manage a rogue than a fool."

He stepped to the door, which he had come such a roundabout way to reach, and rung the bell. In a moment more he stood in the presence of the relict of Paul Partington. Her face was radiant as the sun, while her cap-border encircled it like a ray, presenting no mean picture of that august luminary.

"I'm sure I'm glad to see you, sir," said she, shaking

him warmly by the hand. "Did you find any deficiency in finding the place?"

"*Deficiency!*" replied he, "not a bit of it; there was rather too much of it, if anything. I should have been here half an hour ago, if a young villain — whom I strongly suspect to have been Ike himself — had not sent me a mile out of my way to find you. He told me to turn this way and that way, and by stupidly following my nose I found myself just where I started from. I could have thrashed him for sending me round on so warm a day as this; but, madam, he is, after all, merely a boy, true to the boyish instinct of fun. The boy is not true to his nature who is not mischievous. Why, I was a boy once, myself, incredible as that may seem, and a wilder dog never wore satinet and a felt hat, or got flogged for misdemeanors that he *did n't* do, than myself; but here I am, — no matter how old, though confessing to thirty-seven years, — and, as people say, not one of the worst men in town, either."

She had conducted her guest into the little sitting-room, where the spinster was waiting very anxiously for the promised presentation, Mrs. Partington having previously begged her not to be "decomposed" at meeting him, for he was very "congealing" in his manner, and a "perfect Apollyon for politeness."

"Allow me to present you with Miss Chatterbody," said she, as they gained the centre of the room.

"Chatterton, sir, at your service," said that lady, coloring slightly, as if it were a coloring matter.

"I assure you, Mrs. Partington," said he, politely bowing, "you could n't present me with anything more agreeable."

The dame begged him to be seated, and he attempted to do so, but the chair unfortunately possessed but three legs, and the honored guest rolled ingloriously upon the floor. He rose to his feet, in great indignation.

"What does this mean?" said he. "It seems to me that everything is conspiring to try my temper — naturally very sweet. Here I am directed a mile out of my way to find *you*, and then find *myself* sprawling upon your floor, — which, though it is remarkably clean, is not a very desirable place for one to sit, in a land where recumbency is not the fashion, — through the medium of an infernal three-legged stool. — Excuse me for using so strong an adjective, but I never was so completely *floored* in my life."

"A thousand pardons, sir," said Mrs. Partington, "but Isaac must have taken that leg to make a bat of."

"And were he here," replied he, "I should be tempted to give him a bat that would make him bawl."

"We should all be willing to be forgiven, sir," expostulated the dame.

"True, true," replied he, recovering his good humor, "and to forgive, likewise. What a world this would be if we found nothing to do in it but to resent fancied wrongs; and more than half that we call wrongs are *but* fancies, and a large portion of the other half but the mere effect of wounded self-esteem, that brooks nothing which conflicts with it."

Mrs. Partington gazed upon him admiringly; and, as he sought another chair, she turned to Miss Chatterton and said,

"If he was the pasture for a parish, he could n't be more fluid."

To this remark the young lady nodded and smiled assent; and the object of the encomium, with the wrinkles all ironed from his temper, sat in the best of humor, imparting such a glow to the surroundings that even the rigid profile upon the wall seemed to bend from its rigidity, and become imbued with the infection of the scene. The jar of a step upon the floor caused a slight tintinnabulation of the old china in the buffet, which appeared like a response to the flow of good humor that pervaded the apartment. The circle was soon increased by the addition of the expected guests. There was an ominous manuscript protruding from Wideswarth's pocket, while his eye denoted an abstractedness, as though all the intelligence it ever wore had been abstracted from it. Philanthropos was calm and exalted, having on his way interrupted a street fight, and suffered the martyrdom of profane abuse from many juvenile tongues. The Brahmin Poo-Poo, with his meerschaum colored to a delightful complexion, and his red cap and black tassel, and satin petticoat trousers, was an object of respectful curiosity. Mr. Blifkins, having attended without the permission of his wife, seemed uneasy and fidgety, as a man must who gets goods under false pretences. The venerable Dr. Spooner was conspicuous among the number, his bald head rising like some tall cliff on which the eagles of thought might well delight to rest. They were all there, and the spinster was introduced to them by every variety of name to which "Chatter" would hitch; and all was moving very happily, when the door-bell rang violently, and Mr. Increase Slow came in, with his face very red and angry. He was the last of those who had been invited. After greeting the company, he said,

"I am sorry to complain at such a time, mem, but I should have been here a full hour ago, but for your Ike.

He is a great trouble to me. He goes on my grass with entire impurity; and, just now when I attempted to rush out and drive him off, — gently like, you know, — I found he had put a chip in the latch of my door, and I was kept shut up there till a policeman let me out. If you are to be his guardian, sir, as I understand, he will require all your care."

"Are you sure it was he, sir?" asked old Roger.

"Certainly, I am. There 's nothing done round here that he is n't at the bottom of it."

Mr. Slow dropped into a seat like a kedge-anchor, and the party grew suddenly grave, as a meadow full of strawberries and birds may, when a cloud comes betwixt it and the sun.

"Mr. Roger," said Prof. Wideswarth, nervously fingering the manuscript in his pocket, "a kindred quality of mirth appears to enter into the whole plan of the universe, and this boy, though roguish, is a human exponent of the quality; and, apropos of mirth, I have here a short poem, that it would delight me to read to you."

"I should be equally delighted to hear it," Roger replied, winking to Mr. Slow, who settled back in his chair, as though fixing himself in a position to sleep, in case the circumstances might warrant.

Wideswarth cleared his throat, twitched out his manuscript, and thus proceeded:

"I sing of mirth! — that boon of bounteous heaven,
Which stirs our bosoms with its generous leaven —
Given mankind to cheer their lot below,
To countervail the smart of pressing woe;
Given the heart the worth of life to prize,
Given to bless all objects to our eyes.
Without its aid the heavens were dark and drear,
The winds were full of naught but boding fear;

The Bob-o'-Lincoln on the bending hay
Would tune his note to dirges all the day;
The grass and flowers, that glow in such sweet guise
Would be but Quaker drab beneath our eyes;
And melody of bird, and bee, and brook,
Would be expunged from Nature's singing-book!
All Nature laughs through the repeating years —
Laughs when the first young flower of Spring appears,
Laughs in the Summer prime of beauteous bloom,
And sends to heaven its echoes of perfume;
Laughs when the Autumn binds its yellow sheaves,
And reddens in the face as Autumn leaves;
Laughs sturdily along November's sky,
And roars in boisterous mirth when storms are high,
Rattles our windows with a jubilant din,
Or, laughing with the sunshine, enters in.
What notes of mirth rise from the shady nooks,
From birds and insects, foliage and brooks!
What peals of laughter shake the concave high,
When thunder rattles through the summer sky!
The lambs run laughing o'er the vernal plain,
And glad sounds tinkle in the summer rain!
Mirth gives a charm to girlhood's fairest grace,
And limns the generous soul on boyhood's face.
Sweet girlhood! changing like the varying wind, —
Now wild for this, and now for that inclined, —
Teasing papa with never-ending needs,
That he 's "dead broke" if half the list he heeds;
Now a piano, now a fan, a ring,
Now a new dress from such a "charming thing!"
He frets — good man — his cash is not a pile,
Refuses — yields — he 's conquered by a smile.
And boyhood, rampant with its fun and noise,
Oft mingles bitter in our cup of joys,
And many an anxious sigh is made to start,
And many a throb to heave the parent's heart,
While watching 'mid the wilfulness of youth
To see the germs of honesty and truth!
O, Ike! thou elf, who dost with pranks abound,
In every home thy counterpart is found;
Thy mischief may at times becloud the soul,
But smile, and half the doubt away shall roll —

But give the music of an honest laugh,
And then will vanish all the other half.
But levity should ne'er its guile obtrude
To mar the cheerful heart's beatitude;
It has no place where genial humor dwells —
Its home is where the voice of passion swells;
Where the red wine glows in the ruddy light,
And turns to day the watches of the night;
Where the hoarse voice, in Bachanalian strain,
Echoes in chorus with some coarse refrain!
Let us be gay, and let our mirth arise
Before the great All-Good as sacrifice.
The source of joy no sombre tribute claims,
Nor priestly rite, nor sacrificial flames;
The heart's outpouring in its happiness
The smile of kindly heaven will ever bless;
So may our purest strains of joy ascend,
And with unwritten harmonies of heaven blend."

The reading was followed by many remarks approbatory. Mr. Slow ventured the observation that, though it was tip-top, it seemed to him strange that so much should have been said about fun with so little fun in it; but Dr. Spooner came to the rescue of the poet, by saying that in this respect, if it were so, it was like many sermons that we hear, all about religion, but which did not contain one spark of it! Philanthropos agreed with the sentiment of the poem, and said he had thought of recommending to the Provident Association the application of laughing gas in neighborhoods where poverty prevailed, in order that privation might be lessened by the infusion of jocularity.

At this point there was a loud ringing at the bell, and presently a tall, spare, seedy-looking individual was introduced, whom Miss Chatterton recognized as Signor Lignumvitæ, who taught music in the neighborhood. Turning to Mrs. Partington, he said, in English a trifle muddy,

"Madam, zat vat you sall call him, ze plaggy Hike, be one ver bad garçon. He no ear for ze music, but ven I blow ze horn, and play ze grand opera, he toct he's hands, so,"— making a trumpet of his hands and tooting,—"and mak all ze music no worth nossing. I can no stand it. Eferybody laugh at me. Zey touch zar nose, so,"— putting his thumb to his nose,—"so mosh as to say, 'Ah, ha! you be von humboog!' You sall leek zat plaggy Hike!"

"This is a fine opening for a guardian," thought Roger, as Mrs. Partington turned her eyes towards him. She went out with the Signor, and Roger remarked to Miss Chatterton that there were times when he did not regret that he had never been a parent.

She replied that she deemed none could properly direct children, as teachers or guardians, who had not children of their own. He thought a moment seriously, and then admitted the general correctness of the remark.

"I don't know what I should have been," said he, "surrounded by a family,— perhaps a pater-familias of rare virtues,— but my heart is whole. I never saw occasion to leave the charmed circle of single blessedness."

"Were you never in love?" she questioned.

"Once," said he, affecting to sigh; "everybody, they say, is in love once. When I boarded at 101, a young and gallant fellow, there was one fair creature to whom I paid many attentions, and some money for certain buttons that she attached at sundry times to needy garments; and she gave me, as I thought, indications of regard beyond that of a mere landlady's daughter, as she was,— a regard usually included in the weekly board-bill. I determined not to be cruel, and leave her to suffer on account of my indifference. Fortune fixed the flint of my affection. 'T was on a night in summer, and the gentle air swept across the back-sheds, and through the parlor windows of 101, over three consumptive geraniums that attempted to bloom there. As I entered, I saw a female figure, clothed in white, by the open window, that my heart told me was Seraphima's! I stepped noiselessly towards her, over the tufted second-hand carpet, that Seraphima's mamma had bought at auction. A moment, and my arm encircled her neck, and —— I kissed her! In another moment I was rolling on the floor, with one of Seraphima's flower-pots broken upon my head. My heart had deceived me, and I had unfortunately kissed another man's wife, which, in those days of innocence, was deemed a sacrilege! An impression was made by that blow which will never be effaced. It is here to this day," — pointing to his head. "From that moment Seraphima became obnoxious to me, — all my love for her was knocked out of me, — and she died, some fifteen years afterwards, of a broken heart and tight lacing."

"It is a wonder," said Mrs. Partington, who had returned in time to hear the close of the story; "it is a wonder that it did not give you a suggestion of the brain."

"It did, ma'am," replied he; "and that suggestion was, to leave the women alone."

The door-bell here rang again, and Mrs. Partington came in with a queer little, bald-headed man, whose appearance denoted an acquaintance with fluids of an inflammatory character. He was somewhat confused on finding himself in so large a company, and turned to go out, when the motion revealed a human face drawn roughly in black on the bald scalp behind, like that funny picture of Johnston's. He turned again, with his nose blushing very red, and addressed Mrs. Partington:

"Madam," said he, "I 've brought myself here to complain of your Ike. I looked bad enough before, but he has made me look a great deal worse, *behind*. I am a double-header, — a man beside myself. A pretty object, are n't I? I 'm only fit now for a politician who wishes to be on both sides of the fence at the same time. You see, I was a little overcome by the heat of the day, and, sitting down a moment in the shade, fell asleep, when along comes Ike, and, as you see, he made a marked man of me. Everybody says it must be he who did it. Could I see with the eyes he has given me behind, I might, like some other people, laugh at my own fun, which privilege is now denied me."

Mrs. Partington cast a look full of despair upon Roger, as she escorted the man to the door.

"This is certainly a very pleasant young man," said he, "with an excellent chance for improvement, and considerable of it. I am delighted with my prospect."

"Should you have to resort to corporal punishment," said Philanthropos, "I should suggest the brier-rose twig, as it will bring the rebel sooner to penitence, as Colt's pistols and steam guns tend sooner to bring about peace."

"I hope you will administer chloroform before you apply it," suggested Dr. Spooner; "and, as in the new materia medica the efficacy of medicine is tested by the doctor's taking it himself, allow me to recommend, Mr. Philanthropos, that you have it tried upon yourself. I would be delighted to do it gratuitously."

"A capital idea!" said Wideswarth; "it is worthy of a sonnet."

"Perhaps he could bear the flogging better than he

could the sonnet," said Roger, in an under tone, punching the Brahmin in the ribs, who sat smoking his meerschaum. The Brahmin responded by a grave bow. Mrs. Partington returned, holding in her hand an open note, which she handed to Roger, in much confusion. He read:

"MISS PARKINSON: Your boy has been and tied a culinary utensile to the caudle appendidge of a canine favorite of ourn, an indignity that wee shall never submit to. He is a reproach to the neighborhood, and you must punish him severally. THE MISS TIMMINSES."

He crushed the paper in his hand, and said, "This is a precious litle rascal, to be sure; and, according to present appearances, the chances of finding any good in him are about as limited as would be those of finding strawberries growing on the top of Mount Washington."

At this moment the door opened, and the subject of their animadversion entered, throwing his hat into a corner, and tumbling down along side of it.

"Isaac," said the dame, tenderly, "you are causing me a great deal of unhappiness. Do you do all the mischief there is done in the neighborhood?"

"No, I don't, neither," replied Ike; "I don't do half so bad as they make out."

"Did n't you fasten me in?" said Mr. Slow, coming forward.

"Yes, sir; but I should n't have done it, if you had n't been so ugly. No boy would ever trouble you, if you 'd be kind to him."

"True," said Dr. Spooner, "there 's a good deal of human nature in a boy."

"Kindness is better than spring guns as a defence," said old Roger, "but the lad seems incorrigible. Here comes another complaint, I dare say," as the door-bell rang again.

Mrs. Partington held up her hands, as she went to see who was at the door, and returned with a poor-looking woman, who wore a widow's dress.

"I 've dropped in, ma'am, though I 'm a stranger," said she, "to thank your manly little boy for taking the part of my lame son, when he was imposed upon by the bad boys in the street, just now. He drove them away like a hero, and punished them for their cowardly conduct. And he was not content with this, but he gave him a bright silver dime to buy some oranges with. A boy with such a heart as his must be a treasure to you, and he will prove a comfort to you in your old age."

"There," said Roger, gleefully, rubbing his hands, "that one act compensates for all the rest. Had I a son like that, I should prize him more than mines of gold. Such a boy would make ten years of hard matrimony endurable. Madam, here is a ten-dollar gold piece for your information."

She received it very thankfully, and passed out, invoking on him and the house the widow's blessing.

"And do you forgive him?" said Mrs. Partington, smiling with gratification.

"Yes, madam," he replied; "and boys should be forgiven far more than they are. A boy that does n't love fun is n't always to be trusted; and the one who has his wits about him, and does not take to fun, will, depend upon it, take to something worse. Parents mistake when they put an unyielding check upon a boy's conduct; when he gets his way, he will, nine times in ten, go differently from his direction, and covert sin will work insidiously, maugre all interdiction. I can't bear to see a parchment-faced boy, with a ledger in his glance at ten. Give me the lad with his soul speaking in his laughing eye, and thrilling in every nerve of his animated body. That is your true boyhood. Where there is no malice, mischief is not sin. The boys commit it as the kids eat fruit-buds, or the birds pick Mr. Hovey's strawberries, — it is their nature."

The speech was received with applause by Ike, who had donned his guardian's hat and gloves, and was standing leaning on his gold-headed cane. Mrs. Partington was astonished; Roger was disposed to be indignant, but he fortunately remembered what he had just said, and contented himself with seeing Ike take them off.

Mrs. Partington bustled about, and in a short time announced that tea was awaiting the company in the room "contagious" to the sitting-room, where the company sat down to the table. Roger was seated directly opposite Miss Chatterton, at Mrs. Partington's right hand, while by her side Ike had taken his accustomed position. The rest of the company took their places agreeably to their hostess' invitation to "derange" themselves as they could make it convenient.

There was pleasant music around the board, and happy faces beaming amid the steam of the fragrant souchong. There was much agreeable conversation among all the parties. It was general and discursive for the most part, though one particular incident gave it, to some parties, a tender interest. Ike had observed a disposition on the part of his guardian to speak low and confidential things to his opposite neighbor, Miss Chatterton, and his foot, as he sat by her side, just reached that of the old gentleman. He thought to himself what a prime thing it would be if he could touch his toe and make him believe that Miss Chatterton did it, and resolved to try it. When the doughnuts were handed round, Roger selected one that was heart-shaped and handed it over to his vis-a-vis, with the remark,

"This, my dear Miss Chatterton, is the 'heart that never loved.'"

The lady received it with the reply, "Indeed! and yet, you see, it is broken;" breaking a piece of it off as she spoke.

"A melancholy fate," said he, "for that which was wholly yours."

He was surprised, as he uttered this, to feel a gentle pressure upon his foot beneath the table. It was a light and careful touch, and bore no semblance to accident.

"As much so as it was the young lady's at 101," said she, archly.

He felt another touch as she spoke, which assured him of its origin, and gave him a thrill of pleasure. He beamed upon her like the sun upon a planet.

"And how would you have acted," said he, "had you been in her place? Would you have died in fifteen years of a broken heart?"

"Can't say that I might not have died before that, of some other disease," she replied.

He felt the touch under the table again, which operated upon him like a jar full of electric eels.

"Were you ever in love, Miss Chatterton?" said he, in a tremendously deep whisper, as low as G.

"Never with any one but myself," replied she, smilingly.

The touch followed the remark, as the sound follows the flash.

"How would you like to be?"

"I can't say."

The touch succeeded, to his infinite delight.

"Miss Chatterton," said he, reaching over, so that his remark might not be heard by any one else but her, "you have made a deep impression upon me. Indeed, I may say that your foot has touched my heart, — given it, so to speak, a finishing touch."

"My foot touched your heart, sir! I don't understand you."

"Not perhaps literally," he continued; "but the little touches of your foot beneath the table have touched me very sensibly."

"I have not touched you," replied she, very much surprised.

"I see how it is," said he, in some confusion; "it is another instance of the trickery of that plaguy Ike. But, be that as it may, you have much interested me, and I shall place this evening among the happiest of my life."

Ike, as he saw the dénouement of his plot approaching, had made his escape just in time. During this scene the other members of the party had been busily talking.

"Yes," Wideswarth at this point was heard to say, "in petty trials are summed up most of the sorrows that beset us here. We brace up against large trials, and support ourselves by props of resolution; but the little worriments, like the dropping that wears the stone, undermine our temper, and down it comes with a crash, and a confusion of oaths and tears. Please listen to a sonnet I have to-day written regarding minor trials:

Bigger vexations, like a 'fresh' in spring,
Assail the soul in their impetuous wrath;
The fierce tornado on its course doth wing,
Dashing obstructions from its chosen path!

But little troubles, like a nibbling mouse,
  Gnaw slowly from our comfort, as 't were cheese ; —
Take you a smoky chimney to a house,
  Or scolding wife, perpetual bane to ease,
Or grain within the eye, or gouty feet,
  Or debts unpaid, — exchequer running low, —
Or hurdy-gurdy grinding in the street,
  Or six-cent Cubas that you can't make go."

"Allow me," said Roger, "to propose, as the two concluding lines, the following:

Or one sweet foot of an illusive joy,
Made less than nothing by a roguish boy."

"I have no objection to the lines," replied Wideswarth, "excepting that of irrelevancy. I cannot exactly understand —"

"My dear sir," said Roger, "that should be no objection; for who ever thinks of asking what a sonnet means? I appeal to yourself. We take it for granted that a poet sees his own meaning, and out of compliment ask no questions."

"I could have suggested a minor difficulty to have added to the number," said Philanthropos; "the ingratitude one is liable to meet with who tries to do a good act. A few days since I saw a dog going along with a heavy basket in his mouth, and, thinking of relieving him, I attempted to take it from him, meaning to carry it myself, when the canineite snapped at me as though he suspected my motives."

"I was much annoyed, a few days since," said Dr. Spooner, "by a trifle which very much disturbed my equanimity. I was passing a lady whose dress spread over an area about equal to that of a load of hay, when I accidentally stepped upon her flounce. An unmistakable tear followed, at which I looked round to apologize. But my contrition and shame all vanished before the look she gave me. It was the concentration of spitefulness, and, instead of apologizing, I asked myself the question if she were not the aggressor in protruding herself upon my path, and so I passed on; but it disturbed me."

"A nervous wife," said Blifkins "is a consideration in this direction." He said it timidly.

"All fade away before rheumatism in the ankle," said old Roger.

"Are you subject to romantic affections?" inquired Mrs. Partington, with anxiety in her tone and a spoon in her hand. "My poor Paul was terribly infected by them one winter, when we lived contagious to the marshes."

The door-bell rang violently, and the old lady went out to see who caused the alarm. She came back immediately.

"There was nobody there," said she. "Well, as I was saying, he had an affectation in his back, and an embargo in his head, and a vertebra all over him. He could n't move without resistance."

The door-bell rang again, which she attended to with the same result.

"I 'm shore," said she, "I don't see who it can be. Well, as I was pretending to say, our minister sent for him, right in the midst of his trouble, to come and cut up a pig for him. Nothing would do but he must go. So he crawled out, and just as he was going up over a little hill, holding on to the fence —"

The door-bell rang the third time.

"Well," said Mrs. Partington, as she rose to go, 'bells can't ring without hands, unless they 're rung by the spirits. Perhaps it 's them."

"Well, by all means ask them in," responded Roger; "it will give new spirits to our party."

"I can't see, for the life of me, what it means," said she, coming back from the door; "but, as I was telling you, as he was going over the hill his feet slipped, and he was prostituted from the top to the bottom. He got up, strange to say, as well as he ever was in his life. The remedy is very simple."

"So it is," said he, "and I think I'll try it, some time."

The fact that Ike came in just then, coupled with the recent ringing, gave evidence of the cause of the latter, and Roger looked at him with an expression denoting a guardian's feelings.

"Ike," said he, "come here; I am to have a hand in your bringing up. Now, I have to tell you that you must toe the mark; be obedient, dutiful, and respectful, or —— you villain! that is my toe you are kicking."

"Is the touch as tender as the one you just now received?" said Miss Chatterton, with a sly manner.

"No more of that," said he, smiling amid his pain, "if thou lovest me. That illusion was a pleasant one, which may yet, I hope, through propitious fates, become a reality."

The party had by this time arisen, and, as he uttered the significant expression, he took her hand, which she did not withdraw, and whispered in her ear,

"It is a strange thing, — but there are many strange things happening all the time, — that an obdurate old bachelor should have been thus subjugated, and by such means; but I am confident that it is a good fate which has brought us together, for which I must thank that plaguy Ike."

She touched his foot, — not the gouty one, — and smiled, and the conquest was complete.

The party now rose to depart, but before they went expressed their undivided delight, Dr. Spooner averring that he had, for a long time, been seeking for the delectable, but had never come so near its attainment before; proposing Mrs. Partington's health, which was drunk, "paregorically," as she afterwards expressed it.

She returned thanks, stating that she was very fulsome with her emotions, and ready to make any sacrament for their happiness. And this was the way the guardianship for Ike began.

AUTUMN.

Hail! beauteous queen — (not literally, please!
 Thy reign I 'd rather signalize in verse;) —
My full heart drops in homage on its knees,
 The while thy glories it would fain rehearse.
Blest of Pomona, thy redundant horn
 Is full of fruitage, and around thy brow
Bright vines are twined, with berries that adorn
 Thy golden ringlets with a ripened glow!
Ceres her trophies brings, and at thy feet
 Pours out the bounteous harvest's golden rain,
And gushing wine, in pipes, makes music sweet,
 While sturdy Plenty dances in thy train.
O, Autumn! I could sing a song sublime
In praise of thee, from now till Christmas time.

TWENTY YEARS MARRIED.

Yes, twenty years have winged their flight,
Since that mysterious word I spoke,
When, on a beauteous summer night,
I first assumed the flowery yoke.
I long had craved the blissful chain,
And cheerfully subscribed the vow;
Perhaps I 'd do the same again —
Perhaps — though I am older now

Ah ! well do I recall the time
When she, now pensive by my side,
Stood, in her blushing morning prime,
A tender, sweet, and bashful bride;
And I, so proud of that dear hand,
Could scarce contain myself for bliss; —
I 'd bought a tract of fairy land,
And sealed my purchase with a kiss.

For happiness we trimmed our sail,
My darling little bride and I;
Hope's breezes blew a pleasant gale,
And gently smiled the summer sky.
The world seemed made, for her and me,
All bright wherever we might turn,
Our life to be a tranquil sea —
Sweet innocents ! we 'd much to learn.

For soon did Care's disturbing breath
Its baleful influence impart,
And bitter sorrow, born of death,
O'ercast the sunshine of our heart;
But still, as trouble round us rose,
Each closer, fonder, clung to each,
Blessed with the strength of love's repose,
Enduring all that grief could teach.

We 'd much of joy, though small our sphere,
And craved no more extended fame,
For children made our dwelling dear, —
'T was wonderful how fast they came ! —
"The more the merrier," we said,
And in them every wish was blest;

A part in our embrace have staid,
  A mound at Woodlawn tells the rest.

Those twenty years have left their trace
  Upon her brow, then smooth and fair,
And stolen, some say, the witching grace
  That once her features used to wear;
But still I see the same kind eyes
  Beam on me with a light as true
As when, in love's young paradise,
  I first their inspiration knew.

And I — well, well — we 'll let that pass; —
  None more than I time's changes see,
Each day I shave myself, — alas!
  My mirror does not flatter me;
But if I 'm changed for worst or best
  I cannot answer, on my life,
And leave the solving of this test
  To such as choose to ask my wife.

This lesson we have fully learned:
  Pure happiness that men have deemed
Is but a hope soon overturned,
  A vision but in fancy dreamed;
That all of happiness below,
  Pursuing which the life is spent
In mingled scenes of bliss and woe,
  Is measured by the word CONTENT.

Though fortune may withhold its smile,
  As it has done in time before,
Content shall still our way beguile,
  And rest the future landscape o'er.
The future! — who its tale may tell? —
  But for it we 've nor doubts nor fears,
And like our life that 's past so well,
  We 'll try another twenty years.

Aug. 15th. 1858.

WHOLE-SOULED FELLOWS

"SPEAKING of this class," said Dr. Spooner, "I am delighted to acknowledge their excellence, and would go far to shake such by the hand; but perhaps my estimate of the whole-souledness of the individual might be different from yours, for my comprehension demands quality, as an essential element of the whole. A whole-souled man, as some of you seem to regard it, is one of warm, impulsive nature, open-handed and lavish; qualities, I grant ye, that are essential,—for soul is feeling, and not a merely cold mechanism; but generosity must be a thing of principle as well as natural impulse — the spiritual man in harmony with the natural man. This leads to acts that insure the title of whole-souled fellow. In one case, a fellow may be whole-souled in companionship, and spend money as freely as water with you, but his soul is vitiated; another may be generous to a fault, and an admiring world approve him and say he is a whole-souled fellow, but look through him a little, and you will find a great under-current of selfishness, that, were it known, would detract from the general admiration. I know one who bears the reputation, who is really a very good fellow, socially, that employs hundreds of girls at starvation rates in the manufacture of garments, and makes a princely salary at the expense of their life and comfort. Though nominally a whole-souled fellow, any man who thus for his own gain will sacrifice others is egregiously flattered by the imputation. So of those who give largely of money that they cannot spend. There is no soul in it. There is *craft* in it, that assumes the form of soul, which men materially cased regard as soul, through their dim spiritual spectacles. The widow's mite that was cast into the treasury swells to a mountain, in comparison with such an act.

The whole-souled fellow that I believe in is he who, warmed by natural kindness, blossoms out and fructifies in justice and right, ignoring self, and struggling continually for human betterment, from the betterment law existing in himself — whose life is a continued example of persistent generosity." Well, what 's the use of talking about what everybody knows? And yet there may be some whole-souled fellows who are not entitled to so generous or good an appellation.

BEHIND THE SCENES.

COULD we get behind the scenes of life, and observe the workings of the machinery, and the various traps and shiftings and changes that are taking place all the time, we should be half inclined to distrust the absolute virtue of much that passes for such, and see, faintly at least, through a great deal of villany, some good, that the removal of the whiskers and washing off of the paint might reveal. Behind the scenes and before them is exhibited pretty much the same thing; the counterfeit seeming the real, and much of the real being nothing but counterfeit. And, speaking of going behind the scenes, to one unacquainted with such locality as the stage of a theatre the first permission to enter that mysterious province is the open sesame to many wonders; revealing to him how it is all done: — how the roses of health and happiness may glow on cheeks pallid and hollow with care; and how the lines of sorrow may appear, from the adroit touches of paint, upon brows not yet marked by a wrinkle; how fierceness and malignity may flourish on faces where the kindest spirit rests, through the magic of burnt cork and false mustachios; and how injured innocence and rank villany are allied, when a little soap and water bring them together at the close of the drama! He sees men at the wings, like special providences, controlling the different moods of scenic life; here shifting a house of comfort and affluence to a beggar's hut, and there producing upon what was a "blasted heath" a bower of roses. He sees the elegance that from the front gleamed in the beauty of scenic art transformed to a mere daub, the paint apparently thrown on by the handful; and architectural magnificence but a mere frame-work of rough pine, held up by props from behind. It is a new emotion to him, such a queer admixture does it present of all sorts of life in one little world—the grave and the gay, the good and the bad, mingling together with a freedom of manner very different from the marked antagonism of the outward presentment. He wanders through the ins and outs and labyrinthine turnings of the strange place, puzzled at a thousand new things, and half regretting that the illusion should have been dispelled in whose deception he has so long happily lived.

WOMAN'S SOVEREIGNTY.

We 're swayed a thousand ways by woman's wiles,
And every day admit her sovereign power:
We bend, delighted, to her potent smiles,
We bend when tears outpour in plenteous shower;
Her witchery of grace bows low our hearts,
Her winning voice has conquest in its tone,
We yield us captive to the myriad arts
That round our pathway hem us like a zone.
By her sweet lips we swear our lives away,
We vow eternal homage to her eyes,
The raven curl round her white neck astray
The magic of her power intensifies!
But most we bow beneath sweet woman's sway,
When walking 'neath a clothes-line on a washing day.

PETS.

It is an amiable human weakness, is the love of pets; and the one who "crunches" them in his heart, as Gruff and Tackleton did the crickets on his hearth, has little affection for anything else. The love that one expends on pets is auxiliary to a higher and holier affection, and does not take from it; as it may be classed with loves of kindred and friends, that may be infinite in their scope, and yet be consistent with the one grand central affection, and strengthen and sanctify it. Pets come in many forms. The heart loves dogs, and birds, and flowers, and at times queer objects become invested with an interest which almost takes the phase of disease. A sweet little human pet of our own, that now rests in a land where love is the life it lives, unalloyed with the pains that marred it here, had a strange proclivity for toads. The little creature loved everything that lived, but in the summer-time it was her delight to visit the garden and find her uncouth favorites, and watch their ungainly movements with a pleasure that one might expend on a rose or a canary. A little book was published, a few years since, by Grace Greenwood, called "History of my Pets." We have a thumbed and soiled copy of that book, which money could not buy. It was owned by another pet of ours, who, years ago, went down the dark valley and left us. It was a solace to him in all his hours of trouble and pain. The sight of that book mollified his grief, and his sobs would subside to smiles as his eyes rested on the pictures. The fancy has been cherished that the loving spirit still rests about the book, and hence it becomes a pet in itself, sacred from the contamination of use. From its pages the beautiful brown eyes seem to look up, and the cheerful laugh sounds again in the glee of delighted childhood, and we renew again, for a moment, the old-time presence, until the dream dies in the light of material care, and the book is laid sacredly in its niche again. Those pets that come in the human form, how we cling to them and idolize them, to have them, alas! fade from our arms in exhalation, as the dew fades from the flowers, seemingly crushed by the intensity of the affection with which we enfold them. But the heart follows them, and we hear a voice that speaks comfort to our soul, saying, "These pets ye shall behold again!" and we still look in the way they have gone.

BY CHANCE.

THE venerable Mrs. Partington asked us the question, once, if we believed that everything was foreördained beforehand in advance, and we were compelled to answer that sometimes we did, and then again we did n't. Some time after, we were sitting looking over the papers, when the door opened and Mrs. P. stepped in. There was a smile on her face, and the old green umbrella in her hand. After welcoming her and requesting her to be seated, she said, "Well it 's all lubricated now; just as clear to me as crystial." — "What is?" we queried, a little puzzled to know what she meant. — "That about foreördination, you know, and chance, and all that, which we were talking about." — "Ah, yes; well, how was it?" — "Why, I 'tended the lectur' last night — one of the eternity course." — "Fraternity," we suggested; "who spoke?" — "O, Mr. what 's his name — he that made the refrigerator, you know, for warming houses in summer and cooling 'em in winter — Emerson — T. P. Emerson." — "You mean R. W. Emerson," we hinted; "did he lecture on refrigerators?" — "O, dear, no!

'twas on chance; and sich a lectur'! I thought I'd heerd lecturs before, but that succeeded 'em all."—"Indeed!" we said, somewhat interested, though there were eleven letters unopened on the table, "tell us about it." —"Well," she continued, "it was about chance, and he is sich a queer man that you have to watch every word or you can't understand him. If you lose one word, it's jest like a stitch broke in a seam made by some of the sowing-machines — the work is good for nothing. Well, he said there was no sich thing as chance, and that every thing was planned out beforehand. And, to prove it, he spoke of a ship on the sea, knocked about by the winds and waves, and showed, just as loosed as anything I ever saw, that she was not there by chance, or that she was, and I declare I don't know which." The old lady reached down into her spacious pocket, and, taking out the old Constitution and Guerriere handkerchief, wiped her specs, as though she wished still for more light, while Ike amused himself by trundling Lion round the room, by his two hind legs, like a wheelbarrow.

MRS. PARTINGTON AND THE RUSSIAN HELMET.

"Is that a tropic of the Chimera?" said Mrs. Partington, pointing to a Russian helmet that a friend had brought from the Crimea. — "That, Madam," said we, "is a trophy of the Crimea, that fearful battle-ground, and it seems to bear about it the odor of strife in the perilous deadly breaches, and the crash of contending forces." She looked at it attentively. "Yes," responded she, "and not only the breeches, but the rest of the uniform besides." It was evident that she had made a slight mistake.

WHO IS VILE?

"SHE 's a vile creature," said the severe woman, looking very red in the face. The conversation had been upon the propriety of recognizing one who had fallen from virtue, if fame were to be believed, and the severe woman, whose purity could not be questioned, closed her side of the argument with the remark commencing this paragraph. Dr. Spooner arose from the table and stepped behind his chair, as children do in schools when called upon to recite. "The term vile, madam," said he, looking at the severe woman, " is a very strong one coming from human lips, and those who utter it should be very sure that they stand on sure ground themselves. Because great imperfection may be imputed to any one, it does not follow that the whole body is corrupt. There may be beneath all this corruption a stratum of pure soil, in which good seeds may grow, — in which, indeed, they may be now germinating, — that may not shoot their leaf up through the crust of sin and degradation that keeps them down, but may throw out the tendrils of an undying principle, that, deeper than the flesh, will one day find an outgrowth in other airs, and shame those who, wrapt in their own sensuous perfectibility, have not allowed a spiritual seed to grow. Vile, indeed! The expression comes with a poor grace from any unless they have the scale and balance by a special patent from heaven with which to weigh human wrong, and it should be carefully used. I once knew a case where a good woman and a bad woman made custards for a sick person, and both met in the sick room — the one with a proud spirit that she was not like the wicked one, the other humble and retiring, as if ashamed of herself. But the good woman's custards were made of skimmed milk and sweetened with brown sugar, and the bad woman's were made very deliciously; and the sick one fancied that the souls of both those persons were seen in the custard-cups; and in the comparative estimate he found more intrinsic excellence in the bad woman than in the good woman, and believed, as he still believes, that many transgressions, that spring from human weakness, will be forgiven, for the sparks of love that may be still smouldering deeply within. I see you laugh at my homely illustration; but it is a life-picture, treat it as you may. Let us call them unfortunate, rather than vile, and humble ourselves to regard them with charity."

The severe woman looked very red, but said nothing further till the doctor was gone.

THE HOUSEHOLD GHOST.

BEING AN ACCOUNT OF A VERY SINGULAR VISION SEEN FROM BENEATH THE BLANKETS ON A COLD NIGHT.

WITH a silent foot, unshod,
In the mystery of the night,
Light the flitting phantom trod,
Glimmering in ghostly white

Cold the north wind blew without,
Scattering terror as it sped,
Rattling at the crazy spout
And the clattering tiles o'erhead.

On the window-pane at hand
Grew the web the frost-sprites spin,
But 't was very summer-land
Where the ghost kept ward within.

Here and there amid the night
Eye the mystic form could trace,
Floating in its garments white,
With its anxious-looking face;

Bending o'er the nestlings' couch
  With a kiss so sweetly given,
That the sleepers felt the touch
  As a token dreamed of heaven.

Such a mighty power was there! —
  Waking, by a single breath,
Smiles of happiness most rare
  On the lips of sembled death!

Far amid life's later night,
  Sad and dark with sin and pain,
In its drapery of white
  Will the phantom walk again.

With its calm eyes true and clear,
  And its finger raised above,
Breathing in the troubled ear
  Accents of a *Mother's* love.

MRS. PARTINGTON PATRIOTIC.

"Hurra!" said Ike, as he read the fact in the papers, "here 's O'Regan admitted to the Union." "A furriner, I should jedge," remarked Mrs. Partington, looking very wisely at the steam that rose from the tea-cups and formed in one cloud near the ceiling; "but I 'm glad they 've let him come in to enjoy our political rights and lefts, and other perogatives. There 's room enough, and the rear of our institutions should be distended. I don't believe a man should be cut off because he was n't born in this country for twenty-one years, which of course was n't any fault of his, for everybody would be born here if they could have their own auction con sulted."—"It means," said Ike, "a new State."—"Well, child," replied she, "the odds is only the difference — States or men, 't is all the same. Let 'em come into our grand consternation, where the eagle shall spread its broad opinions over 'em, and make 'em happy in an unlimited bondage of brotherhood, like the Siamese twins." She had not taken her eyes from the steam that rose from the cups, and joined in one cloud, that seemed to represent the Union she was depicting. Ike had a better illustration, for he took the five preserved peaches on the plate, and put them all into one.

WEANING THE BABY.

THERE 's trouble in the house, and Bub in arms
  Protests, with stentor lungs and brimming eyes,
Against this greatest of his earthly harms,
  The order cutting off his small supplies.
With stormy brow — a tempest in a bowl —
  He bellows with a most determined might,
Disclosing fierceness in his infant soul,
  That in the Infantry may some day fight.
We speak of sorrows — what are they to Bub's,
  And the maternal's, half disposed to yield?
'T is hard to find, amidst earth's minor rubs,
  A trouble near so sad as is revealed
Where the accustomed lacteal rations stop,
And infant lungs, like Divés, bellow for a drop.

HOME MUSIC.

AN old square piano — "Chickering, Boston" — has occupied a corner in a moderate home for a number of years, and been regarded as a necessity. It has been a true friend, for its influence has ever tended towards harmonization. However discordant other elements may have been, — and there may have been times when some of the dust and pins of life got in among the human organism to produce temporary jarring and inharmony, — the old piano has rung ever truly and cheerfully, responsive to the touch. It has been a household pet. Practised fingers have picked sweet melodies from it; but all, the unskilled as well, have tried their hand at it. Even the youngest is great at fingering. It has been a pleasant thing with him who is the ostensible head of the household to sit, in the repose of the evening, the care of the world shut out with the closed curtains, and hear some one, in the unstudied grace and glow of home inspiration, unlock the gates of melody with the piano-keys, and trip away over melodious meadow fields and gather the humble flowers of song to wreathe in a garland about the hearth-stone—none of the lofty and high-studied themes, that arouse mighty plaudits where Thalberg or Lang is their exponent, but just a simple melody or two, awakening fond memories of old times, or thrilling with the consciousness of a new pleasure. Ah! this is the acme of musical delight, though there be those who revel in high-seasoned opera, and turn up their august noses at the humble home-strains alluded to. There is a pleasure, besides, when one is in his remote corner, busied with book or pen, to have a strain come to him of some remembered song, fraught with gentleness and happiness. His task is forgotten, as he listens, and he beats time on his palm, gazing abstractedly at nothing, and yet how much he sees! No wonder that his thought should run to rhyme; and of late, when thus held by a spell, and diviner melodies entered his soul through the opened doors of fancy, the following rhapsody came to "the writer," and wrought itself in form upon paper; and this is the guise in which it revealed itself:

Essence of love divine!
O'er my soul like the spirit of wine
Thou stealest, and in rapt dream
Sense merges in that stream

Of resonant delight we deem to flow
From God's own presence, where we know
The Harmonies abide, and music fills
The broad heavens, as the blood thrills
Through these terrestrial veins ;
And where celestial strains
Are thought and language that impart,
In quick accord from heart to heart,
The golden sympathy which there obtains !

Music ! — O, subtle mastery
That sets my spirit free
From the tired body and its care,
Which, light as bird in air,
Rises upon the joyous wings
That buoyant melody brings —
Finding sweet sympathy with flowers
In the everlasting bowers,
And with fair earthly blooms
That fling their rich perfumes
Over the summer days,
And with the genial rays
The sun in his loving temper sheds
Upon the spring-time flower-beds,
And with bees and running brooks,
And quiet, pleasant nooks,
Where the birds sing, and the breeze
Is busy with the gossipy trees,
And with all that 's beautiful and bright
And loving, given for man's delight !

I yield me to thy power,
Great spirit of the hour !
Bound by thy magic spell,
My heart, responsive to the swell
Of thy wild measure, swings
In its turret, and my whole being sings
In unison with that which wings
Its way o'er vibratory strings
Of subtle air, whose pulsings greet
My ear in this remote retreat,
As I list to mark the fading feet
Die out in distance of the last cadence sweet

MRS. PARTINGTON AT THE BALLET.

"WHEN is the bally troop coming on?" said Mrs. Partington, after watching the dancers at the Boston Theatre about half an hour. — "That is the ballet troupe," said Augustus, with a smile, pointing at the beautiful sylphs that were fluttering like butterflies about the stage. She looked at him incredulously for a little while, and said: "Well, I believe in calling things by their true names; and what they call them a troop for, I don't see. I thought it was a troop of horse, such as they had in the Contract of the Ganges." She levelled her new opera-glass at the stage, and looked long and earnestly. "Well," said she, "if there ever was anybody that needed sympathy, it 's them! Worn their dresses way up to their knees by dancing, poor creaturs! and by and by, at this rate, they won't have nothing to wear." She stood beating time as the waves of gauze moved hither and thither in illustration of the poetry of motion, while Ike amused himself by tearing up his theatre-bill, and putting it into a lady's silk hood, which hung over the back of the front seat.

FLOWERS.

DIDST ever think how simple flowers bloom,
And shed their beauties on the summer air,
Each giving forth its measure of perfume,
Or gladdening earth by its effulgence rare —
Unheeding aught that flattering lips may speak,
Nor taking airs upon themselves at praise,
Doing their duty with a carriage meek,
And cheering all their little life of days?
No jealous rivalry contention brings,
As in more beauteous circles far than these;
No pride impels the blossom as it swings
To make some humbler sister ill at ease:
But each one blooms with its own charms content,
Nor, if excelled, cares it a single scent.

INVOLUNTARY.

An amusing instance of an involuntary performance happened, some years ago, in a church not far from Boston. The organist was a splendid musician, but had an infirmity with which, we are glad to believe, very few of his brethren are now troubled, — he would crook his elbow after dinner, and was too ready to "look upon the wine when it is red." It made very little difference, however, in his playing, even though he had dipped in "potations pottle deep." One Sunday, he came to church remarkably hilarious. There was an unusually bright sparkle in his eye, and his white fingers ran over the keys in most profuse liquidity, producing sounds that, while they were very beautiful, were so undisguised that even the dullest could not but understand that there was something queer about the organist, and that their own solemnly-dedicated organ was playing anything but the legitimate airs of their Zion. People nudged one another, the more rigid with frowning looks, some with surprise, and others, of the undevout, with an appreciating grin. The pastor hesitated when giving out the first hymn; but the organ never did so well, and redeemed itself from the obloquy of its recent suspicious conduct. The congregation rose for the prayer, — the people did so in those days, — when, just at the hush of the performance, while all were intently listening to catch the voice of the pastor, as it emerged from the hoarse whisper of the opening, the organ gave a frightful scream, that smote the ear like the laughter of fiends, echoing from every nook and corner of the old church. The pastor stopped in his prayer, and opened his eyes; the audience turned round, and every eye was bent on the organ-loft. The organist had risen with the rest, but his efforts to preserve his equilibrium had proved unavailing, and he had tumbled over upon the key-board, producing the fearful "involuntary," as he reached his hands out to save himself. Conscious of the disorder, and confused by the looks turned upon him, he recovered himself, and, holding out his hand towards the minister, said in an unsteady but patronizing voice, "Or ri, sir; drive on!" This broke the back of all propriety, and it was thought that the prayer which followed did the audience but little good. Another organist was engaged before the next Sunday.

SIGNS OF FALL.

THE curious wind comes searching through the street,
With bodings bitter,
Whirling around the quick pedestrian's feet
Whole heaps of litter.

The traders all withdraw their fragile stock
Of lace and muslins,
Unable to withstand the testy shock
Of Autumn's tusslings.

Delaines and thibets float upon the air
In tempting manner;
And Balmorals are dancing everywhere,
Like many a banner.

And winter furs come on us unperceived
Of fitch or sable,
And madam and the girls, their cloaks achieved,
Are comfortable.

And little Tommy takes his winter boots
From where he 's thrown them ;
Alas ! he tries, and finds that neither suits,
For he 's outgrown them.

The vine looks sickly on the trellis high, —
The leaves all curling,
And every breeze that hastens rudely by
Sets them to whirling.

The old spout, hanging by a single nail,
Laments and mutters,
As if in meek remonstrance with the gale
That threatening utters.

The summer birds have left their breezy haunt
Among our branches,
And moved upon their regular annual jaunt
To warmer ranches.

Huge heaps of coal defile the sidewalk way,
And we — confound 'em ! —
Must o'er their yielding heights a path essay,
Or travel round 'em.

And many bills thrust in their leech-like length,
With items fearful,
Testing the purse whose corresponding strength
Is never near full.

The biting airs the shrinking flesh appall
By sharp incisions,
And everything proclaims the approach of Fall,
Except provisions.

IKE'S SPRING MEDICINE.

"ISAAC, what is the matter?" said Mrs. Partington, in the morning, as Ike bounded into the room, jumped over a table, kicked down a chair, and concluded with turning a somerset, by which operation he succeeded in knocking two plates from the dresser. "What ails you? Are you possessed, or what? Such abolitions of feelings are not pretty." There was a severity in her tone, and she stood looking at the boy through her spectacles, as a pair of Lutheran windows might look down on a Bantam chicken. Ike stopped as she spoke, but looked up roguishly in her face, while he replied, "Did n't you tell me to take my brimstone and molasses three mornings, and then skip three? This is the first morning to skip, and I 'm a doing of it." The dame smiled slightly, as she replied, "You must be more apprehensive in going through the world, or you may get apprehended, my dear. It would make you too sulfurious to take your spring medicine every morning, so I thought you might pass over three mornings." — "Should n't I be a Jew," said Ike, feeling the shape of his nose, "to *passover* three mornings?" Mrs. Partington, whether she was aware of the atrocity or not, said nothing further, and Ike and Lion went out for a roll on the grass.

PARTING.

We speak of parting o'er the opening grave
  Where weary nature finds a fitting rest,
The while, to anxious doubts and fears a slave,
  Dire anguish clouds the sunshine of the breast;
We speak of parting when we bid farewell
  To some tried spirit kindred with our own,
And 'gainst the fortune doth the heart rebel
  Through whose obtrusion those we prize have flown;
But, O! how feebly does the word convey
  The thought of that black severance of fate,
When those we 've loved have torn themselves away
  And merged their friendship 'neath the clouds of hate
That living death, from dull indifference born,
That knows, to follow it, no resurrection morn.

ASSIMILATION

A WORD about diet — the matters that we eat, and their effects upon us. We are made from the dust of the earth, not by being shaped in the human mould and pushed upon the stage to enact our part, but by eating dirt-pies, made up in the several forms of beef and mutton and vegetables, and grow to our limit of physical life by the accretions of dust, in some form or another, that we pick up as we go along. This is all that it amounts to, and, however we may disguise it with nice condiments, and lay claim to a higher origin than dust, the fact is, nevertheless. Whether in form of choice wines or rich preserves, or dishes whose delicacy is the acme of desire, it resolves itself to this. The question, then, comes up, like Sam Weller's of the red-nosed man, with regard to the particular kind of vanities that he preferred, which sort of dust is best? Here is a chance for division, where individual tastes will take issue. The lovers of beef and the lovers of macaroni will contend for the mastery, — the animal and the vegetable. It is, we think, an established fact that a man partakes of the nature of what he eats. The man who eats beef, for instance, becomes of most oxlike and sinewy ponderosity, according to this rule, while he who partakes of the delicate flesh of the marsh nightingale must become indued with the flexibility of a dancing-master. Feasters upon wild game and swift fish are fast men, those who cotton to pop-corn are remarkably snappy in conversation, while those who indulge in apples or acid articles may be known by the acerbity of their character. Narrowing the rule down to sausages, those who fancy this sort of food are remarkable for no particular trait, though their conduct

5*

is somewhat highly seasoned with a strong tendency to the sage. It is not ascertained that eating tomatoes will induce redness of the cheeks, or parsley any particular facility for learning grammar, or walnuts any higher aspirations; but this much we may be sure of, that gross feed is inimical to clear thought, and moderation in diet is a great helper to spiritual and intellectual advancement.

COMPARISON.

I SAW a Nun, upon a day, who moved,
  In queer attire clad, and eyes cast down;
As though to breathe God's air were task unloved,
  I gathered from the shadow of her frown.
Beside her walked a maiden bright and fair,—
  A lovely one, with cheeks of ruddy hue;
Young loves lay nestling in the twining hair,
  That round her head in sweet luxuriance grew.
A smile was on her lip, a contrast great
  With the unbending parchment of the face
That by her gloomed, and on her seemed to wait
  The blest attendants of a loving grace.
If which were holiest I were called to say,
The holiness of beauty would decide the day.

MALAPROPOS.

"I DECLARE," said Mrs. Partington, as Miss Waggles, the daughter of the green grocer, looked in upon her in the full feather of extreme fashion; "you look as if you had just come out of the upper drawer, and smell as sweet as the balm of Gilead." Miss Waggles smiled, smoothed down her stiff silk,—just bought,—and tossed her head daintily, on the back of which hung the new bonnet that she had come in on purpose to show

How long is it, Dear, since it was dyed and turned? P. 55.

"Does that calico wash, dear?" asked the old lady, without taking her spectacles from her forehead. She did not see the blush that suffused the Waggles as the green grocer's daughter informed her that it was silk. "Dear me," exclaimed she, taking hold of it; "so it is; how well you have kept it! It looks as good as new. If some girls had worn it, it would have all been in rags before now. How long is it, dear, since it was dyed and turned?"—"It is new," said Miss Waggles, suppressing a hoop and extending a spiteful feeling at the same time.—"Is it, indeed?" responded the dame. "Well, my visionary organs do deceive me so, that I believe that I am growing near-sighted; but are you going to have a new bonnet to match?" This was putting the agony on too thick; it was the grain that broke the back of the camel. Miss Waggles remembered that she had a sudden engagement and rose to go, and a strange smile played around the mouth of Mrs. Partington as her visitor sailed out of the door like a line-of-battle ship. Ike watched her, and thought what fun it would be to see her go up.

MRS. PARTINGTON ON SURPRISE PARTIES.

"They 're all very well, surprise parties are," said Mrs. Partington, laying her knitting-work in her lap, and putting her specs up on the roof of her cap. "They 're all very well where folks are prepared for 'em; where they have the sandwiches and cold ham all cut and dried, with the lemonade in the goblins, and the coffee in the tureen all ready to be turned out; but where they come like an army, hungry as bears and hypothenuses, and ready to eat one up, with no provisions made or cooked for 'em,—heaven help us! it is trying. People may smile as much as they may, and say they are dreadful glad to see 'em, and all that; but my opinion is that they would be glad to see 'em a good way off, all the time. But when they carry things with 'em, as they do to ministers, and surprise 'em with donations of doughnuts and silver plates, that is a different matter. When our minister lost money in railroad shares, that cut him off short, his perish gin him a surprise party, and helped him along surprisingly. They are good when they 're managed like that." She stopped as a beam of reflected sunshine came into her eyes with blinding force, filling her with surprise, as the sun lay by the west; but could she have seen the sly look which Ike bore, on the opposite corner, as he thrust a piece of looking-glass into his pocket, she would have no longer wondered. That boy was evidently a party to her surprise.

INDIVIDUALITY.

"I LOVE to stand at the street corners," said Dr. Spooner, as he was standing, with his cane behind him, on which he was leaning, looking up and down the street. "Did the fact never occur to you," continued he, "that every one of those persons moving before you was an individuality, an atomic component in the great aggregated humanity, and yet an isolation, a microcosmatic existence in a world of existences?" He looked at us a moment, as if expecting an answer. Overwhelmed by the profundity of the question, we remained silent. "Yes," continued he, lifting himself up by his cane, "each individual is an individual world. All the love, hope, ambition, hatred, and devotion, revealed in the grand macrocosm before us—the world—is enacted in each little globe that moves by us,—forming the microcosm—the individual. It is a grand study, sir. Man, abstractly considered, is a broad sweep of the human horizon with the glass of truth; individually considered, the telescope is reversed,—revealing man infinitely less, but still the same. I have stood here, by the hour, reading the faces that have moved by me as the planets move round the sun, presenting varied phases,—one little world presenting the mirthful phase, another the sad, another the anxious, another the fierce,—but how distinct and beautiful the individuality! At such times I think of the music of the lines describing the 'solemn silence' with which the planets revolve,

'Forever singing, as they shine,
The hand that made us is divine.'

These sing to me in their distinctness and silence, and"—A boy passing at the time touched the Doctor's cane, and, it being just when he was drawing himself up to give emphasis to his sentence, he fell backward, with considerable violence. He smiled as he gathered himself up. "Human weakness," said he, "may fall, but eternal truth must stand."

MISAPPREHENSION.

"COMMON TATERS!" said Mrs. Partington to herself, as she waked out of a little nap in which she had been thrown by a soporific preacher. "What has common taters to do with the Gospel?" The preacher had alluded to some commentators, the odd sound of which tickled her ear and wakened her. "Common taters!" she continued; "well, all sorts of taters are bad enough, and many of 'em are rotten clean through; and if he is calling his hearers such names, heaven knows where he'll stop. Common taters, indeed! I'll send him a peck of uncommon ones to-morrow, and show him that all of 'em an't alike." She left the house with a very indefinite idea of what he meant, but determined to set him right on the potato question.

HOME MUSIC.

Music, in the concert-room, in the theatre, in the church, is very excellent. In loving oneness with it, the spirit is lifted up and made better through its influence. But it is at home that the influence of music exerts its greatest power, where from lips that we love come the sounds of song in home strains, that fill the house with celestial harmonies. When the day's endeavor is over, and the mind, harassed with care, seeks the relief of home; then, when, in slippers, we dissolve connection with the world for a time, and shut it out with the closing shutters, and we longing pray for the nepenthe that shall lull us into forgetfulness, for a brief season at least, of perplexing and vexatious business, steals in upon us the voice of wife or child in some sonnet of domestic tenderness, and we melt to tears, as its mellifluous note trembles upon the sensitive ear like the song the angels sing. Blessed exorcist of blue demons is this domestic song. How they vanish in the clouds that leave the brow and the heart! The room is redolent with the frankincense of cheerfulness thrown abroad from melodious censers by the invisible agencies, who surround us with constant surprises of good, and love to abide with us when we open our hearts to them.

"But when the heart is full of din,
And doubt beside the portal waits,
They can but listen at the gates,
And hear the household jar within."

Enchanting power of domestic song! Greatest and best of instrumentalities! The magnificence and stately grandeur of genius may sound on loftier strings, but in the littleness of song, the sweet wood-notes of home delight, the heart finds its truest solace, and asks for nothing more.

HARVEST HYMN.

God of the harvest! unto Thee
With grateful sense we bend the knee,
While to thy throne our thanks arise,
The full heart's earnest sacrifice.

God of the Seasons! God our trust!
Thy loving kindness from the dust
Has quickened with a living birth
The flower and fruitage of the earth.

Thy care has sent the sun and rain
To ope the bud and swell the grain;
Thy lavish hand has filled our store,
Till with thy gifts it runneth o'er.

O, may our hearts, dear Father, be
A field devoted more to thee,
Wherein may never dare intrude
That poisonous weed — ingratitude!

The seasons, as they come and go,
Thy constant love and goodness show!
O, may they, like the sun and showers,
Call forth our souls' divinest powers!

MRS. PARTINGTON ON HORTICULTURE

"So you take an interest in the science of the soil?" said the neighbor, leaning over the gate, as he saw Mrs. Partington with a bran-new garden-trowel, she had bought of Curtis, hovering over some plants that she was endeavoring to "set." She arose from the dust of the earth, as though so great a question should be answered perpendicularly, and, wiping her hands on her apron, said, smilingly as an open dandelion-blossom, "Some." — "You have many fine varieties, I see," continued the neighbor; "they display excellent taste." — "They smell better than they taste," replied she. "Some helly-o-tripes, over there, are very odious." — "Many fuchsias?" asked the neighbor. — "Some confusion," replied she; "but as soon as the borders are deranged I think it will be very ambiguous. I do love to see things growing! I think that is the beauty of a garden, don't you?" The neighbor assured her that he thought very much as she did, and deemed a garden that had nothing growing in it must be a very dreary place. "A perfect desert of Sarah," said the dame, breaking in like a sunbeam on a fog. — "Are your plants not too near together?" the neighbor asked. — "O, no," she replied; "they are more sociable when they are near together, and there 's no room wasted. It is very pleasant to have grounds of one's own to cultivate; and, if the cats don't tear it up, my garden will bloom by and by like a Paradox." She struck the trowel in an upright position, like a note of admiration, as she concluded, and the neighbor went along. The cats trouble the old lady's gardening operations, though Ike has bought more than four quarts of torpedoes tc throw out at them.

A BIT OF NONSENSE

THE sun was brightly shining down,
  And there I saw him stand;
Upon his brow a darkling frown,
  A lantern in his hand.
Anon he moved along the track,
  And every face did scan;
I thought the cynic had come back
  To find an honest man.

"Ha ! old Diogenes," cried I,
  "This light your search bespeaks;
But is it here as vain to try
  As 'mong the ancient Greeks?
Is honesty a thing as rare
  As when in Athens' street
You first began your lamp to bear
  The precious gem to meet?"

He turned about and grimly stood,
  And held his lamp to me;
I marvelled at his surly mood,
  Such impudence to see.
Said he, "Old chap, you 've quite mistook,—
  I an't the one you s'pose;
I 'm he who has to overlook
  The gas-pipes when they 're froze.

"But this I 'll tell you while I can,
  That you may heed as true:
Whene'er I want an honest man,
  I shall not trouble you."
I marvelled more such words to get
  From that disgusting clown,
And took my tables in a pet,
  And wrote the rascal down.

CHARACTER.

How many gleams of character a man gives, without saying a word, by outward involuntary indications! The vane does not show which way the wind blows with more certainty than do the little idosyncrasies of exterior habit denote the quality of the interior man. It was the remark of some one that a man of sense could not lay down his hat in coming into a room, or take it up in going out, without discovering himself by some peculiarity of the motion. You may dress a boor up in purple and fine linen, but the boor will reveal itself. So will the gentleman, even through rags. He need not speak to do this. The Lord Duberlys will declare by their acts the primitive shopman, even though their tongues be tied by never so many conventional prescriptions. A gentleman moves invariably as to the manner born, which education may scarcely impart. He holds his title direct from the hand of Nature, and finds a living voucher for it in the educated character, which combines urbanity, dignity, good sense, and kindness, irrespective of dollar consciousness.

SELF-RESPECT.

Self-respect is an excellent thing, but, like many other excellent things, it is susceptible of being overdone. It sometimes takes the form of a disease, and runs to self-inflation, on the one hand; or, if poor, to self-immolation on the altar of pride. People have starved to death rather than confess to being poor; and very often, if we could lift the veil from many homes, we should find bitter distress that friendship and love would have been glad to relieve, had not pride shut friendship and love out of its confidence. Minds so affected call for pity. Beneath the exterior of cheerfulness, and prosperity, and hope, the darkest despair is lurking. The heart hardens in the aching of ever-present misery, and feeds on its silent bitterness. Such pride, were it rational, would be the height of wickedness and folly. Of what use are friendship and love unless they can be appealed to for sympathy and aid in the dark hour! In them, if rightly regarded, are deposits which may be drawn upon, and will not be refused, when the trial comes. This is the case if we are true to the principles of friendship and love, and from a just appreciation make our deposit, so to speak, in the proper institution, as we would make a money deposit. The right to receive aid where the one asking it has ever been ready and willing to be drawn upon at sight, is no more a compromise of pride than would be the asking for one's own that had been loaned.

LOVE.

Love is divine, — unselfish, asking naught,
  But winning it by the attractive force
Of generous trust and sweet unfearing, fraught
  With the grace of tenderness to mark its course
Harshness and doubt cannot abide with love.
  Doubt is from selfishness, and that can ne'er
Yoke with the sentiment that from above
  Was sent, which Scripture sayeth casts out fear.
Love has no limit, — 't is the God in man,
  Broad, universal, deep, and evermore
The same, as when the stars their song began
  Of sweet accord, when Time creation bore.
O, could we feel *what* Love is, passion free,
Then God the good, indeed, with us would thronéd be!

FRENCHMAN'S LANE.*

'T WAS a brave old spot, and deep was the shade
By the fast-locked boughs of the elm-trees made,
Where the sun scarce looked with his fiery eye,
As he coursed through the burning summer sky,
Where breezes e'er fanned the heat-flushed cheek, —
Old Frenchman's Lane, up by Islington Creek.

Most lovely the spot, yet dark was the tale
That made the red lips of boyhood pale,
Of the Frenchman's doom, and the bitter strife,
Of the blood-stained sward, and the gleaming knife,
Of the gory rock set the wrong to speak,
In Frenchman's Lane, up by Islington Creek.

But the grass sprung green where the Frenchman fell,
And the elder-blossoms were sweet as well,
And the pears grew ripe on the branches high,
And the bright birds sang in the elm-trees nigh,
And the squirrels played at their hide and seek
In Frenchman's Lane, up by Islington Creek.

The blessèd shade on the green sward lay,
And quiet and peace reigned there all day;
The fledglings were safe in the tall elm tops,
More safe than the pear-trees' luscious crops;
For the pears were sweet, and virtue weak,
In Frenchman's Lane, up by Islington Creek.

But at times when the night hung heavily there,
And a spirit of mystery filled the air,
When the whispering leaves faint murmur made,
Like children at night when sore afraid,
Came fancied sounds like a distant shriek
In Frenchman's Lane, up by Islington Creek.

And gleaming white at times was seen
A figure, the gloomy trees between,

* Frenchman's Lane was the scene of a fearful murder, where a sailor belonging to the French fleet that lay at Portsmouth, N. H., nearly a century ago, was found with his throat cut. Hence its name, and the mystery connected with it.

And fancy gave it the Frenchman's shape,
All ghastly and drear, with wounds agape!
But fancy played us many a freak
In Frenchman's Lane, up by Islington Creek:

For lovers' vows those dark shades heard,
Their sighs the slumbering night-air stirred,
And the gleaming muslin's hue, I ween,
Was the ghostly glimpse, the limbs between'
There was arm in arm and cheek by cheek
In Frenchman's Lane, up by Islington Creek.

Ah, blissful days! how fleet ye flew,
Ere from life exhaled its morning dew,
When children's voices sweet echoes woke,
That often the brooding stillness broke,
As the meadow strawberry's bed they 'd seek,
Through Frenchman's Lane, up by Islington Creek.

Those days have long been distant days,
Recalled in memory's flickering rays,
And the boys are men, with hearts grown cold
In the world whose sun is a sun of gold,
And their voice no more in music will speak
In Frenchman's Lane, up by Islington Creek.

And Frenchman's Lane has passed away:
No more on its sward do the shadows play;
The pear-trees old from the scene have passed,
And the blood-marked stone aside is cast,
And the engine's whistle is heard to shriek
In Frenchman's Lane, up by Islington Creek.

But, true to ourselves, we shall ever retain
A love for the green old Frenchman's Lane,
And its romance, its terror, its birds and bloom,
Its pears and the elderblow's perfume, —
And a tear at times may moisten the cheek
For Frenchman's Lane, up by Islington Creek.

THE FIRST SUIT.

Not at law, good friends.—We mean the boy's first suit of clothes, as he emerges from the semi-fix of boyhood into the realization of frock-coat, vest, pants, and boots, and walks out among men, a *man*, in his own opinion. Indeed, it might not be safe for one to insinuate that he was any longer a boy; and even parental rule is materially restricted, in view of the consequence assumed with the clothes. What an air of exaltation marks his steps as he moves along! and he looks at everybody that passes as if expecting to hear some remarks about his improved appearance; for, of course, he thinks they are all looking at him. He will not exactly cut his former acquaintances, who remain in jackets, but he will let them know their places. There is an impassable gulf of broadcloth now between them, and theirs is but a satinet condition, that can properly claim no sympathy with his. He looks at the young ladies now patronizingly, and has a half-idea of regret at the killing nature of his attractions, wondering which of the number he shall select as his particular flame. His habits change. He talks now in a different key, and his childish treble is no longer discernible. He thrusts his hands into his pockets, and fingers his keys in a maturity of style that receives universal admiration. He speaks of his father as "the governor," of his mother as "the old lady," of his grown-up sisters as "the girls;" and of his brothers, two or three years younger than himself, as "the small fry," telling Tommy, with considerable authority, to black his boots for him, and Mary Jane to adjust his neck-tie. He soon learns to say "us men" with the greatest freedom. Such are the first steps in progressive manhood, too often marred by rowdyism in the secondary stages, where impudence is mistaken for smartness.

MORAL TENDENCY.

"WHERE is your little boy tending?" asked the good man, as he was inquiring of Mrs. Partington with regard to the proclivities of Ike, who had a hard name in the neighborhood. He meant the direction for good or ill that the boy was taking. "Well," said the old lady, "he is n't tending anywhere yet. I thought some of putting him into a wholesome store; but some says the ringtail is the most beneficious, though he is n't old enough yet to go into a store." — "I meant *morally* tending," said her visitor, solemnly, straightening himself up like an axe-handle. — "Yes," said she, a little confusedly, as though she did n't fully understand, but did n't wish to insult him by saying she did n't; "yes, I should hope he'd tend morally, though there's a great difference in shopkeepers, and the moral tenderness in some seems a good deal less than in others, and in others a good deal more. A shopkeeper is one that you should put confidence into; but I've always noticed sometimes that the smilingest of them is the deceivingest. One told me, the other day, that a calico would wash like a piece of white; and it did just like it, for all the color washed out of it." — "Good-morning, ma'am," said her visitor, and stalked out, with a long string attached to his heel by a piece of gum that had somehow got upon the floor beneath his feet.

SYMPATHY WITH RASCALS.

BYRON says, "a fellow-feeling makes us wondrous kind," and we sometimes are half inclined to accept this as the reason for a latent and deep-seated sympathy we entertain for rascals. The confession causes us no shame, as we think, if there is one class of men more than another that needs sympathy, it is these. The principal reason for this is that they receive none. The rascal — the legitimately-recognized and found-out rascal — stands alone, comparatively. A woman or two, in the form of mother, wife, or sister, may cling to the rascal, and love him better that he is debased, and follow him to the scaffold, may be, but beyond this he is alone. Rascals have no sympathy with each other beyond a mere sense of mutual danger, and the master of them all leaves them in the lurch just as they most need his help. The antecedents of rascals are to be looked at, and herein is much cause for sympathy They were, perhaps, born rascals by psychological entailment, and could n't help it any more than they could help being squint-eyed or club-footed; or, perhaps, by wrong influences, — insidious and hard to be resisted, — the best qualities of their minds became perverted, and were led to run in the wrong channel. From the very earliest indications of his rascally proclivities, every hand is raised against the rascal, and society "puts into every honest hand a whip to lash the rascal naked through the world." The law is against him, and his life is literally fenced with constables' poles and policemen's batons. His only teacher is his fear, and his only preacher the criminal judge. Of course, this sympathy only extends to the detected rascals. There are many great rascals who never get found out. These

"Non entendez," said he again, still smiling at her, and turning away at the crank.
"Not in ten days," she mused. P. 69.

only should be detested, — the devourers of widows' houses, the disturbers of the poor, the extortioners, the slanderers, — but not one spark of sympathy should be extended to them. It is to the wicked, hunted, benighted, fated, tempted, and fallen man that the sympathy belongs, who has such odds against him, — who, with Ishmaelitish instinct, has his hand raised against every other man, seeing in all his enemies. How far he is from happiness! How much need he has of sympathy! We do not love the rascality the rascal commits, — that is ever to be deprecated, — and its hideous character is another call upon our sympathy for the rascal who is impelled by the insidious whisper of the devil to commit it, and to be committed for it. Verily, the way of the transgressor is hard, and sympathy with him is called for in the same degree that his lot is hard.

ORGANIC.

"Will you please to play Apollyon crossing the Alps?" said Mrs. Partington, reaching out of her chamber window, as an organ-man was turning his crank with a persistent arm beneath. — "Non entendez," said he, looking up, and smiling at her. — "Can't you play it in less than ten days?" replied she, in an elevated key. — "Non entendez," said he again, still smiling at her, and turning away at the crank. — "Not in ten days," she mused; "I suppose he means it will take more than ten days to learn it so as to play it exceptionably." She gave Ike a five-cent piece to carry down to him.

SCRATCHING FOR A LIVING.

Mr. Nighthewind is a utilitarian. Everything around nim has to scratch, as he expresses it. He had to scratch, he says, to get along, and he means that everything else shall, that he controls. Mr. Bounderby was not more exultant or boastful of his beginning than was Nighthewind of his scratching. A morning caller found Mr. N. out in the yard in his dressing-gown, busily engaged with his hens, chasing them from corner to corner, and acting by them in a very mysterious manner. "What are you doing?" said his visitor, thinking him a little mad. — "Doing?" said he; "why, these hens" — shying a stick at a big rooster — "won't scratch, as I had to; and I'm determined they shall scratch for a living. They are so pampered with luxurious feed that they don't seem disposed to scratch. Shoo! you rascals! why don't you scratch?" and Mr. Nighthewind went again into the energetic demonstration; but so obstinate are hens that they did n't seem to profit by it.

ODORLESS ROSES.

A rose of rarest beauty met my view,
  Half in the verdant dewy foliage lying;
I strove to reach it, but too high it grew,
  And the fair flower escaped my earnest trying.
At last, a ladder gained, I plucked the prize,
  And deemed myself well paid for toil expended;
Alas! I found it only pleased the eyes, —
  No fragrant odor with its beauty blended!
And then this moral crossed my vision's disc:
  That there are human roses brightly blooming,
For which men neck and peace together risk,
  But find when gained, no gentle heart-perfuming, —
No breathing sweets amid the flower they've won,
And feel the sense of being severely "done."

THE PRITCHARD HEIRS.

CHAPTER I.

THE venerable Pritchard, for a thousand years, more or less, head of the firm of Pritchard, Smead, & Raikes, merchants, had finished his business on a pleasant Saturday evening, in the summer before the beginning of the present century, and retired to his old homestead, which he had occupied for a great number of years, and which, like himself, was apparently strong and good for many years to come. He had lived so long in this house that it seemed as if he were a part of it, and was in complete sympathy with its brick and mortar components, though to all else it was a stupid old pile enough, — a ghostly and ghoulish thing, — that the timid heard strange sounds issue from, and hastened by with all celerity. It was brimful of odd closets and odd traps, the uses of which had outlived their generation; and it was said that a secret communication existed inside, with underground passages, conducting to the garden behind the house, and that the house had, in its day, served as the head-quarters of an expert smuggler, who drove a lucrative business through the medium of the viaduct aforesaid; though this was merely a supposition, as, when the old house was pulled down, to make way for a new block of granite stores, no trace of the secret passage was to be found.

Mr. Pritchard entered his house, swinging the heavy oaken door to behind him, which awakened dull echoes through the ancient fabric, hung his three-cornered hat on a peg in the entry, and deposited his cane in its accustomed corner. After which, he turned the brass knob of the old parlor-door, and entered, his feet making scarcely any sound upon the sand-strewn floor. He seated himself in his arm-chair, to which he had been long accustomed, and, laying back, seemed deep in thought.

Mr. Pritchard had been what the world understands by the term, a good man. He had been as honest as circumstances would permit; had never been detected in any flagrant violation of law or equity; his word had long been law among the merchants of his day, and, at the close of a long mercantile career, marked by some shrewd speculations, including the purchase and sale of a large amount of continental money, he was said to be worth several hundred thousand dollars. He had not wasted his substance in riotous living, nor in extensive charities, though he gave freely at times to objects connected with public benefit; and when collections were taken in the church where he attended, the return of the contribution-box from over the door of the faded blue-lined wall-pew where he sat disclosed always a bill lovingly hovering over the heads of the coppers that lay at the bottom of it, the admiration of all who saw it. Some said he was pharisaical about this; but we know there are envious and slanderous people in the world, and the very best of us are liable to feel the force of their malignant and depreciating remarks. With our statement of Mr. Pritchard's position and acts, we leave him in the hands of the reader. He has gone, long ago, with his faults and his virtues, and the opinion of men cannot affect him one way or the other.

He had been several years a widower, his wife having died in giving birth to his youngest child, who, at the time of which we write, was about twelve years old, a fair and sensitive boy, with a heart full of loving feeling for every one, but especially for his father, who was very dear to him, and who bestowed upon this, his youngest born, as much love as a man absorbed by business and the world can feel. The boy resembled his mother, and in the old man's tender moments the thoughts of her would stream down into his heart with a touching influence, and invest her child with new claims to his regard.

It was in one of these moods that Mr. Pritchard made a will. He had drawn it up himself, and had it witnessed by two men of substance, one of whom had died, and had placed it away carefully, in a nook which he knew, where it was to rest until called for, at his death. There was nothing unusual in this mode of proceeding; but those who witnessed his signature — those to whom he necessarily confided the secret of his making the instrument — had not the most remote idea of the character of its provisions, or who were to be benefited thereby. But the angel that prompted the will, and was looking over his shoulder when he wrote it, one dark night, saw the pleased smile that mantled his face as he recorded the name of his youngest son, Henry — named for himself.

The two other boys, James and Thomas, were of a different character from the youngest. James, the oldest, possessed all his father's shrewdness and much of his own, and he early showed a disposition to pursue a course likely to make him a leading mind in the community. He was ambitious and persistent, and not too regardful of the rights of others; a disposition that had revealed itself in many acts of youthful littleness towards his companions and playmates, which now, at twenty-one, gave him the reputation of being the sharpest young man in town. He had been with his father since he had left school, and had become conversant with all the modes of making money then existing. His only affection for any one was through their money, and his father formed no exception to the rule. The second boy was a dreamer, and exhibited no business proclivities: better content with a book and quiet, at sixteen, than with all that the mart could afford, obtained through strife and endeavor.

The only one of his sons to whom Mr. Pritchard made any mention concerning a will was to his youngest, as he stood by his knee the morning after.

"How shall I name you in my will?" said the old man to him, patting him upon his head. "Shall I leave you enough, so that when I die you will be rich, and never have to work any, and will have plenty of servants, and coaches, and pretty things, as you wish for them?"

The boy looked up in his father's face, and his eyes filled with tears, as he said he would rather work and forego all that had been named, so that his father might live; and the old man let the will remain where he had placed it, and never referred to it again.

We left him in his arm-chair, with the house hushed and still; and he was sitting with his head laid back, deeply thinking, perhaps, of past times, and perhaps, thinking of the future, towards which he was hastening. His two boys were at school, his eldest son at the store, and the housekeeper, who had filled that position for many years, was in her chamber, in a remote part of the old pile. Was Mr. Pritchard asleep, that he sat there so still? It was unusual for him to sleep thus; but the weather was warm, and the cool air blew in from the garden, freighted with the odor of flowers, and imparted somniferous influences. He slept well after the fatigues of the day, and his breathing was so gentle that the ear was pained by the effort to catch the tone of its rise and fall. His eyes were open, as if the outward senses were still awake, though his weary spirit was steeped in forgetfulness. Still he sat there in the venerable chair, saved from other generations, and moved not, though hour after hour crept by, and the stroke of the old clock on the stairs proclaimed the passing time. It was a waste of time for Mr. Pritchard to sit thus, when there were many papers to adjust before bed-time, and a letter upon the table, involving a sale of many goods, must be answered before the morning mail.

"Father!" cried a joyful voice, breaking the silence, "Father!"

Mr. Pritchard moved not, though the voice was one that he loved to hear when awake. How soundly he slept, not to hear it!

"Father!" and Henry Pritchard, awed by the silence, moved towards his father's chair, and placed his hand upon the arm that lay extended upon the velvet covering. A moment more, and his cries rang through the house, and "Father is dead!" reverberated through the still rooms like a voice in a tomb. Mr. Pritchard slept the long sleep of death!

There was a great parade at the funeral. The bells were tolled, and the flags upon the shipping were hoisted at half-staff, and a long train of respectable mourners followed the remains to their last resting-place. A funeral sermon was preached upon the virtues of the deceased, and the papers of the day were full of eulogies upon the great man fallen in Israel, and elegiac poets sang his praises in the most approved verse. His death pointed a moral for many discourses for a long time, and was used beneficially to illustrate the fact that the rich and the great must die as well as the poor; and a superb monument was erected to his memory, bearing upon its tablet the inscription, "An honest man 's the noblest work of God." Mr. Pritchard slept.

CHAPTER II.

"It was always a mystery to me what Pritchard did with that will," said a corpulent old gentleman, with very white hair and a very red face, to another old gentleman, with whom he was conversing. "He made a will, I know, because I 've got a memorandum of having witnessed it a year before he died. Let 's see, that would make it more than thirty-five years ago. How time does fly away! Pritchard was a very careful man, and that the will was n't found seems very strange."

"Perhaps he destroyed it," said the other old gentleman. "Some folks don't like to think of dying, and after they have made their wills they destroy 'em. They 're kind o' superstitional like."

"Well, Pritchard was n't one of that sort. He knowed he 'd have to die; and he was a very careful man. I do wish it had been found. I guess that oldest son of his would n't have fared so much better than the rest."

"I guess not," said his shadow; "and how he 's managed to get it all into his own hands, away from Thomas, who is worth forty of him as a man, is more than I can tell."

"Why, 't is the same old story," says the red-faced man; "Thomas must foolishly go to speculating, and ruin himself in that way; and then his *kind* brother relieved him by paying half of what his share of the patrimony is worth. It 's plain enough. Then his younger brother, that he had sent off in one of his ships, dies in the Indies, and he steps in for the whole of his share on a pretended will from Henry. He must be dead; for he has n't been heard of for more 'n thirty years now."

"Hush!" said the other; "here he comes in his coach, with his wife and daughters, as proud as peacocks."

The coach rolled by them as he spoke, and James Pritchard bowed coldly to the old friends of his father, who returned it for the father's sake, but not for his own.

"I han't got no patience with that fellow!" says the one whom the red-faced man had been speaking to, striking his cane on the ground. "He was the last, I know, in his father's regard, and is now enjoying all his money. It 'll make the old man unhappy in his grave, if he knows anything about it."

"I guess he does n't care about it," said the red-faced man; "where he 's gone our exchange is n't negotiable; but sometimes, as I pass the old house, there, that 's been shut up so long, I almost expect to see the old man step out of the door. I wonder why James does n't tear it down."

"He dare not do it, it is thought," replied his companion; "for they say that the housekeeper, before she died, hinted to him that when he pulled down the old house, he would fall with it. It has doubled in value since Pritchard died."

"Good-by," said the red-faced man. — "Good-by," responded his friend; and they separated, rattling the bricks with their canes as they moved away.

It was at the close of the day on which the above conversation occurred that the family of James Pritchard were seated in his magnificent drawing-room, supplied with every luxury that wealth and art could produce. The feet sunk in carpets wrought on foreign looms, luxurious couches wooed repose, heavy curtains gave a grandeur to the apartment, exquisite pictures graced the walls, costly candelabras glittered upon the marble mantelpieces, and large mirrors multiplied on every hand the splendors collected there.

"James, who were those gross-looking people who bowed to us as we were riding, this afternoon?" said Mrs. Pritchard, as her husband sat, with a half-abstracted air, reading the paper.

"Old Varney and Slade," was his reply, somewhat abruptly, and a little harsh, "old friends of my father's."

"Well, what claims have they upon *your* attention, if they were only *his* friends? I think their presumption in speaking to you unbearable. You should respect your daughters' feelings, Mr. Pritchard, if you have no regard for your wife's, and not encourage any such familiarity. Poor things!"

"One was such a horrid fat man!" said the youngest daughter, raising her jewelled hands.

"And the other was so terribly gaunt!" said the elder, with a tone of horror.

"Why, really, ladies," said Mr. Pritchard, with a chagrin that he vainly strove to conceal, "you treat my father's old friends with considerable freedom. They are very respectable citizens, and, besides, they are very necessary people to me — or those whose good-will I would fain secure, though I half suspect, from their coldness, that I have n't got it."

"Very well," said his wife; "I suppose it will always be the case that a woman is to have no voice in determining who her husband is to be intimate with, though she herself must be circumspect in *her* acquaintance. At any rate, the mother of your daughters will try to retrieve what their father loses."

His brow contracted, and his heart prompted a bitter reply, — no unusual thing in that household, — when the door-bell rang, and Mr. Varney was announced. With a half-imprecation, he ordered the servant to admit him; and, as the haughty wife and daughters swept in stately pride from the room, our fat old friend of the afternoon's conversation entered.

Mr. Pritchard welcomed him with a shake of the hand, marked by assumed heartiness, and conducted him to a seat, at the same time taking his hat from his hand. But Mr. Varney held to this most tenaciously, for he was a humble man, and it rather took him aback to witness the splendors which he saw around him.

"Thank'ee — thank'ee!" said the old man; "your father, Mr. Pritchard, was a very polite man — very. I never went into the old house in my life that he did n't order up the best his cellar had in it, to drink General Washington's health."

Mr. Pritchard rang the bell. The servant appearing he was ordered to bring a bottle of the best wine from the cellar, and glasses.

"I did n't speak on that account," said Mr. Varney; "but it sounds so like your father! and, as I 've been walking pretty brisk, I will try a thimble-full."

The wine being brought, Mr. Varney imbibed rather

more than his stipulated amount, and, placing his glass upon the salver, he said,

"I 've come up, Mr. Pritchard, in this odd way, not exactly on my own account. You see, about an hour or so ago, I was sitting on the corner opposite, where your father's old house is standing, when a stranger came along, who stopped and looked at the old building, and asked me who it belonged to. He seemed mightily taken with it, and went over and tried the door, as if he wanted to go in. I told him who it belonged to now, and who used to own it.—Lord bless your father! I can see him just as plain as if it were yesterday!"

Mr. Pritchard looked over his shoulder, with a troubled expression, as if he expected to see some sight which he did n't want to, and said,

"Well, Mr. Varney, this man?"

"So I told him," continued Mr. Varney, who was warmed up by his wine, "all that I knew about the family, and about your father's making a will, and about my witnessing it, and about how it never was found, and much of the same sort, when he asked me if I did n't think you would sell the old house. I told him he had better come over here and inquire: but he asked me to come, as I was somewhat acquainted with the family; and so I 've come."

"Very well, Mr. Varney, you have done your errand very handsomely," said Mr. Pritchard. "You may tell the one who sent you that the old place is not to be sold; and I may as well say to yourself that a repetition of your visit on the same errand would be very disagreeable to me."

The old man had poured some wine from the bottle, preparatory to taking another "thimble-full;" but, as

Mr. Pritchard finished speaking, he placed it upon the salver untasted, and, taking his hat, turned to go. He was politely bowed to the door, and left the house with a figurative brushing of the dust from his feet as he departed.

"I could n't have drank it; it would have choked me," said he, the thought of the sparkling fluid dancing through his mind, as if to tempt him into a regret for his self-denial.

Soon after his departure, the house of James Pritchard was illuminated with a blaze of light, and merry sounds of music and the laughter of glad voices came from the open windows. It was a reception night, and fashionable forms moved here and there amid the splendors revealed without. Poor people went by on the other side, and looked up wistfully; but there was no atmosphere there, they knew, wherein the virtue of charity could grow, and they passed on.

A different scene was enacting, at the same moment, in an obscure part of the town, at the home of the other of the Pritchard heirs.

Thomas Pritchard sat in his little parlor alone. He was a man apparently fifty years old, and his iron-gray hair denoted that care had not passed over him lightly. There was a gentle expression upon his face, and an eye indicative of great kindness; but there prevailed at the same time an expression of indecision and of shrinking back in his manner, as if from extreme sensitiveness. His bearing was that of the gentleman, and his kind voice had a sympathetic and loving tone that bespoke a heart attuned to rightful feelings. He was a fine-looking man, intellectually, and his countenance altogether was prepossessing in the extreme. Such was Thomas Pritchard. His home exhibited none of the extravagance of wealth, as seen at his brother's; but, though humble, an air of neatness prevailed on every side, and competency was evident throughout. A neat and somewhat extensive library occupied one side of the small parlor, a piano found a place upon the other side, some beautiful pictures in water-colors graced the wall, and a portrait of old Mr. Pritchard smiled down from above the mantelpiece. A fine taste was perceptible in the arrangement of a vase of flowers upon the table, and a stranger might guess that the hand of woman had given the touch that lent such an air of neat cheerfulness to the scene. Mr. Pritchard had been a widower for several years. He had had a number of children, but they had died, one by one, and none remained of his family but one young boy, and an adopted daughter, whose education he had mainly attended to himself. Her works graced the walls, and her fingers could awaken sweet tones from the instrument which held its place in the room. He had adopted her at a time when, involved in troubles, he had scarce a hope of being able to give her a support; and it was a source of joy to him, ever after, that he had done so. He had cultivated her mind himself, and trained it in a manner to repay him ten-fold for the care bestowed; and now that his days were weary with the thoughts of those he had lost, her voice broke through the gloom to cheer him, and her hand ministered to his comfort, as though hers was the reflected love of that which had fled, returned from the brighter sphere to soften the sorrow of this.

As we have said, he sat alone. The shadows had fallen gradually around him, and he was scarcely sensible of the darkness, when the door opened, and a beautiful girl entered, clothed in white, and bearing a light. The sudden glare startled him, and he shaded his eyes with his hand.

"Madeline," he said, "this gloom is more in keeping with my present feelings than the light. Carry it away, my dear child, and come to me."

She obeyed him, and, returning to where he sat, threw her arms around his neck and kissed him, with all of a daughter's tenderness. Laying her head upon his breast, she looked up into his face as though earnestly endeavoring to pierce the gloom resting there, and devise some means for its banishment.

"Father," said she, in a sweet voice, sinking to her knee by his side, "shall I sing for you? My voice, you say, soothes you when your spirit is troubled."

"No, my child," replied he, placing his hand tenderly upon her head; "this is a time when I would not have my thoughts interrupted, even though they are very sorrowful ones. Your voice is very sweet to me, my child, always. This is the anniversary of my father's death, and the thought comes to me of the strange fate that has attended his sons — that — "

He ceased; and the whole tide of feeling for the wrong done him by his brother, and his own humble condition, rushed through his mind, but found no expression. He would not wound the gentle ears inclined towards him with the bitterness swelling up in his own heart, and he pursued the theme no further.

"This home is too poor for you, my sweet girl," said he, kissing her forehead. "A refinement that would grace a palace should not be hid in obscurity like this."

"Dear father," cried she, starting to her feet, "you, who have given me this refinement, know that its first desire is to minister to your pleasure. What other companions do I want than yourself and my dear brother and the circle that I call friends? What more of gratification do I want than my music and my painting? I desire nothing, but to make you happy."

The fond girl threw herself into his arms as she spoke, and the father and daughter momentarily forgot their sorrows in a loving embrace. They were disturbed by a voice at their side, which called out,

"Hallo! what courting 's going on here? Who 's this? You, Pritchard? Ah, yes, and here 's my little pet, Miss Madeline. Bless you, my darling! That 's right, love your father."

This was all spoken in the hearty tones of our old fat friend Varney, who caught Madeline, as she extricated herself from her father's arms, into his own, and kissed her voluminously before she escaped from the room,—vanishing like a spirit through an opposite door.

Mr. Varney chuckled as she disappeared, and then, with a renewal of his hearty tone, said,

"Mr. Pritchard, I ask your pardon, but I 've brought a gentleman here, who wants to make some inquiries about the old estate yonder,—if you know anything about its being sold—if it 's ever going to be."

"We will have a light," said Mr. Pritchard, rising.

"No," said another voice beside Mr. Varney's, "no light is necessary. I merely wished to make inquiry concerning the property, as I am pleased with its situation, and would like to purchase it for building purposes."

"I have no longer any interest in it," said Mr. Pritchard, with strong emotion: "my *brother* has got it all now (there was a strong emphasis on the word brother), and he will not sell. He believes the downfall of his fortune depends upon that of the old house, and he dare not do it."

"Has he no other brother?" asked the stranger.

"No," replied Mr. Pritchard; "he never had but one, beside myself—a little brother, who died abroad. He was too good, and too frail, for a hard world like this."

"Well, sir," said the stranger, "having ascertained concerning the property, I will now take my leave. Good-night, sir."

He passed out as he spoke, but Mr. Varney remained behind a moment, just to say that the stranger seemed as rich as a Jew, and that he did n't, for the life of him, know who he was.

CHAPTER III.

TOWARD the close of the day after the one we have described, a pedestrian, dusty and weary, walked up the broad street that led by the stately mansion of the oldest of the Pritchard heirs. He appeared to be upwards of forty years of age, stooped in his gate like one prematurely old, and was evidently a stranger, for he gazed at the lofty dwelling of James Pritchard long and earnestly, as if admiring the beauty of its architecture.

"Whose residence is this?" he asked of one who was passing at that time.

"Pritchard's," was the reply.

"Pritchard's?" reëchoed the stranger; "the name is not familiar to me. Is he a native of this place?"

"Yes," said the man, "he is one of the sons of old Pritchard, the merchant, that died here many years ago, and he has contrived to get all the old man's property into his hands. Got a brother over here, humble enough." And he passed on.

The stranger stood looking at the house, when a gay

party came tripping down the steps, consisting of the two daughters of James Pritchard, and a young and fashionably-dressed man, whose likeness to the sisters was sufficient evidence of his relationship. It was their brother, a petted and only son, the heir to the name and fortune of James Pritchard. As they passed the stranger, the youngest of the sisters whispered to her brother,

"O, Richard, what a horrid-looking creature! What can he be staring at our house for?"

"I can't say," replied the young man. — "Look here, old fellow," said he, addressing the stranger, "what concern have you about the house, yonder, that you stare at it so? Do you think of a midnight visit to it, and a robbery of plate? The young ladies don't like your looks, and you had better move on."

"Don't be so severe, Richard," said the young lady; "he may come and murder us in our beds."

The stranger made no reply, but looked upon the party with a strong glance of contempt as they moved away, and then mounted the steps that led to the elegant mansion. He rang the bell with a feeble pull, which was speedily answered by a servant in livery, who stared upon him with a supercilious expression, and then demanded why he had not gone round to the back door.

"Because I want to see your master," said the stranger, with a weak voice.

"Well," replied the domestic, "go round to the back door, and I will call him."

The stranger walked slowly round the house, looking up at the windows, as he went along the gravelled walks, that made his weary steps more slow and painful. Reaching the door designated, he sat down upon the step to await the approach of the proprietor of the mansion. At last the servant appeared, and requested the stranger to walk into the library. Mr. James Pritchard was sitting at his table writing, as the man entered.

"Is this Mr. Pritchard?" he asked.

"It is," was the reply.

"You had a brother Henry, sir?" continued the stranger.

"I had," replied Mr. Pritchard, with a sudden flush upon his face. "Why do you ask?"

"Because, sir, I knew your brother in India, and was with him in his last moments. He enjoined a promise upon me, if ever I came to his native place, to call upon his brothers, assuring me of a warm welcome. It is many years ago, but I have not forgotten the promise. Fortune has gone rather hard with me since, and I am induced to ask your aid for my old friend's sake."

"Indeed, my brother's friend, you have a strong memory, to retain the matter so long."

"I never can forget him; he was so generous. I remember that he left his share of his father's patrimony to your brother."

"There your memory fails you," said Mr. Pritchard, with irony in his tone, rising at the same time, and going to his secretary. "This, perhaps, may refresh your memory," unfolding a paper, "if you are the one you represent yourself to be. The property is willed to me."

And there, in unmistakable tracery, was the name of James Pritchard as the legatee of Henry Pritchard. The stranger grew pale with emotion as he looked upon the paper, while the legatee watched his face with sharp inspection. Resuming his composure, he said, with a sigh,

"True, true, time plays sad freaks with our memory; but is the other brother of my friend—is *your* brother alive?"

"Yes, he lives," said Mr. Pritchard, with embarrassment; "but an estrangement has grown up between us. Family difficulties have led to non-intercourse, and we rarely meet. But our conversation is growing irksome, and, as I have pressing business, you will please excuse me if I bid you good-evening. Take this for your needs, and, as a reminder of painful things is what I cannot bear, owing to a too sensitive nature, I beg you will not call again."

He placed a five-dollar bill in his visitor's hand, and, calling a servant, directed him to show the stranger to the door. The bill was quietly laid upon the corner of the table, and an expression of pain was visible upon the man's face as he left the door of the inhospitable mansion. On leaving the house, he strolled pensively along, apparently unheeding as to where he was walking, when he entered the street where the old Pritchard house stood in its decay, with its low-browed windows, its heavy cornices, and its immense stacks of chimneys. The stranger paused a moment to look at it, and moved away in deep thought. He turned a corner at the end of the street, and, in a moment more, was at the house of Thomas Pritchard. Knocking at the door, it was opened to him by the charming Madeline, who ushered him into the parlor, as he expressed the wish to see Mr. Pritchard, who was not in, but was momently expected. The stranger's humble and weary appearance won her sympathy, and her kind voice bade him be seated till her father's return. She arranged for him the softest seat, and showed such a solicitude to please him that he was profuse in thanks for her kindness. At length Mr. Pritchard returned, and was informed that the stranger awaited him. Entering the parlor, he courteously saluted him, when, rising to his feet, the stranger stood in the broad light that broke in a flood from the west, and held out his hand. Mr. Pritchard took it, and, looking full in his face, with a disturbed air, asked him who he was.

"Thomas Pritchard, don't you know me?" was the reply.

The voice was a voice from the dead, — the voice broke the gloom that hung over a remembrance of thirty years, — the voice was a renewal of fraternal joy in his breast,— and, with a cry of "Henry, my brother!" he held the stranger to his heart.

The sound had attracted the fair Madeline and her brother Henry into the room, who were made partakers in the joy of the reünion. The mystery was explained. He had been very ill in India, and, in the belief that he was about to die, had made a will bequeathing his portion of his father's estate to his brother Thomas, whose name, as he had just seen, had been erased, and that of his elder brother substituted. The vessel to which he was attached had sailed, leaving him, as it was supposed, to die. Reviving soon afterwards, a rich native of the country, attracted by his friendless condition, had taken him to his own home, where he had been cared for with the greatest tenderness, and his life saved by the most unremitting attention. He at last so ingratiated himself that the old man adopted him as his son, he taking the name of his new father. His remembrance of home, at first vivid and mingled with regretful feelings at leaving the spot he loved so well, became dimmed by the lengthening absence. Communication between the portion of the country where he was and his own land was rare, and at last indifference gained complete mastery over him, and he had devoted his energies to business. He had married young. His wife and family were living, and had come with him to the adjoining town, where he had stopped on account of cheapness of accommodation; for "you must judge, my brother," said he, pointing with a melancholy smile to his faded garments, "that I am not quite equal to our aristocratic brother, with whom I had an interview this morning."

His kind brother assured him that he was most welcome to such as he had, and asked a description of that interview, which was given him. Thomas Pritchard heard it with a downcast face, and when he raised it there was a cloud upon it; but no word escaped him of censure for one who had done him such wrong.

"And now that I have come to life again," said Henry Pritchard, in a lively tone, "I shall be the executor of my own will, and adjust the slight mistake of a name that has somehow occurred."

"Not for the world," said his brother; "let him have it all, as he has got all the rest. I wish not to contend with him for it."

"Well, then, for the present let it remain as it is," said Henry; "and for the present let me remain the stranger that I was an hour since, for a purpose of my own. I will be your guest for a day or two."

Madeline busied herself in preparing the evening meal, and the Pritchard heirs spent a long hour at the board, talking of old times and scenes, and the thousand things that come up to interest those who have been long separated.

"And now, Thomas," said Henry Pritchard, "I want to get peimission to visit the old house again. There is a strange feeling in my mind with regard to it. I am not superstitious; but, if ever a man was visited by a denizen of the other world, our father has paid me a visit. He came in a dream, and I thought he revealed the old room to me where he died. Doing so, he seemed to point to a closet which I do not remember to have existed, but without a word of explanation he disappeared. Three times the vision appeared to me, and there was a troubled appearance upon the face that disturbed me. It revived the interest in my home, and the new desire that brought me here. How is this entrance to be gained?"

"Our neighbor, Mr. Varney, will get permission for me," said his brother, "and you can accompany me."

Mr. Varney was sent for, and our old fat friend came soon after, waddling into the room. He started as he saw the stranger with Mr. Pritchard, who placed his fingers on his lips in token of silence. The desire to visit the old house was stated, and Mr. Varney undertook to procure the necessary leave in the name of Thomas Pritchard. This he succeeded in doing the next morning, and the three proceeded together to the old pile, that had been deserted for many years.

The massive oaken door grated harshly on its hinges as the brothers entered, and their footfalls and subdued voices wakened strange echoes through the rooms. It was with deep emotion they entered the room where their father had died. Several articles yet remained of what then filled it, and for a short time the main object of visiting the place was forgotten in the tender reminiscences of the past that were awakened. An exclamation from Henry Pritchard at last attracted attention, and, pointing to a panel in the wainscot, he said, in a whisper,

"The very spot the ghost revealed to me!"

An examination showed that the panel was a secret door, secured to the floor by small hinges, and at the top by a spring, which was hid in the deep moulding. The rust of years prevented an immediate removal of the panel, but after some little exertion it was done, when a large amount of old papers was found, and in a case by itself a paper, labelled "THE LAST WILL AND TESTAMENT OF HENRY PRITCHARD."

As the paper was unrolled, the eye of Mr. Varney fell upon the names of those who had witnessed the will, and he shouted out, in a tone that made the old house ring again,

"Found, at last!—found, at last! I told 'em there was a will. Found, at last! 'Witness, Simon Varney,' as plain as your hand."

The will was written in a clear and distinct manner, and the tenor of it was, that the eldest son, James, having been fitted for business, should enjoy his position in the firm of Pritchard, Smead, & Raikes, and that the property should be equally divided between the brothers, Thomas and Henry Pritchard. The instrument abounded with kind expressions for his children. It was thought advisable to return the papers to their hiding-place, and the panel was restored as before. No sooner was this done than the door opened, and James Pritchard entered. His brow was dark as night, and the expression of his face cruelly forbidding, as he looked upon the assembled group in the little low parlor. He took no notice of his brother Thomas, but, turning to the stranger, whom he recognized as his visitor of the day previous, he demanded, in an imperious tone,

" By what right, sir, do you enter here without my permission ? "

" By permission of Mr. Pritchard, sir," was the stranger's reply, in a humble tone.

" And by what right has he permitted you ? " cried the imperious man, with increasing violence.

" By my right as one of my father's heirs," said Thomas Pritchard, in a voice firm and distinct, as though the occasion had given him new powers.

" Then leave, all of you," said he ; " for the house is mine."

" James Pritchard," said Thomas, with a firmness of tone that was unusual, " you are yourself an intruder here, and remain but by our sufferance. Our father made a will, deeding his property to myself and our youngest brother. That brother lives."

James Pritchard laughed scornfully, and his laugh sounded fearfully in the old house.

" It is too late a day," said he, " for such an assertion, and assertion is not proof."

He stamped his foot as he spoke, and the panel, but feebly secured, fell with a loud sound at his feet, revealing the secret closet.

" Our father speaks to you, James Pritchard, from the tomb," said Thomas Pritchard, holding the will towards him, " and affirms my truth ; and here, by your side, is one from the grave to claim his right. It is our brother Henry."

The color fled from the haughty man's cheeks, as though a ghost had, indeed, risen and was standing before him. He clutched at the air, as if to seize something with which to support himself, and gazed upon the stranger with an eye in which hatred and fear seemed combined.

"I deny his identity!" at length he found voice to say. "I deny his identity, — he is an impostor! I have twenty witnesses of my brother's death. Your credulity has been deceived. The will is a fabrication."

"I was one of the witnesses, myself," said Mr. Varney, as though this were the greatest event in his life; "no cheat, sir! See there, 'Witness, Simon Varney.'"

James Pritchard left the house, saying, as he left,

"I deny the will, and deny the scheme trumped up by a fool and an impostor to deprive me of my right."

The younger brothers held a brief conference as to what course to pursue. To establish their claim would require money, of which they had apparently none at command, while the one who was to contest it with them had abundant means. In this strait they appealed to Mr. Varney, who, after revolving the matter for some time, gave it as his opinion that the one who had proposed to buy the property the day or two before would advance money to aid their cause, through hope of obtaining it. He said this with a significant glance at Henry Pritchard, who nodded in reply; and Mr. Varney was left to consult with the stranger, when he should see him. The next morning Mr. Varney informed the brothers that the stranger would advance them money to any amount, through him, though desirous of remaining unknown in the matter. This seemed to remove one difficulty from the path, and, having retained eminent counsel, the cause was submitted entirely to his hands. The town became interested in the affair, and public opinion divided upon the question, a large party siding with James Pritchard; but the will was too well authenticated to admit of doubt, although the second brother had long since sold his right in the property unconditionally to the elder, which shut him out from his interest in the will, and the denial of the identity of the younger seemed hard to prove, which rendered the case apparently a safe one for the possessor of the property. But there were those engaged in the cause, backed by the wealth which came from the invisible friend of the Pritchard heirs, who met the fierce contestant of their father's will with a powerful force. Evidence was introduced to prove the death of the young Pritchard in India, — the one who had brought the will, — and the probability of his decease argued from after circumstances. On the other side, the cause was left to the evidence of personal resemblance to the deceased, attested by old people who remembered the elder Pritchard, and by the memory of his brother Thomas. After great difficulty and the occupancy of months of time, the case was decided in favor of the Pritchard heirs. This decision was made at the close of a fine day, and Thomas Pritchard, sad at his success, went home with a clouded brow and a weary heart. Henry Pritchard had gone to inform his family of the result.

Since his return he had acted very mysteriously with regard to his family. To the repeated invitations to bring them to his brother's house, he had invariably replied that they were very well where they were, and from his evasion it had appeared that he was desirous they should remain in present obscurity.

Thomas Pritchard was received by his children with affectionate regard, and they learned from his lips the intelligence of his success. He sat down in his armchair, and leaned his head upon his hand, with the air of a man who had been defeated. A knock at the door aroused him, and in a moment more James Pritchard stood before him. His surprise was great. Neither spoke for a minute; at last, motioning to a chair, Thomas Pritchard asked his visitor to be seated.

"Not," said he, in a manner far different from that which he usually employed, "till I am assured, by my brother's forgiveness of unbrotherly wrong, that I am welcome. Thomas, we have long been estranged. I have deeply wronged you; and during this vexed trial I have thought of that wrong. My father's spirit has struggled with me, and my stubborn heart has yielded. I had, before the decision, resolved to make reparation, and have now come to express that determination, and to beg your forgiveness, and that of my disowned younger brother."

Thomas Pritchard had risen to his feet as his brother was speaking, and before he had concluded he had grasped the hand held towards him, and pressed it to his heart with a fervent embrace.

"And you have my most hearty forgiveness, James," he cried, shaking the hand warmly. "This moment is worth more to me than all the wealth of India. I have never been estranged from you; my feelings have been true to you, with a conviction that you would some day come back to brotherly allegiance. James, you are welcome. I wish Henry were here to share my joy."

The door opened as he spoke, and Henry Pritchard entered, accompanied by Mr. Varney, whose delight in the success of the heirs was great, in the importance that the witnessing of the will had given him. A blank expression fell on his jolly features, as he saw in whose presence he stood, while Henry Pritchard, with no further notice than a glance, passed to the other side of the room. James Pritchard left the spot where he was standing, and crossed over gently to where his younger brother was gazing upon the picture of his father upon the wall.

"Henry Pritchard," he said, laying his finger upon his brother's shoulder, "your elder brother asks your forgiveness. He disowned you from a mistaken belief, and is willing to repair, as far as possible, the injury he has done, by restoring, without further contest, the property he has held so long, — unjustly, dishonestly held."

Henry Pritchard turned and looked upon his brother's face. Its expression assured him, and, seizing his hand, he shook it warmly. It was enough. The Pritchard brothers were at peace!

Mr. Varney coughed and fidgeted to attract attention; at last, when wearied with trying, he spoke, —

"I 've come for you to go with me and see the benefactor who has befriended you, in his own house. He 's sent his coach for you."

The heirs at once obeyed the summons, and invited their elder brother to accompany them, which he assented to, and, getting into the coach together, they drove away. Through the main street of the town they passed, towards the suburbs, and, after riding about ten miles, they arrived at a splendid mansion-house, embowered in trees, and everything about it denoting affluence and taste. The coach stopped, and the party alighted. They were met at the door by a lady of about forty years of age, in whose complexion the effect of an ardent sun was visible, who, in elegant terms, bade them welcome, ushering them into a parlor, richly but neatly furnished. She told them her hus-

ard stood before them, and was introduced to the astounded brothers as "General de Main," the proprietor of the mansion in which they then were. They had not missed him from their side, and the surprise was complete. He smiled at the puzzled expression they wore, while Mr. Varney chuckled and rubbed his hands gleefully, as if the matter was nothing new to him, and he was aching to tell all he knew about it.

"I am here," said their host, "in four capacities: as the East Indian General de Main, Henry Pritchard, the unknown benefactor of the Pritchard heirs, and your host,—in all of which I shall endeavor to do my duty; and this, my sweet wife, shall make up for my deficiencies." He touched a bell, and folding doors unclosing, disclosed a rich banquet, spread for a large party; and there assembled were the family of their host,—the oldest, a young man of about twenty-two, and four young ladies, of ages varying from sixteen to six years, —as beautiful as their mother, and as vivacious as they were beautiful. And there, among them all, to the astonishment of Thomas Pritchard, were the sweet Madeline and his son Henry, who, through the good Mr. Varney, had been brought there before them, he having transformed himself into an ancient Ariel to bring about results on which his heart was set. He looked upon the scene with tears in his eyes, and his great sides shook at the fun of the thing.

The party welcomed the guests, and James Pritchard, though his heart smote him for what he had done, experienced a pleasure he had not known for years,—the first return for sincere repentance. He was cordially welcomed by his brother, and every attention shown him that could make him at ease; and Thomas

Pritchard, in his new-found joy, made all happy by the magnetism of his presence.

"And how could you so hide yourself from us?" asked Thomas of his brother Henry.

"Through the aid of my father's old friend, Varney, whom I remembered. I sought him, and through him learned all of our family affairs, and proposed the purchase of the old house. Then I visited you in the dark, the night before I disclosed myself to you; and the idea suddenly occurred to me to preserve my incognito. My friend Varney assisted me in it all, and through his aid, in spending my money, I am located here, where I shall remain for a season."

Mr. Varney smiled blandly with new importance, and smoothed the napkin upon his lap with nervous delight.

The party sat long, and separated with the promise of renewed affection, which promise was fully redeemed. The Pritchard estate was settled; *how*, the world knew not, and Mr. Varney, who knew all about it, would n't tell; but things remained relatively with the brothers as before, with the exception that Thomas Pritchard's house was enlarged, and more beautiful pictures graced the walls, and more books swelled the library, in which he took delight; and neater and more roomy grounds appeared about the house, in which the fair face of Madeline was often seen of mornings in the summer time, bending over the blossoms less bright than the glow upon her cheek. And the blush was brighter when young Frank de Main pressed her hand and whispered into her ear tender words, not unwillingly heard. The families mingled, although the haughty wife and daughters of James Pritchard reluctantly consented to associate with those they had despised; but the General and his wealth reconciled all difficulties, and even the humble Thomas, reflecting the glitter, became a visitable brother. It was a moment of mortification when the daughters and son discovered in their India uncle the one they had feared as a robber; but they were of the class that are willing to be forgiven, and forgot it, as their uncle seemingly did.

There was a grand family party, the next year, at the house of Thomas Pritchard, on the occasion of the marriage of Frank de Main Pritchard and the charming Madeline; and the papers of the day, which we have consulted, bear testimony to the gallantry of the groom and the beauty of the bride, of which we have no doubt. The superb set of diamonds, given her by James Pritchard, was scarcely less beautiful than the costly products of the India looms with which she was presented by her husband's mother. But neither gift was so precious to her heart as was the blessing of her father, as he placed his hand upon her head and invoked upon her the richest of heaven's bounty for her dutiful regard, and kissed her brow as the amen to the prayer. The amen was echoed by Mr. Varney, who took her in his arms, and kissed her vehemently, much to the disgust of the fashionable portion of the family, who looked with aversion, as they had at a time previously, on the horrid fat man. Mr. Varney did n't know what they thought, and did n't care. He was as happy as though he had been made the possessor of all the Indies, and acted accordingly. Some thought it was the wine, in which he pledged the bride's health eleven times. The last act of folly which he committed was to punch the aristocratic James Pritchard in the ribs, in a great style of familiarity, which that gentleman overlooked in the hilarity of the occasion.

The old house was torn down, soon after, by general consent, and a fine block of stores was raised upon its site, that long was regarded an ornament to the part of the city where it was located, and even now, though some thirty years have transpired, is looked at with pride by the older merchants.

If the reader see no other moral in this story than the simple struggle for money that forms its basis, then the writer will feel that his real effort has been over looked, and that his work has been in vain. But he hopes its true meaning will have been observed, and in this hope he leaves in their hands the story of the Pritchard Heirs.

DON'T FRET.

What is the use of fretting? Better take
  Things coolly, nor allow ourselves to fume;
To growl about it cannot better make
  A thing that 's wrong, nor darkened spots illume.
We have, we know, but little time to stay,
  With everything around us to enjoy:
What sense were it to waste our time away,
  And leave the real gold for its alloy?
Fret not, O, fret not! — be a jolly soul, —
  That is to say, of course, be if you can;
Yield not yourself to anger's fierce control,
  But let good-nature's sunshine warm you, man. —
Now, may perplexing mischief haunt the life
Of that performer on that wretched fife!

THE DICKY.

VERY much of human happiness depends upon the dicky, — more, perhaps, than we are aware of, or are willing to admit. Harmony is made to respond with the vibration of its strings, and those strings draw at times closely about the heart, as well as the neck. We challenge philosophy to maintain itself against a refractory dicky-string or a treacherous button. The placidity of temper that might bear a man along above and defiant of other accidents, shakes to its centre when tested by accidents that pertain to the collar. He becomes, perforce, choleric at once. It is not every one who knows how to wear a dicky: upon some it is never becoming, sitting as ungracefully as the sides of a wheelbarrow. Such people adopt the demi-dicky, that presents the suspicion of a shirt, but gives people a strong idea that the wearer is undergoing a choking sensation. Gracefully worn, the dicky is eminently ornamental, — the mirror before us gives assurance of the fact; but such as have not been provided by Providence with necks adapted to the wearing of dickies, should never essay it, but stick to turn-over collars instead. Wyars was a melancholy instance of the folly of such ambition. His head had, for some wise purpose, been placed upon his shoulders without the intervention of a neck, and he aspired to wear a dicky! But it was the sort of ambition that o'erleaps itself, and condign punishment attended such gross infraction of the law of fitness His dicky, as if sensible of the folly of trying to be respectable, broke through all restraint; and, meet Wyars when one might, the dicky showed symptoms of eraticism: now about two points off the wind, now at right angles with the body, and one day he appeared with both points of the dicky peeping very quizzically from under the hind part of his hat, he looking for all the world like the man with the turned head. He gave it up shortly afterwards, and now wears an extended binding of his shirt for a dicky, that comes up under his jowls like a splinter for a broken leg, keeping his head in a perpetual perpendicularity, like a martinet on parade.

HEATHENISH.

Radbod, the pagan chief, had bowed his head
To teachings of the holy word, and then
He came the last grand offering to perform, —
Within the holy font to wash away
The trace of heathen sin that yet remained.
He turned him to the priest: "Pray tell me true,
O, man of God, where are my fathers now,
Where are my kindred, and the loving ones
Snatched from my bosom by remorseless death?"
One foot immersed, he stood the fate to hear
Of those whose memory still was priceless held.
"Alas, my son, they lift their eyes in realms
Where unbelievers shall forever dwell!"
Then Radbod said, as proudly he looked up,
His dark eye flashing with the loving light
That burned within, an ever-constant flame,
"Where'er my kindred bide, there too will I, —
Whether within the blest abode of those
Redeemed and singing their celestial joy,
Or where the darkness is forever felt
In depths of an unutterable woe.
As God loves me, so do I love my race."
No more; he straightway from the font withdrew
His dripping foot, nor could entreaty move
His faithful soul to forfeiture of love
And union with his kindred in the land
Where soul meets soul, — and so the heathen died.

BRINGING UP CHILDREN.

WITH regard to the management of children, said the philosopher, a few wholesome rules may not be amiss. As Solomon said, "spare the rod and spoil the child," it is your duty, at the outset, to impress upon the mind of your child the idea that force alone is to be your measure of family discipline; but, as it may be troublesome and require time to apply the switch, the next best thing is *tongue.* The tongue is easily applied, takes little time, and is very salutary. As soon as your children are up in the morning, or get into the house from school, begin to find fault with them, and blame them about their looks, gait, and behavior. Speak to them tartly, if you want them to mind you; there is nothing like a good sharp parental voice in making a child start quickly. It would be unbecoming weakness to ask them to do what you wish, and a tone of displeased authority is very efficacious in inspiring feelings of respect. If they do not start quickly, — particularly if a boy has his boot half on, or a girl her head half combed, — threaten them with dismemberment, decapitation, or any other equally trifling penalty, if they do not jump, and the willing haste they will show in minding will astonish you. If children are teasing round you from hunger or whim, yell at them lustily, and threaten them with whipping. No matter whether you execute the threat or not, — persevere in threatening, and after a while they may be led to believe you will do it. It may take some time, but stick to it. It will not do to gratify any little desire of theirs at once; it will look too much like bending from parental dignity. It is best always to refuse them at first, and work their feelings to turbulence, and then to comply; this will give them a sense of their dependence, and your self an opportunity of throwing oil upon the troubled waters. It is a fine experiment, when well managed; and it is, besides, a practical application of the text, "through much tribulation," &c. If one of your children cry, through the teasing propensity of another, first look round, as if searching for something to throw at the head of the culprit, then, with an angry eye, dart upon and give him or her a rap. It will be remembered, you may depend. Don't waste time in counsel. This would derogate from the parental authority. If your children are noisy, it is an ingenious expedient to feign extreme distress, and threaten to go away or jump overboard; by appealing to their affections thus for a few times, they will get so as to believe it. If this fail, go up stairs, or anywhere in the cold, under pretence that your head is "splitting open" from their noise. If a child is disposed to sing, check it at once; it is a boisterous practice, and should be discouraged. As if heaven had not given it more use for its lungs than a bird! It is a good way to cry out "Stop that noise!" It prevents the formation, by the child, of a too exalted opinion of its own vocal ability. The same rule may apply, if the child is disposed to dance. What can be more ungainly than a little child capering about a room, with no more consideration than a lamb? If a child is disposed to be affectionate, don't return it; remember that we should not love the creature more than the Creator. Don't show that you love it too well; it is best to repel petulantly all little acts of endearment; to encourage a child in kissing is apt to lead to bad results. If your children make mistakes, and are not ready to learn, it is a beneficial plan to rail at them for their stupidity, and present a microscopic view of their failings; this latter, particularly, if a neighbor or play mate chance to be present. Disparaging comparisons are very apt to encourage them to persevere. Be careful and do not praise them for good qualities they may possess; this would tend to make them vain, and vanity is sin. Having yourself arrived at what you know by intuition, or divine inspiration, of course it is of no use to instruct your children how to do anything. Let them find out as you did. You will get along a great deal better in your management if you have some grandparent or maiden-aunt to assist, especially if they take views opposite to yourself in everything. The balance is thus beautifully preserved. A good grumbler is invaluable among a family of children; the grumbler will prevent their dying from a surfeit of jollity. Depend upon it, said the philosopher, the advice I have given, if it be rightly understood and rightly applied, may be made profitable. The interests of time and eternity depend upon judicious family training; and yet how few there are who know how to bring up children in the way they should go! Almost all read the Solomonian injunction, "Train up a child and away he 'll go," — and they go it.

UNMET CONFIDENCE.

MUCH of the evil of life springs from hiding ourselves from each other; and that we do hide ourselves is the result of a want of confidence in each other, that would allow us to give and receive with kindness. We dare not tell one of his faults, though they may be very apparent, because we fear to offend him. He sets us down as his enemy, at once, when we wound his self-esteem by intimating that he is not infallible. So when others are spoken of in whom we have interest. An intimation of their possible imperfection excites us against the one breathing the suspicion. We know the charges are wrong; we feel that we cannot have been mistaken in the individuals who so much engross our esteem, and hence we cast off those who, by the very act of daring to incur our displeasure, have proved themselves our best friends, and the most worthy of our friendship. The charges may be false, groundless, but they should be made, in orker to be met and refuted, and the motive of their being submitted canvassed, and its sincerity established. In domestic matters the want of this confidence is severely felt. The tart and scornful reply to a confided thing checks future candor in that direction. No man, if he have any spirit, will incur the danger of getting snubbed twice in the same way. Hence when, after many days, scandal bears tales to ears that should have heard them long ago, tears and bitterness make a dismal episode in life, that never would have occurred if those who weep had known the secret of securing their own happiness. An ingenuous spirit should be met with equal openness and candor. To cramp such a spirit, and still its warmth by reproach, or innuendo, or indifference, is a fatal mistake, and lays the foundation for a healthy growth of misery in the time to come, when love and confidence are most needed. Men speak in very severe terms, and justly, of deserted homes and domestic wrong; but, could they become acquainted with the facts that led to such desertion and such wrong, they would find, maybe, that their sympathies are due in a different direction from that in which they have been solicited. This is a lesson which will admit of much thought, and, as the old gentleman remarked when he laced the boy's shoulders with an ox-goad, we hope it will do good.

THE DEAD SAILOR.

His sails are furled, his voyage is done, —
  Now may the gallant sailor rest;
The peaceful port his bark has won,
  No hostile storms shall more molest;
Life's boisterous course he has bravely run, —
  Lay him away, with his worth confest.

Ay, throw above him the starry pall
  He loved so well in his hours of life;
He has seen its gossamer shadow fall
  Where the spirits of ocean waged their strife,
Has waved its folds round earth's huge ball,
  His soul with its sovereign glories rife.

'T is a fitting shroud, and he loved it well,
  But his beaming eye is glazed and cold
And his manly heart will never swell
  To see it in starry pride unfold;
Yet place it there, — its stars may tell
  The shining deeds of the sailor bold.

It may tell the tale of a generous heart,
  That never refused a friend's appeal;
It may tell of tears that dared to start
  From founts that pity bade unseal;
It may tell of a bolder, a sterner part,
  Where duty claimed his nerves of steel.

All, all alone! not a kinsman near
  To see the earth receive its own;
No gallant messmate by his bier,
  To mark his frail wreck where 't is thrown;
The winds sing o'er him an anthem drear,
  And the heavens their tears outpour alone.

But naught he cares: nor rain, nor cold,
  Nor ill of earth, doth the body know;
His spirit eyes on scenes unfold
  Surpassing all he has known below;
Around and above him are joys untold,
  He ne'er would exchange for mortal woe.

Then lay his hulk where the bright flowers bloom,
When the bitter winter storms are fled,
Where the apple-blossoms shall give perfume,
And the grass its emerald beauties spread,
Where the stars he loved shall ever illume
With gentle rays his lowly bed,
And birds all the summer long shall come
And sing o'er the sailor dead.

THE COOLIES.

"WELL, what if they did?" said Mrs. Partington, as the visitor was condemning certain parties for the transportation of coolies. She glanced at the thermometer, as she spoke, with the mercury indicating ninety degrees, at the same time inhaling a pinch of Col. Rhoades' rappee. "I think they ought to be praised," continued she, "for trying to get a little coolly anywhere, such times as these. How hot it is, to be sure! It is almost equal to the horrid zone;" and the old lady fanned herself energetically. — "But," said her friend, "I mean the coolies, brought from the East." — "Well," responded the dame, "it does seem like an interference with the plans of Providence to bring them here; but when the wind sticks at the south all the time, they should n't be blamed for trying to get the east winds to cool the people off with, anyhow." Her friend looked at her with compassionate benignity, but attempted no further explanation, while Ike sat endeavoring to make the sundered parts of the old lady's cooler stick together, as he had seen Signor Blitz do.

10

TALKING HORSE.

It is very amusing, during a trotting season, to observe the horse-bent of conversation at the grounds, and outside, among those, small and large, who are interested in horses. It seems as if every man was thinking horse, and by sympathy had become half horse. Indeed, one might be excused for watching the mouths of those speaking with the expectation of having them neigh like horses, as those who come from sections where lobsters are caught become so imbued with lobster as to partake of the peculiarities of that excellent fish. Passing round from group to group, it appears like hearkening to the same conversation, divided into sections. In each section the same matters are discussed: horse genealogy, horse manners, horse points, horse riding, and horse raising — the latter so frequently that a general equine resurrection seems the main point of horse belief. One would think, at such times, that there was no other animal in the world than the horse, and that the whole of human progression, with its weight of moral and social interests, was to be helped along on horseback, or upon a spider-web vehicle, weighing but about seventy-five pounds. A man who cannot talk horse, then and there, is floored — is nowhere — is obsolete — is done up. Though he should speak with the tongues of angels and of men and have no knowledge of horse, he is as nothing. The merest tyro of the curry-comb turns up his nose at him. It is well to affect horse, at such times, though one may not know the mane from the tail, or the snaffle from the side-saddle. Some pursue this course, and win a great reputation by listening and looking. Looking at a horse appreciatingly and admiringly is about half equal to speaking about him, and some have by this course been able to pass as respectably under the eyes of the initiate as though they were born and educated in a stable.

PICTURES.

We don't care whether pictures abound in a house from pride, fashion, or taste, so that they be there. If there is insensibility in the proprietor, he may be the means of gratifying taste in others, or of awakening a taste where it was lying inactive before. It is more delightful, of course, where good taste prompts their supply; then the pleasure of the exhibitor is added to the gazer, be he never so humble, and the two realize a better brotherhood, — not before recognized, perhaps, — in the broad avenue of natural taste. How cheerful the walls of a home look with them; and, by the rule of opposites, how cheerless without them! It is a garden without flowers, a family without children. Let an observing man enter a house, and ten times in ten he can decide the character of the proprietor. If he is a mean man, there will be no pictures; if rich and ostentatious, they will be gairish and costly, brought from over the water, with expensive frames, and mated with mathematical exactness; if a man of taste, the quality is observable, and, whatever their number or arrangement, regard has evidently been had to the beauty of subject and fitness, with just attention to light and position. In humble homes, when this taste exists, it still reveals itself, though cheaply, but the quick eye detects it and respects it. We have seen it in a prison, where a judicious placing of a wood-cut or a common lithograph has given almost cheerfulness to the stone walls on which it hung.

THE OCEAN.

Thou art jolly in thy mood, O, playful giant,
  Hurling us here and yon, despite our will,
To all entreaties deaf — to all defiant —
  Holding no moment, at our bidding, still.
The poets praise thee — those upon some mountain,
  From which their optics thy bright face can see,
Dipping their cups in the Castalian fountain,
  Pouring libations soft in praise of thee.
O, treacherous sea! how sweet thou look'st but now,
  And smooth, as is the cheek of maiden fair; —
There are ten thousand wrinkles on thy brow,
  And anger's fury in thy hoary hair.
Let poets sing of thee — 't is my conviction
They 'd sing another tune, if 'neath thy jurisdiction!

FATALITY.

"Did you ever notice," said Dr. Spooner, "the fatality that attends upon the name of Atwood? Meet with it where you will, oysters may be found connected with it as closely as barnacles to a ship's copper. It seems the most natural thing in the world. Atwood seems as much made for oysters as oysters for Atwood. I can't understand it, any more than I can spirit rapping or the aurora borealis. It is one of those mysterious phenomena of the universe that cannot be fathomed by the usual rules of interpretation. Should I go to England, I should expect to find Atwood engaged in the oyster business. Were I to go to France, I should be greatly disappointed did I not find Mons. Atwood opening the bivalves to my order. Were I to find my way to China, I should look for Atwood with a long tail to supply me with oysters! It is very strange, and I never look at the sign bearing the name without thinking of this des tiny — this *oystere* destiny, if I am allowed the privilege of indulging in a little pleasantry — that chains them to a specific calling, like old Sassafras that rolled the big rock up the mountain."—"I have myself noticed this fatality," said the imperturbable, who sat smoking in the corner, "and your remark about meeting the name in foreign parts I myself have tested. I have met it in Paris, in Amsterdam; and once, when in Cairo, Egypt, as I was taking some oysters with a friend, I had the curiosity to ask the name of the one who kept the place, with a view to establishing the fact of which we are speaking, and the name was given of ——" — "Atwood, of course," said the Doctor, breaking in. — "No, sir," replied the imperturbable, "it was Tomally, an Egyptian as black as your hat." He kept on with his smoking, while the Doctor pulled on his glove and went out, evidently troubled at the smile that greeted his discomfiture.

A SERIOUS CALL.

What of the night, O, watchman on the walls?
  Dost see the day-star through the mist arise?
Hears't thou the herald voice of God, that calls,
  Speaking as once it spoke from out the skies?
Has man aught further on his journey passed
  In the dark shadows of the dreary night?
Will his horizon long be overcast,
  And thick the veil that keeps from him the light?
What of the night, O, watchmen? See yon gleam
  Shoot upward from the darkly-curtained east!
It is the day-star's radiating beam —
  Now from its thrall will manhood be released!
What of the night? — O, why this silence deep? —
No day-star beams to them — the watchmen are asleep.

THE BARON OF BOSTON

The Baron he liveth a happy life —
  O, a happy man is he !
For his mind has no shade of care or strife,
  And its fancies are bright and free.
No acres broad doth the Baron boast,
  But his heart is rich as a king's,
And that dominion he craves the most
  Is what good fellowship brings,
      As he laughs,
      As he quaffs,
  In the light which his happiness flings.

And the bold Baron sits in a regal way —
  His retainers are friends most true,
And he rules them at will by the magical play
  Of his fancies rich and new.
His sceptre 's a Cuba, of title proud,
  Betipped with a glowing star,
And his crown is a circle of fragrant cloud,
  More graceful than jewels are,
      As he puffs,
      As he snuffs
  His odorous, sweet cigar.

No malice he bears in his genial breast,
  No bitter thoughts he knows ;
So full of his own broad friendship blest,
  No room has he for foes.
He welcomes a friend with a loving cheer,
  With the clasp of a generous hand,
No human ice in his sunshine clear
  Can ever unmelted stand ;
      And he smiles
      And beguiles
  By the heart's own kind command.

And long may the Baron his rule preserve,
  And his castle doors be stout,
With garrisoned larder and cellar to serve
  To keep the enemy out ;

And when in the evening of life the gale
  Shall bear him from Time's rough coast,
May he speed o'er the sea with a willing sail,
  To the haven desired most,
    And his elegy
    The world shall see
  Recorded in the Post.

SWEARING.

ALMOST every one accustomed to smoking, who has a proper regard for the little courtesies of life, asks, before he indulges in his propensity, if it may be offensive to any. Suppose the same question were asked with regard to swearing, by those who are disposed to indulge in the luxury of blaspheming. There are times when good taste is fearfully shocked by the introduction of words and sentiments that should not be spoken by the members of any circle; and, though not disposed to claim for ourselves a very great measure of sanctity, there are times when we have been offended — to use a very mild term for the feeling — at expressions which good manners should have suppressed, and good morals should never have allowed to enter the mind of those who uttered them. We think the time has gone by when profanity is generally regarded as an essential adjunct of wit, and that a story loses nothing of its piquancy when the profanity is left out. It is very offensive to have an obtrusive head, with an oath ever between its teeth, thrust among decent people, and it is a wonder that sensible men, themselves, who speak profanely — and there are too many such — should not see the probable disagreeable nature of it to those who hear them, and suppress it. At least, they might preface their remarks with the question, "Is swearing offensive to you?" If, as in nine cases out of ten where the same question is asked about smoking, the answer is in the negative, then the swearer can blaze away with his anathemas and imprecations till the teeth of everybody chatter to hear him. Many seem to swear unconsciously, the oaths coming in as naturally as italic words in the emphasis of conversation; and, like the boy who declared that he did n't whistle in school — that it whistled itself, they might give the same excuse for it. There is something very unsatisfactory in swearing, and after a man has indulged in his profane stories, and has made crowds laugh by them, he feels, when he gets by himself, that he has n't much to brag of, after all, and that

> "The atheist laugh 's a poor exchange
> For Deity offended."

THE PRIMA DONNA.

"Did you like her vocalization?" asked the amateur, reaching over the seat on which Mrs. Partington was sitting, as a young lady finished the singing of a favorite piece of music, in a manner that set every heart thrilling with pleasure to hear her. — "What did you say?" said she, turning partly round. — "Did you like her vocalization?" he repeated. — "Yes," replied she, with animation, beating the time on her umbrella-handle, "and I liked her singing too." She kept on, like a jolly old wheelbarrow — "Why should we send to Europe and England and France and Fiddledee for executioners of music, when we can find such voices at home by our own fireplaces? It seemed to me while she was singing that we were getting over the bars of heaven, and had come to a rest on top when she stopped. The music of the spears can't be no better. But do look at that boy! I declare I believe he will be a prodigal of musical talons, by and by, if he lives long enough." She pointed at Ike, who had secured a long-handled contribution-box out of the deacon's pew, and had transformed it into an imaginary violoncello, playing upon it with the handle of a deceased palm-leaf fan, the fragments of which strewed the floor.

MISANTHROPY.

THE picture in Bleak House, representing "the young man Guppy" in the theatre, with dishevelled hair and desperation upon his brow, after being rejected by Esther, is very ludicrous. The young man feels that fate has done him a deep wrong, and he defies fate. He challenges fate to hit him again. The milk of human kindness has dried up in him, and he is now lacteally farrow. Guppy is one of a class that we meet with almost every day, who, through large self-esteem and a sovereign belief in their own importance, become misanthropic at the first breath of ill-luck, and resolve to punish the world, that they conceive has injured them, by leaving it to its own destruction. We 'll have nothing to do with this ill-natured world, they say, which has so far lost sight of its own interests as to treat us, its brightest ornaments, so badly, and then see how it will get along! We abjure it, we leave it, we wash our hands of it. In this spite they regard the world, and bore the ears and plague the hearts of all who listen to their complaints. They see, however, the great globe spin on, to their utter disgust, and find that, after all, they are acting very foolishly; that growling does no good, and that a cheerful acquiescence in the dispensations of Providence, and humble trust, are far better than breaking one's head in futile buttings against destiny or accident. Nine times out of ten, those who growl the most against the world have most reason to growl about themselves. They make, by their own stupidity or improvidence, the fortune they deprecate, and have no more reason to quarrel about it than they would have to complain that destiny gave them a sore finger after they had put their finger in the fire. Could people who attempt the misanthrope but look at the ridiculous Mr. Guppy, it would seem that they should be cured of the disease of overvaluing themselves.

MEASURING LOVE.

"Brief, brief at best is all the love of man!
  A word, a promise in a moment broke,
  As evanescent as the wreathing smoke
That melts in air ere we its form may scan."—
Nay, loved one, nay, speak not the cruel word,
  For recently, when on the railway train,
  My fleet thoughts fleeter flew to thee again,
And love for thee my heart's emotion stirred:
More ardent grew the faster that we flew,
  And every mile the passion warmer burned,
  And every mile my heart the fonder yearned
To pour for thee its offering warm and true.
Talk of the length of love! Why, all this while
My love you might have measured by the mile.

PLEBEIAN PRETENSION.

THE doctor said it was a case of the gout — a clear case. This was surprising to everybody, and everybody smiled hugely at the idea; for beyond the most frugal limit of appetite, including occasional tea, the sufferer had not gone. There was a great flutter in the family on account of it, because a case of the gout, they deemed, brought respectability with it. Sir Leicester Dedlock, in Bleak House, had the gout, and gloried in it, because it was a disease that had been in the family for many generations, and he had it by descent. But here was a case where it had left the charmed circle of the aristocracy, and had planted itself directly upon a plebeian toe; — painfully, it is true, and the flesh cringed and groaned in the utter misery of it; but it was "respectable," and a grateful posterity, it was deemed, would look back reverently to the one who had introduced the gout into the family blood. That doctor was regarded as a marvellous man, whose science had penetrated through the rheumatic and erysipelatic indications, and had singled the gout as the actual disorder, then gnawing like a vicious devil at the mortal extremity; and it was with a thrill of pride that inquirers for the health of the sufferer were assured that the gout was the malady. Then old plates in Gentlemen's Magazines were sought, by which to define the true position for the gouty patient, — to determine whether the foot should rest at an angle of forty or sixty degrees, or on a plane with the horizon, — the difficulty being dispelled by an old habitué of the theatres, who prescribed a flowered dressing-gown, plenty of flannels, and the foot upon a common cricket, as the theatrical position, and it was forthwith adopted. The world affected to laugh about it, — it was such a glorious joke! — the world always jokes when it affects to sympathize. Here was a claim to gentility; here was an attempt to overstep, with a gouty foot, old landmarks, by one who had no legitimate right to the position, and men were alarmed; but, though they tried to sneer it down as rheumatism, and roar about it till they were red as erysipelas, the doctor, who ought to know, said it was the gout, and the sufferer, standing on his crutches, swore he would cut his toe off before he would abate one nail of his claim — that it was *so*.

THE FRANKLIN STATUE.

"Did you see the statue?" we asked of Mrs. Partington, the next day after the inaugurative procession. An expression of disappointment passed over her features, as she answered, "No, I did n't; it must have gone by when I went down stairs to get some water for the children. A three-cornered gentleman, with a cocked hat, on a cart, I took to be it; but I found out that it was one of Franklin's contemptuaries, an old printer. But the occasion was very obtrusive," continued she, brightening up like a jolly old warming-pan, "and if I did n't see the statue, somebody else did; so it 's just as well." She smiled again, and subsided into a calm, while Ike, with three chairs, and Lion harnessed to a table, filled with a clothes-basket, four chairs, and a water-bucket, was "making believe" a car in a procession on his own account. Lion did n't seem to enjoy it.

A WAY TO BE HAPPY

THE study to be happy is a momentous one, and its pursuit is one of the great rights that are laid down in our political decalogue. How to be happy is just what we all would like to know. A few suggestions on this subject may not be amiss; and if they should not be deemed exactly the thing, try the opposite course from the one recommended, and see if that will secure the desired end. Get up in the morning scolding and fretting with everything and everybody — it will be an excellent discipline for yourself, and give your family an ardent appetite for breakfast; and if the fault happen to be with your wife, make no apology — it is a lesson put in in advance, and will operate prospectively. Growl about the expense of dinner, and hint about being ruined through home extravagance; this will, of course, secure economy, and help bring about perfect peace in the household. Kick the dog, if he is in your way, and if he bite you it will afford excellent evidence that things are working. Refuse to acknowledge your neighbor's bow; he is a wretch that some one has been talking about, and hence deserves to be cut by one of your superior purity; of course, your contempt will break his heart. Complain to the widow next door that her son is a disgrace to the neighborhood, and hint to her about the Farm School and the poor-house; it will tend very much to cheer her. When you come home and find the floor scoured, plant your dirty feet upon it; the cheerful phenomena attending this experiment will be very novel. Be crabbed as a bear to employés, and find all the fault you can; nothing gives such a delicious flow to the spirit, and secures such willing service, as good wholesome censure. Always assert your own superior claim to wisdom, and prove your companions' stupidity by measuring their little corn in your big bushel; it will give them a very exalted opinion of you. If a boy come into your store to sell you anything, drive him off, and threaten to set the dog on him; it will encourage him to persevere in an honest calling. We have laid down a few propositions, which may be added-to. Should one follow these carefully, he would soon, undoubtedly, attain the ultimate of mundane bliss.

NEW ENGLAND'S LION.

A LION 's in our path, but not like him,
  In Eastern climes, the monarch of the wood,
Whose roaring echoes through the jungles dim,
  In which he lurks in sanguinary mood,
Waiting to lay his predatory paw
  Unprayerfully on what may come as prey,
And by the force of his own mighty law
  Make all pay toll who cross his royal way.
New England's lion greets us by our path,
  His bright eye, golden in its rim of green,
Flashes not on us with a glance of wrath,
  But e'er in sweet placidity is seen.
Between the lions of the East and West,
The Dandelion I proclaim the best.

UNNATURAL FATHERS.

THE conversation had somehow turned upon parents in plays who were depicted as turning their children out of doors for disobedience, and incidents were cited in actual life where the same thing had been done. These were pronounced very unnatural, and much indignation was expressed at their occurrence. One instance, in particular, was named that seemed like the recital of an old-world tale, where a tyrannical father had shut his door against his daughter for the offence of loving and marrying one obnoxious to him, and she had sickened and died with not one word of forgiveness or message of love from his cold lips, and he had denied her even the honor of a formal attendance at her funeral. "Shame! shame!" was the cry; "how unnatural!" Dr. Spooner raised his finger. The glove was off, as though he were fearful the intervention of thread would disturb the electric force of the gesture. "Not unnatural," said he; "pardon me, but to my view the conduct of such a father is the most natural thing in the world. *Why*, do you ask? Because the relation between such father and daughter is entirely natural, without one ray of spiritual light to illumine it, without one feeling of spiritual sympathy to cement it. Such fathers are the Dombeys, who are incapable of sympathetic feeling; who marry and raise families, and cultivate pride for affection, which is tested in scenes like the one named. Their marriages are conventional, and their offspring partake of the same conventionality. They are proud of their children, as they might be of their horses, and the world calls it affection; but at the first breath of opposition to their rule or inclination, from a child that dares to love, the offended pride turns the child out of doors, and has no remorseful feelings afterwards for the act. Love does not thus. It may at times storm and rave at opposition, where the hopes of a lifetime are blasted by wilfulness — inherited wilfulness, maybe — on the part of children; but where true affection is, obdurate pride, anger, frustrated intention, everything yields to its gentle pleadings, that never plead in vain. Depend upon it, there is nothing unnatural about the case you have named."

A DIFFICULTY.

"DOMESTIC difficulties," said Mrs. Partington, "comes in different guys, — some is quarrelling, some is poverty, and some is something else; but this is the greatest of 'em all." She pointed to a paper, as she spoke, which chronicled six children at a birth. "There 's difficulty," continued she; "and how the poor mother will overcome it is more than I can imagine. Only think, six mouths to feed, six dresses to wash, six heads to comb, six cases of chicken-pox to take care of, six measles to look after, six to pull out of the water, six to keep from getting run over, six to buy books for, and six to get places for when they grow up. I declare I don't see how she can ever get over it." No wonder that she saw the difficulty, when she found it so hard to manage one, who even then was trying the experiment, that he had seen Blitz perform, of balancing a plate on his finger, to fall in a moment to irremediable smash.

LOVE.

THE pulse of life is Love, — without its throb,
Men were but mere machines, and poor at that,
And all life's duties but a weary job,
Like these, my rhymes, — unprofitable, stale, and flat!
Love is born with and in us and around,
It lights our cradle with its ray serene,
It follows us in sorrow's depths profound,
It shrinks not, howsoever drear the scene;
Stronger when woe's dense cloud of trial lowers,
Its voice is heard still breathing in the gloom,
As the sweet herb of night expands its flowers,
And sheds amid the darkness its perfume!
Yet Love too oft feels not the gentle mesh
Of olden thrall, but sighs for pots of flesh.

HEIR-LOOMS.

How sacred a thing is made, by the lapse of time! A stick that one of our remote ancestors has carried in his hands may have been handed down to us; and though he is one with whom, in the world of matter, we have nothing in common that we know of, unless it be a common name, and that perhaps changed in the spelling, we are brought near to him by this simple twig — a meaningless thing in itself — to which, by some strange process, the spirit of its original owner has imparted itself. Why not? No thought is lost, and why may it not be that our venerable ancestor's thought, that prompted him to cut the twig we prize, and cherish it, and trim off the knots and make it so comely and shapely, and to guard it for many a year, may still in some way — we 'll not say how — protect it, in order that it may be a connecting thing between himself and his descendants, thus preserving a sympathetic *rapport* between the past and the present? It has always seemed to us that heir-looms were imbued with this old spirit, for this purpose. And that they have their effect is manifest in the way that they are cherished by those people who are governed by the "sentimentality" that recognizes the value of a thing above its market price, and set more by an old cocked-hat, or a pair of small-clothes, or a faded dress, than by a thousand new things, with no association, beyond the fact that they may not yet have been paid for, to commend them. What sacredness attaches to an old chair, for instance, whose arms have held many a generation that still speak to us! Our ancestors embrace us in the antique and queer frame, and we repeat the assertion of Miss Eliza Cook that "we love it." It would bring perhaps, twenty-five cents at au.tion, and everybody but ourselves would laugh at it; but every sliver of it has a value that money cannot offset. Heir-looms have good influences about them, inasmuch as they come down from good people. Things thus transmitted bear some evidence of person or deed that is pleasant — representing, in this direction, one combining many virtues, and in this some act that it makes us better to know, though generations removed from the time and scene of its occurrence. A knife or a halter would not be preserved as an heir-loom, nor the memory of crime-stained life be very particularly cherished, outside the annals of justice. So we honor our ancestors through transmitted timber, old crockery, or old pictures, or keep alive patriotic emotions by collecting canes from old Ironsides, Independence Hall, or Mount Vernon.

DON'T LOOK BACK.

How some men dwell and ponder on the past;
  Like ghosts come back 'neath glimpses of the moon
Sighing o'er hopes and joys too bright to last,
  And happiness departed all too soon!
Like owls they live, delighted with the night,
  Or brood in hollows where the sun ne'er cheers,
Shutting their eyes perversely to the light,
  That broad before them evermore appears.
O, men, throw off the sombre pall which hides
  From your soul's vision the bright land *To Bé*,
And sail on hopeful o'er the flowing tides
  That tend toward the everlasting sea!
This counsel heed: that track 's the rightest one
That brings our vessel's prow the nearest to the sun.

GOOD RESOLUTIONS.

"THIS is the season of good resolutions," said the young man, in answer to Dr. Spooner's wish for a happy new year. "Nominally," replied the Doctor; "there is something in the commencement of a new year that naturally suggests thought of habits contracted or pampered during the year that 's past, and, as we see them clinging to us like vampires, sucking the marrow from our moral or physical bones, we plant our feet with something very like resolution, and say we will turn over a new leaf. And we are honest in the determination, and mean to stick to it; but, alas! with the waning year resolution wanes, and we find that our promises, like pie-crust, are very easily broken. Like a man full of wine and meat disavowing a desire for victuals, so we, with appetites satiated, for the nonce deem that appetite is an easy thing to overcome; but we find that we cannot throw it aside with our tobacco. It becomes an importunate thing, that, like Banquo's ghost, obtrudes itself in our hours of pleasure, and everywhere. It is an ever-present thing. Memory battles with resolution, and the diseased fancy clothes the banished with a thousand fascinations, and we become its victim, till a new year brings new resolutions, to be broken again in after time. When a man leaves off a habit and resumes it again," continued the Doctor, "I am reminded of the scripture where the evil one goes out of a man and seeks rest in dry places, but, finding none, he returns to his old apartments that have been cleaned up during his absence, to follow the simplifying rule laid down by my friend Dr. Sawyer, and the latter days of that man are worse than his first. Habit and appetite once established, they are about as hard to throw off as was the little old man of the sea, who volunteered as a neck-tie for the renowned Sinbad. Stick to your resolution, my young friend, for one month, and you will deserve a medal as big as a griddle for your moral heroism." — "And did you ever find it thus hard?" the young man inquired; "did you ever have habits thus hard to overcome?" — "*Did* I?" repeated the Doctor, twitching at his gloves nervously. "Who is there that has them not? Habit takes a thousand forms, and he who rails the loudest at you for using tobacco or wine may have a habit of cormorantish appetite dragging him down in another direction." The Doctor went out, leaving the young man standing with meditation in his eye and a paper of silver-leaf tobacco in his hand, the open stove-door before him.

MRS. PARTINGTON ON MUSIC.

"MUSIC is one of the greatest attractions of home," said the teacher, leaning his left hand upon the table, and elevating his right, with the fore-finger protruding, like a lightning-rod. "The greatest attraction," he repeated, drumming upon the table with his sinister digits, as if he would enforce his remark by a practical example. — "Well," said Mrs. Partington, smoothing down a seam in some garment she was making, "I believe it is, and when our neighbor, Mr. Smooth, got his new pioneer fort for his noisy children, it seemed as if they had added forty detractions to home, for they were always quarrelling like dog's-delight to see who should play on to it. The way to make home harmonious," — and she looked up with an expression of great wisdom, as she said it, her eyes glancing through the western window at the

Old South vane, that gleamed in the sunshine, as if catching the ray of her own inspiration, — " the way to make home harmonious is to organize it — to buy a hand-organ, and hire somebody to play on to it. The noise of it would soon put a stop to all the family jars, depend upon it." She bit off the thread of her discourse and her cotton at the same time, while her listener smiled faintly, either at the misapprehension she was evidently laboring under, or at the newness of her theory with regard to the harmony of home, but made no further remark.

SACRILEGIOUS.

" SICH corruption in the church!" said Mrs. Partington, bringing her hands down severely on a paper she was reading, containing an account of an Episcopal dedication somewhere. There was instantly great attention. " I read here," continued she, " that the archbishop came in with his mitre and *stole;* and, if stealing is n't corruption, then I don't know what is." She looked round upon the circle, and there was a smile perceptible upon the faces of such as understood what she was driving at. Just as one of the party was going to explain to her that she was lying under a misapprehension, Lion rushed in with Ike on his back, and the harmony of the circle was interrupted.

AN OLD FABLE MODERNIZED.

I GLEAN this fable from jolly old Rabelais,
Who ne'er marred a story by telling it shabbily.
And I earnestly hope that my versification
Will give to its moral a plain application;
Which moral will show that by acting too speedily,
And grasping and striving for aught over greedily,
'T will end most likely in signal disaster
(Reward from the ancient particular master),
While we who are modest, and not any covetous,
Taking all quiet, as Fortune may shove it us,
Will make out better, be sure, at the last of it,
And in its enjoyment make ample repast of it:

One day, when the gods, in high debate,
Had waxed quite warm on concerns of state,
And Jupiter Tonans wiped his face,
As discussion found a resting place—
(For on the nods of the gods, you know,
Depended all matters then below,
And business of merely men or kings,
Or any other terrestrial things,
Must come before the conclave high,
Convened in chambers of the sky),—
That a fearful clamor from earth arose,
Like the accent of a thousand woes,
That broke the Thunderer's short repose.

"What are the sounds that our ears profane?
Mercury! start like a railway train;
Open the windows of heaven, and know
The cause of all this rumpus below."

Then Mercury listened with eager ear,
And smiled to himself the sound to hear,
For in truth it struck him as rather queer:

"O, Jupiter Tonans," a voice cried out,
With tone stentoriously stout,
That rung like a trumpet arraying a host—
"O, Jupiter Tonans! my axe is lost!

O, cruel fortune, thus for to bother one!
O, great Jupiter, give me another one!"

Then Jupiter winked with an ominous leer,
As he the petitioner's prayer did hear —
"Confound the fellow! what clamor he makes!
The very concave of heaven he shakes,
As if he 'd all of creation tax,
By making this muss about *his* axe!
Yet offer him one of silver or gold,
He 'd no longer clamor for this so bold.
Run, Mercury, run! or, sure as a gun,
By this chap's noise we are all undone!
Offer him axe of silver and gold,
And iron — his own choice uncontrolled —
I 'll stake my sceptre that he 'll think higher on
Either the silver or gold than the iron;
But if he choose silver or gold instead,
I say, Mercury, off with his head!"

Jupiter frowned like easterly weather,
And the gods, affrighted, huddled together,
And shook in every wing and feather!

Mercury gave one jump, and flew,
Cutting his way through the ether blue,
And quick as the lightning made his tracks,
Where the man was bellowing for his axe.
"Here 't is, old chap!" then Mercury said,
And threw before him the gold one red.
"None of your tricks," says he, right cross,
"'T is n't for this I mourn the loss."
Then Mercury threw the silver down,
Which suited still less the weeping clown;
But when the iron one met his view,
He cried, delighted, "'T is good as new."
He held its handle, and grasped it tight,
And said, "Old fellow, this ere 's all right!"
Then Mercury called him an honest soul,
Told him for this he should have the whole;
Then left all three with the happy elf,
And went right back to report himself.

Now the clod was rich, and with few words
He bought him houses, and barns, and herds.

His neighbors wondered this to see,
And sought to unravel the mystery;
Nor long did he their wondering tax,
But told the story about his axe.
Then all who had axes vowed to go
And see what luck to them would flow;
And those who had none stopped at naught,
But sold their goods and axes bought,
Then went away, resolved to lose 'em,
And make appeal to Jove's own bosom,
Convinced that he would not refuse 'em.

Their clamoring wakened all the sky,
And angry grew the Thunderer's eye, —
Who summoned Mercury to go
Upon his errand again below —
" These chaps must n't be left to pother one,
Serve them just as you did the other one;
Put the test that then you tried,
Let them for themselves decide,
Give what they ax, and let 'em slide!"

Down went Mercury on his mission
Where they noisily made petition.
The golden axe on the ground he threw.
The first one greedily at it flew,
When, swinging the steel axe in his hand,
The head of the seeker sought the sand;
And so of the whole of the clamorous crowd
Each nose like a coulter the green sward ploughed,
And from this day's ensanguined workery
Arose man's guess of the uses of mercury —
And it undoubtedly a palpable fact is,
Ten medical colleges, all in full practice,
With surgeons awaiting a chance to dissect you all,
Could n't make mercury more effectual,
Or cut men down quicker than Mercury packed his
On this first day of "legitimate" practice.

My friends, ye who read this fable so winning,
Look for the moral at the beginning —
For which, and the story, think just as you may of them,
I have nothing more at present to say of them.

ROBERT BURNS

How little we can see the end from the beginning! Burns was born in a mud cabin on the banks of the Doon, a hundred years ago, — a humble enough beginning, from which no higher future could be presumed through any entailed right,— and to-day the world unites in honoring the one who was then "the babe beneath the shieling," but whose song has since done so noble a work in humanizing man. On the centennial anniversary of the birthday of Robert Burns, wherever the English language is spoken, — and that embraces a very wide range, — men, imbued with a love of the manhood that inspired him, met to do honor to his memory. The high and the low, the learned and the unlearned, save in lessons of heart, combined in ovation to their favorite — their favorite so far as the feelings hold sway over the mere machinery of the brain, for Burns' cultivation was limited, and his song flowed, like "bonny Doon," undirected, save by the great voice of Nature that spoke to him from field and wayside, and brook and flower, and gave freshness and beauty to everything it approached.

It was necessary that he should be born poor. Like the mavis, he sprang from the dead flat of life, and rose to sing among the stars. His spirit was ever reaching far out into the spirit of the universe, and drinking in through its thousand fibres the life that filled it — that burned in his denunciation of wrong, scathed like the lightning in his satire, melted in his lays that had the human heart and the ingleside for their themes, or laughed in the songs that gushed under the inspiration of John Barleycorn. He was not divine;

that is cherished as a glorious thought — for he is made our brother through his imperfection, and men love him for his humanity. There is no writer since Shakespeare that has lived so much in the sympathies of the people as Burns, and herein is the secret of his fame; he was the poet of the common heart, which received him and prized him. He was a prophet, and, with thoughts a hundred years in advance of his time, he denounced wrong then in the ascendant, and the stigma attached to him that ever attends upon such; but the years are doing him justice. The cloud becomes light in the admitted right of his prescience, and his frailties, "where nature stepped aside," are forgotten in the simple grandeur of the truths he sung.

The following was written for the Burns centenary celebration, at the Parker House, Boston, Jan. 25th, 1859, and sung by a member of the Burns Club:

WHAT 'S A' THE STEER?

What 's a' the steer makin'? what 's a' the steer?
The PEASANT BARD first saw the light this day a hunder year;
An' a' our hearts expand blithely — a' our hearts expand
Wi' honor o' his name that 's known in every land;
  For 't was a blessed thing, surely, 't was a blessed thing,
  Sin' a' the world was better for 't when BURNS began to sing;
  Sae we 'll raise our voices high, in tones of grandest cheer,
  That ROB THE RHYMER saw the light this day a hunder year!

His fame 's brawly won, nei'bor, his fame 's brawly won,
An' a' the lan's unite to crown auld Scotia's gifted son;
They plait a laurel-wreath for him, — his weel achievit bays, —
And bring rich offerings o' mind as tributes to his praise:
  For tho' o' humble birth, nei'bor, tho' o' humble birth,
  His genius gied him station wi' gentles o' the earth;
  Sae we 're a' unco happy, and we 'll mak' a joyfu' steer,
  Sin' ROB THE POET saw the light this day a hunder year!

The humble and the high, nei'bor, the humble and the high,
Combine to glorify the bard whose sang will never die;
In every clime 't is heard wi' joy — in every gentle hame —
An' sparkling een glow doubly bright at mention o' his name.
O, he 's the puir man's friend, nei'bor! he 's the puir man's friend,
An' hoddin gray tak's honored rank, where worth its grace doth lend.
There 's a blessin' on the hour that hauds us captive here,
For Rob the Puir Man's Bard saw light this day a hunder year!

Wide is his clan spreadin' — wide is his clan:
They 're counted wheresoever men most nobly act the man;
Not where the tartans gleam, nei'bor, nor yet the bonnets blue,
But where the heart is tender, and men are leal and true.
'T is nae tie o' bluid, nei'bor, nae tie o' bluid,—
His sangs unite the nations a' in ae braid britherhood;
Sae honor crown the time, and pang it fu' o' cheer,
Sin' Burns the Ploughman Bard was born this day a hunder year!

THE KNOCKING AT THE GATE

FOUNDED UPON A REAL INCIDENT.

'T was the social hour of evening,
And the ruddy fire gleamed bright,
On the grateful tea-urn glancing,
With a fond and loving light,
When our happy circle gathered
Round about the plenteous board,
And those cheerful words were spoken
That contented hearts afford;

And the little voices blended
With the graver tones of love,
And the blest domestic picture
Forecast seemed of bliss above; —
Whilst thus at the table sitting,
Heart and eye and tongue elate,
Came a sound of some one rapping —
Rapping softly at the gate.

The bitter wind without was howling,
Rattling rude the window blind,
And the frost upon the casement
Many a witchy shape defined ;
Whilst the snow in angry swirlings
Darted by like figures white,
Phantoms seeming, adding terror
To the dreariness of night.

Maggy then her form presented,
And thus spoke she soft and mild :
"Please ye, very cold and hungry,
Stands outside a little child,
And for bread the poor thing 's asking
For the ones at home in need ;
Shall I give her, may it please ye?
It will be a Christian deed."

Then our little Mary whispered :
"Tell me, what did Maggy say?
Tell me of the little beggar,—
Tell me all about it, pray."
Then we told her all the story—
How some people wanted bread,
And the fearful, tearful struggle
Where pale famine reared its head.

And she listened when we told her
Of her own far happier state
Than that of the little beggar
Lately knocking at the gate,
Listened like a child, half heeding,
To our dismal tale of woe—
Gravely heard us to the ending,
Rocking gently to and fro.

Long she sat, and we, not noting
Talked again of this and that,
Till sweet Mary, sadly sobbing,
Waked us from our busy chat.
"What 's the matter, darling?" asked we,
And with trembling voice she said,
"I was weeping at the story
Of the child who wanted bread!"

Then our hearts were full of gladness,
  And our eyes were full of tears,
At the words our darling uttered
  In this dawning of her years;
'T was the gush of heavenly pity
  That another's woe unsealed,
And we gloried in the promise
  Its deep sympathy revealed.

MRS. PARTINGTON AND IKE.

"What is your mean temperature here, mem?" said the meteorologist, as he sat in Mrs. Partington's little shaded back parlor, on a warm day, with the cool air drawing through the windows, and rustling the cut paper around the old looking-glass frame that had hung for so long a time on the wall. — "*Mean* temperature!" exclaimed she, with a sharp emphasis on the mean; "mean temperature! we have got no mean temperature here, sir; nor mean people, neither, unless you may call Mr. Grab, the sheriff, one, who pretended he had an attachment for a man, and then went and took all his propriety on a mean process for debt. This was mean enough, goodness knows." — "I mean the temperature of the weather, I assure you," said the listener, dreading the indignation that gathered in her tone like distant thunder on the other side of a river; "I mean what is your medium heat?" — "Well," said she, "as for mediums, I don't know much about 'em, though there was a great heat about one that came here, that told people who their grandfathers was; but it cooled off, arter a while. They could n't make *me* believe that. But, goodness me, look at that boy!" She pointed to Ike as she spoke, who had donned the hat of the visitor, and was making a feint to attack the stove-pipe with his cane, having on his arm a large wash-boiler cover for a shield, and a pair of fierce moustaches painted in soot upon his upper lip. As they looked, a fierce lunge conquered the adversary, and the young hero stood triumphant, brandishing the cane in his hand, and shouting, "Down with the border ruffian!" She checked him gently, and, as her visitor regained his hat and stick, which last had been broken, she turned to him, with much satisfaction in her manner, and asked if he did n't think the boy had talents by which he might "require a reputation;" and the visitor said he certainly thought so. Ike knew what he meant, and kept a safe distance from the cane.

COLD WEATHER.

WE shiver as we feel the biting air,
And think more warmly of the ones who suffer,
Counting how much of change we have to spare
For those who wrestle with Old Frost, the buffer;—
Not he who aldermanic honors gained
By public favor in the late election,
But Jack Frost, who our comfort has profaned,
And now assails the poor, who need protection.
Depend upon 't, cold weather is the time
To set our warm heart's blood in kindness flowing,
To coin itself in many a ready dime,
And make the loan the Scripture page is showing,
For which a four-fold interest is given,
Paid at the eternal banking-house in heaven!

AN ANALOGY.

SHOWING A FANCIED RESEMBLANCE BETWEEN A LITTLE STREAM OF WATER AND A LITTLE LIFE.

A gentle rill gushed from the breast of Spring,
  And flowed in beauty through the summer-land,
Stealing along, just like some bashful thing,
  Half hidden by the boughs that o'er it spanned.

But the wild blossoms in its mirrored sheen
  Beheld themselves in all their rustic pride,
And the tall trees assumed a brighter green
  Because they stood the little rill beside.

So humble was it that the dallying grass
  Asked not the question whence the wanderer came,
And the proud lilies, as they felt it pass,
  Looked down upon the stream of modest name.

Yet tenderly the sweet rill loved the flowers,
  And the great trees that grew upon its brink;
It saved for them the bounty of the showers,
  And filled their empty cups with needed drink.

It asked for no return; unselfishly
  It moved, content that it was doing good
Delighted from its ministry to see
  The gladness of a green beatitude.

Anon a change came o'er the little stream,—
  The loving sun had claimed it for his own,
And, like some fleeting picture in a dream,
  In all its quiet beauty it had flown.

The flowers grew sickly that had erewhile dwelt
  Upon its banks in queenliness of state,
The sturdy trees its unlooked absence felt,
  The lilies withered, beautiful of late.

The grasses sighed in sallow discontent,
  And all confessed the rill a friend most true,
Contrite that its sweet life should thus be spent
  Before its loving offices they knew.

'T is thus we 've seen some gentle loving one
  Noiselessly moving through the paths of life,
Here cheering sadness with her voice's tone,
  There giving tears as mollients to strife;

Singing with bird-like sweetness on her way,
  From the outgushing of her teeming heart,
As the airs blow, or the bright waters play,
  Unknowing the blest influence they impart.

We value not the blessing by our side
  Until, down-stricken by some fatal blight,
We feel it with our joy identified,
  And mourn the star now hidden from our sight.

The noisy consequence of life may claim
  The tribute of attention at our hand,
But 't is the little acts of humble name
  That make our hearts with blessedness expand.

NAHANT.

Nahant! bold battler of the mighty sea,
  My harp would sound one note to swell thy glory
How much of health and beauty dwells in thee,
  Thou hard, solidified old promontory!
I rest me here, and feel thy breezes free
  Filling my ears with their enchanting story;
I hear the sea around me ceaselessly
  Curling about thy base its big waves hoary.
O, beautiful! I cry, delightedly,
  Here would I end my life so transitory,
Climbing the rocks in plenitude of glee,
  Or catching mackerel in a little dory.
Great is Nahant, by Neptune loved and Flora,—
Esteemed by all, beside, whose bent is piscatory

NUMBER ONE HUNDRED AND ONE.

MERELY A LOCAL ITEM.

It is a strange title to a very strange story, which, I should not be willing to swear to the correctness of, if any one but myself had told it. But here is the tale, believe it or not. I am a remarkably sensitive man, keenly alive to the beautiful in nature or art,— have in my lifetime gone miles out of my way to see a beautiful face, and a glimpse of some picturesque scene of sea or shore has driven me wild with delight. I had arrived in Boston from an old bachelor jaunt to the White Hills, solitary and alone. On such occasions I cannot bear to have any one with me. A voice disturbs me, and grates upon my nerves. I have turned almost hermit, and forsworn men, merely because a frivolous fool has cried out some commonplace exclamation upon viewing scenes that nothing but expressive silence could do justice to. An exception to this, however, must be made in favor of the militia captain on Mount Washington, who, in delight at the sublimity of the scene before him, cried, "Attention, the universe!" There must be an exception in this case, of course.

I arrived in Boston, after an absence of some years from it,—almost a stranger in it, though I remembered Faneuil Hall, and the Old South, and the Old Province House, and the Old Jail, that stood where the Courthouse was, and old "101," where I had made my home for several years, in a retired up-stairs back room, that overlooked a large garden, and commanded a fine view of the country round about. Here I returned, and, by good luck, as I thought, engaged my former apartment, which the landlady informed me could be vacated for me immediately. I did not take possession till late in the evening, and reserved my first glance for the objects of my admiration for the morning, as soon as I should rise. I went to sleep dreaming of garden walks and summer-houses, and clustering blossoms, that formed the inner side of a wide horizon of beauty, which I gazed on with uninterrupted delight, when the clatter of a milkman's quart-pot upon a gate knocked me all awake in a moment, and I was conscious that it was morning, and the sun was shining in at my window.

I immediately arose and dressed myself, when, placing my chair close to the window, I drew aside the curtain. What! the garden had disappeared, gone, and the beautiful scene which so long had gladdened me was obscured by a red, flaming brick wall, without a window in it, the back of a block of stores on another street. I reached out of the window and looked down upon a shed where I had in old times seen damsels, in the blush of youth and morning, hanging out clothes; but the shed had disappeared, and a long brick L protruded in its stead, with a glass roof, beneath which I could see workmen in their shirt-sleeves moving to and fro. I fancied, in my first disappointment, that everything which I had regarded was swept away, and, humming to myself some original lines, that just then occurred to me, beginning

> "'T was ever thus, from childhood's hour,
> I 've seen my fondest hopes decay,"

I was about closing the curtain, when I saw, through a little vista between the buildings, a beautiful view of a fair scene beyond, — clear sky, green trees, and distance, — made more beautiful from the difficulty through which it was seen. I thought I should become reconciled in a little while to the loss of the rest, could I retain this. Whenever I was in the house I took my station by my window, and enjoyed with miserly regard my *buena vista.*

But "a change came o'er the spirit of my dream." I found one day a source of extreme nervous anxiety to me right in the way of my enjoyment. Some demon, with a special disposition to torment me, had leased a room in a corner of my vista — the proscenium-box, so to speak — to an unappreciative wretch, who, with a levity that deserved the thumb-screws, had placed a large bust of Shakespeare in the window, and put thereon a red shirt and black neck-cloth, and had covered the head with an old straw hat, making the great bard of Avon look as if he had just returned from some jolly bout in the harbor, or some deer-stealing operation in the country. I shut my window in disgust. The next day I looked. The bust was still there, with the addition of a black moustache. I dropped into a seat. The third day a large green patch was placed over one eye. The fourth day a hole had been made through the lips, and Shakespeare was actually smoking a long nine! Shade of Sir Walter Raleigh! but my blood boiled at the outrage upon me and upon Shakespeare. I tried to think of some remedy for the nuisance, and went out to reconnoitre the premises. I found there was a narrow alley leading to the shed which formed the outer bound of the territory where my annoyance was placed, and that from this, with a moderately long stick, I could reach the hated object, push it from its position in the window, and dash it to pieces. My plan was formed, and that night I resolved it should be executed.

About eleven o'clock that summer night, with Tarquin's strides, and a footfall as light as a cat's, I was on my way to my revenge, armed with resolution and a long cane-pole that I had procured for the purpose. The alley-way was dark, which favored me, and I gained my destination without detection. A moment more and I stood on the shed, which commanded a view of the room in the open window of which my bane was resting. A moment more ——

It was a warm night, and, as unpropitious fortune would have it, directly below the window where the bust was resting, the cook was sitting with her lover in the dark, talking preliminary matters incident to matrimony. The oppressive heat had made them drowsy, and, leaning their heads upon the window-sill, they were both fast asleep. They had not heard my step upon the shed. Crash! Down came the bust, red shirt, hat, and all, and planted itself directly between them; and as the lover opened his eyes he was astonished to find a masculine form between him and his dear. His first impulse was carried out, to plump the figure betwixt the eyes; his next was carried out with equal promptness, to let it alone — for his knuckles were hurt. At this instant he caught a view of the outline of my retiring figure, and, bounding through the window, he darted out of the shed-door, meeting me, as I descended, with a warm embrace and an energetic exclamation, which I construed into "*Watch!*" I was much gratified, besides, to hear the windows in the vicinity open, as if a public interest were awakening. Thanks to my science, I had muscle and strength, and here was a field for their operation. I used them with a will. I punched my adversary in the dark, and he was so busy in taking care of himself that he ceased to halloo for the watch. At this moment, a blow aimed at my head by the cook, who had emerged from the shed, took effect on his, and he rolled upon the ground, defeated, while I hastened off.

In a few minutes I was in my room. I looked out, and could see lights moving in the house I had just left, as if the garrison were aroused. I went to bed happy. My object was achieved. The next morning, to enjoy my triumph, I looked towards the hated window. My crest fell immediately, for there, upon the window-frame, was the bust of Shakespeare, with the red shirt still upon it; but, instead of the old straw hat upon its head, *my own hat*, with my name in it, that, I forgot to say, I had left upon the field.

The papers, the next day, were full of it, and reference to the *Columbian Centinel* files for June, 1838, will show the following:

Daring Outrage. — Last evening a burglarious attempt was made to enter the house of Mr. T. Speed, in —— street; but the burglar threw down a bust of Shakespeare in the attempt, which attracted the attention of Mr. Muggins, passing at the time, who pursued the ruffian over a shed, and boldly attacked him in Marsh alley, when the villain drew a pistol and threatened to shoot his assailant, who persistingly stuck to him until a blow from the butt of the pistol knocked him down, and the rascal escaped, leaving his hat on the premises, in which was the name *O. Hush*. Mr. Muggins treated him very severely, and it is believed the atrocious wretch may be detected by the injury he received. The police are upon his track.

It had happened, fortunately, that I was to pay for my accommodations by the quarter. The landlady was the only one who knew my name, and her reply to the questions with regard to it having been simply "Hush," it had been deemed that she wished to keep shady about the matter, and they had hushed. The old lady did not read the papers, and I was safe from her; but I thought it advisable to leave that afternoon by stage for the mountains. Before leaving, I glanced from the window. The bust was still there, and it seemed that the features wore a malicious smile of satisfaction at my discomforture. I slammed the door to with a bang, and bade good-by to *Number One Hundred and One.*

CONTENTMENT.

There is no virtue like it under heaven,
 And he whose life is crowned with sweet content
Is rich as though old Crœsus' wealth were given,
 E'en though, in fact, he be not worth a cent.
There is no bound to man's ambitious schemes:
 His eager palm outspreads as on he goes,
Gold shimmers down through all his daily dreams,
 The verb "*to get*" the only one he knows.
How blest is he who, whate'er may betide,
 Sits smiling at the boon which fortune sends;
Who God's own finger has identified,
 And deems that all he suffers rightly tends!
And I myself am something of this stuff,
Always contented when I have enough.

THE OLD PIANO.

[The following lines are supposed to embody the feelings of one who stands amid the wreck of her ruined fortunes, and finds in the memories of the past a solace for the present. It is not altogether a fancy sketch.]

WHEN the evening falls around me,
  And my room is hushed and calm,
Come to me long-vanished pleasures, —
  Come the wormwood and the balm;
Loving faces smile upon me,
  Faces long beneath the mould,
Loving lips mine own are pressing,
  Lips that long ago grew cold.

O, the voices! how they whisper!
  And I strain my eager ear,
Not to lose a word whose meaning
  All my spirit thrills to hear;
And amid the tones they utter,
  Weaving through them like a thread,
Comes a strain of distant music,
  Echo of a strain long fled.

From amid the brooding shadows,
  And the shapes that come and go,
Hark! the old piano murmurs
  With a note I dearly know;
And my soul in transport listens
  To the keys' familiar tone,
As the shadowy fingers touch them
  With a love they erst have known.

Joyful notes of sweetest meaning
  Tinkle in my wakeful brain,
As upon the parching foliage
  Sounds the grateful summer rain;
Mournful notes of import tender
  Sighingly my heart receives,
As amid the evening breezes
  Sighs the cadence of the leaves.

'T was a phantom, — an illusion, —
  And the voices all have flown,
Leaving me here desolated,
  In my widowhood alone

But the old piano lingers,
  And about its dreamy strings
Rests the memory of fingers,
  And their pleasant utterings.

Now it takes angelic seeming,
  Calling me, with hopeful voice,
From the land where peace and gladness
  Through eternal hours rejoice;
And I feel the hand extended
  Of the loved ones gone before,
Grasping mine amid the darkness,
  With the fervency of yore.

How I love it! — like a sister,
  Ever faithful by my side,
Patient in my fallen fortunes,
  Loving in my hours of pride;
It is not to me insensate,
  And I 'm sure it feels with me,
Sorrowing in my saddened moments,
  Laughing in my hours of glee.

Blessings on thee, old piano!
  While I live we ne'er shall part,
For thy melody is woven
  With the pulses of my heart.
Years may dim my mortal vision,
  And my raven hair turn gray,
But my wasted life is blended
  With the thoughts that round thee stay.

IKE AT CHURCH.

"WHAT do you think will become of you?" said Mrs. Partington to Ike, as they were going from church. The question related to the young gentleman's conduct in the church, where he had tipped over the cricket, peeped over the gallery, attracting the attention of a boy in the pew below, by dropping a pencil tied with a string upon his head, and had drawn a hideous picture

"O, Isaac," continued she, earnestly, "what do you want to act so like the probable son, for?" P. 149.

of a dog upon the snow-white cover of the best hymn-book.—"Where do you expect to go to?" It was a question that the youngster had never before had put to him quite so closely, and he said he did n't know, but thought he 'd like to go up in a balloon.—"I 'm afeard you 'll go down, if you don't mend your ways, rather than go up. You have been acting very bad in meeting," continued she, "and I declare I could hardly keep from boxing your ears right in the midst of the lethargy. You did n't pay no interest, and I lost all the thread of the sermon, through your tricks."—"I did n't take your thread," said Ike, who thought she alluded to the string by which the pencil was lowered upon the boy; "that was a fishing-line."—"O, Isaac," continued she, earnestly, "what do you want to act so like the probable son, for? Why don't you try and be like David and Deuteronomy, that we read about, and act in a reprehensible manner?" The appeal was touching, and Ike was silent, thinking of the sling that David killed Goliath with and wondering if he could n't make one.

SOUNDS OF THE SUMMER NIGHT.

THE soft winds sigh above the slumbering flowers,
  And tremble 'mid the tresses of the trees;
A child's sharp cry disturbs the solemn hours,
  That woman's voice endeavors to appease;
A dull piano's melancholy strains
  Fall faintly on my ear, borne from afar;
A night-key's click the midnight hush profanes,
  And harshly clangs a door's discordant jar;
A dog howls dismally across the way,
  Anon darts through the air a vengeful stone;
And sounds of whispered voices hither stray,
  Revealing lovers' vows by their soft tone;
Yon cat-calls cut discretion to the quick,—
  , that kind fate would grant my hand a brick!

THE HOUSEHOLD SHADOW.

ALL felt badly when the little creature sickened. It was a fearful disease, and the burning skin and the labored breath spoke painfully of danger. The voice was hushed that uttered the word *danger*, and the heart was pained as the ear caught the fearful sound. Danger to the darling that love so clung to, and surrounded, and hemmed in! and alarm awakened more vigilance, and more loving care. But day by day revealed the inroads of the insidious disease, burning at the foundation of the precious life; and hope, that was at first strong in spite of fear, grew day by day weaker. How dear she grew! — how much dearer than when in the fulness of health and beautiful activity; when every impulse was a joyous outburst of conscious existence; when her little arms entwined in fond conjunction with loving arms, and her tender kisses were rained upon ready lips, as the sacrifice of innocent love! She seemed doubly dear; and the imploring look for aid, in paroxysms of pain, sank deep into hearts rendered sad by a sense of inability to help. At last the crisis came. The shadow deepened with every moment, and hope grew less and less; and, when the darkness that comes before the light of morning rested upon the earth, another little spirit was added to the multitude that had gone before, like fruit untimely plucked. Then was the shadow most opaque and dismal, and the household was very dreary. But anon the morning broke, and the sun came up; the gloom of night vanished from the clear heavens and the bright earth, and it was day. So with the shadow over the household. A voice came from the shadow, speaking peace to the saddened hearts. It spoke of love and trust, and gave sweet assurance that it was no tyrant's hand that had smote the household, in the wilfulness of power; but that a loving Father had lifted up the lamb from the weakness and imperfection of human trust to the eternal fold, above the storms and sorrows and sins of time; that behind the darkness of death shone the clear sun of eternal life, and that the morning would break, and the dreary shadows of the night, now obscuring its glory, would flee away; that the loved within the veil were walking beside us in our darkness, to bear us on and up, their loving hands still clasped in ours! Then the household shadow changed, and a holy light played around it; and, though it was still a shadow, and hid the loved from view, a trust born of faith said, IT IS WELL, and the stricken spirits bowed submissively to the will of Heaven.

CHARACTER.

"DEPEND upon it, madam," said the schoolmaster, "that, with a moral basis, men may risk themselves with any temptation, and come out triumphant." Mrs. Partington placed her hand gently on the cuff of his coat, and just three grains of snuff made their mark upon the broadcloth. "There's where all the deficiency is," said she. "'T is the moral baseness that does it, and temptation melts 'em as the sun does the grafting-wax, and the buds don't take root, however strongly they may seem to be set, and they find, after all, as the best of us do, that we are none too good." The schoolmaster brushed off the snuff as she removed her hand; but the lesson remained, as though her words had been India-ink, and her finger-points the needles that wrought them in enduring form upon the memory. Ike was engaged in twisting a fishing-line upon the big wheel.

A LEAF FROM A RECORD.

I STOOD on Salem's wizard hill,
  My sinking soul by terror daunted;
The summer wind blew strangely chill,
My fluttering heart would not be still,
  Upon that upper land enchanted.

I felt a Presence by my side —
  Old Roger Conant touched my shoulder:
My heart sent back its rushing tide,
As I that awful touch descried,
  And the cool breeze seemed growing colder.

Then spake the Presence — not by word,
  But by what people call impression:
My soul alone the language heard,
For Roger's lips no moment stirred
  From long accustomed grave possession

" I welcome you to this fair scene,
  Endowed with beauty, grace, and riches;
Few brighter spots than this, I ween,
You 'll find our nation's bounds between,
  Yet this was once the hold of witches.

" Around you dusky shadows glide
  Of those who made a bloody story·
Yonder is Burroughs sanctified,
With Mary Easty, grace denied,
  And here is sturdy old Giles Cory.

" And angel Martha Cory 's nigh, —
  No saint in heaven's courts is sweeter, —
With Alice Parker standing by;
And old George Jacobs here doth hie,
  With Margaret Scott and Ann Pudeater.

" The list is large, but not a whit
  Of anger now is felt among 'em;
And often round this hill they flit,
Or here upon this summit sit,
  In friendship with the ones who swung 'em.

" E'en now, my friend, while here we talk,
Witch-hangers round among us gather:
Yonder old Parson Paris stalks,
And Justice Hathorne hither walks,
Locked arm in arm with Cotton Mather.

* * * * *

" They carted them to Gallows Hill,
Without a tear, or sigh, or blessing;
And then around, as I am still,
I saw their cup of sorrow fill,
But could not change their fate distressing.

" And yonder were the locust-trees
On which were seen their bodies swinging,
While pious prayers from bended knees,
And sacrifices God to appease,
Rose from this spot, toward heaven winging.

" You know, of course, the matter dark,
For Upham 's told you all the story,
And Poole's bright muse has made its mark,
And 'lumed with wit's effulgent spark
That page inscribed with letters gory.

" But don't condemn those men severe,
Nor by your bushel their grain measure;
As honest they to me appear
As you in this enlightened year,
Who knowledge, wealth, and power, treasure.

" God's glory was their guiding aim,
Much more than yours, who 've often spurned it;
And, though to you it seem a shame
To kill a witch by cord or flame,
The word was plain as they had learned it.

" Please not a word — one single thought
Annuls all cavilling and stricture:
Those darksome times, with horror fraught,
Round which such hideous tales are wrought,
Are shadows to a glorious picture.

" Your landscape were but tamely shown
'Neath everlasting summer weather;

Grand and effective 't is alone
When contrasts in one field are thrown, —
A beauteous whole when viewed together.

"The shadows are of darksome hue,
Not fading out or evanescent;
And bright by contrast is the view
Of beauties that the scene bestrew,
That makes the picture of THE PRESENT.

"There's Salem now, in beauteous guise, —
It does my soul delight to mind it, —
Shines fairer far to thoughtful eyes,
As in its affluence there it lies,
With sombre Gallows Hill behind it."

The Presence clipped the spectral thread
It garrulously had been spinning,
When, nodding with its shadowy head,
It turned about with shadowy tread,
And left me there as at beginning.

THE CABLE.*

The earth is jubilant, and far and near,
From widest east and west, and north and south,
One note of great rejoicing do we hear—
"The cable" is in everybody's mouth.
"Good will to men!"—thus runs the golden line
That thrilled the air o'er the Judean plains,
That loses not its attribute divine,
Though uttered in sub-oceanic strains.
How strange it is! and unbelieving sneers
Die out in silence with the cynic's laugh,
When warm hearts, throbbing in two hemispheres,
Mingle their sympathies by telegraph!
The cable is the best egg ever made —
No wonder all rejoice that it is laid.

* A slight lay to the Atlantic cable; — will answer for any future attemr*

A PLEASANT STORY FOR JEALOUS PEOPLE.

Little Mrs. Staples was one of the neatest, prettiest, and most sensible women in the world; and she had a husband who loved her very dearly, and who strove by every means in his power to make her happy. But there was a lion in little Mrs. Staples' path,—a voracious and hungry lion, waiting at every step to destroy her. Not really to destroy her, but her domestic happiness, which is the life of a true woman. That lion was jealousy; an insidious, lurking, and crafty monster, that Shakespeare endows with green eyes; but of this I know nothing, deeming it, however, very probable, as cats have eyes of a greenish cast. She was jealous, and did not know it; and was all the time conjuring up the queerest fancies about Staples, in which there was a chaotic blending of other lips and eyes and curls than her own, with no distinctness of arrangement; mostly fancies, as indeed were sundry nods and winks, which that same blind horse, Fancy, detected and construed into positive kicks at the domestic peace of little Mrs. Staples.

Little Mrs. Staples loved her husband, Jeremiah, with as much love as she had to bestow; but it was not the love that so fills the heart as to crowd out all fear or doubt of the one beloved; a love which would sacrifice even its own happiness, in order to secure the happiness of its object. Hers was no more unselfish than is the love of nine-tenths of the world's people, which insists upon an equivalent for its sacrifices. But this is a point too nice for our present purpose, as we are only to deal with things just as they are; and little Mrs. Staples was jealous. Of whom? Of no one in particular; of woman-kind in general, I believe. Jeremiah could not speak of a female without an instant imagining of all possible things by the little woman, who, in her pride, deemed that her husband was such a fine-looking fellow that he had but to look at a woman, — the finest, grandest in the world, — and she was his, like a fly caught with molasses. He was, however, but an ordinary specimen of a man to look at, and was by no means a "lady's man," as the world understands the term. True he had many lady friends, and esteemed them for qualities of mind or soul that were congenial with his own; but, so far from being objects of Mrs. Staples' jealousy, they were of a character to subdue such feeling in that estimable lady's heart, had she given them credit for like feelings of honesty and virtue with herself. But it is unfortunately the case with jealous people that the standard of virtue is raised very high by them, and they themselves come up to its requirements in the same degree that the suspected ones fall off. It was astonishing what trivial things would provoke whole chapters of theories in that little woman's brain. A ravelling of calico, a hair, a scrap of paper, anything was sufficient to hang a theory upon, which was speedily and satisfactorily prepared and laid away in some pigeon-hole of her mind for future reference; for little Mrs. Staples did not make much parade of her feelings, and, save an occasional spasm, when Jeremiah was away for an evening in a manner that seemed mysterious, the domesticity of Jeremiah Staples was placid. But the theories laid away in the pigeon-holes must be brought out.

"Who was that lady your husband was walking with, this afternoon, in Washington-street?" said Mrs. Spigh to little Mrs. Staples, one day.

"I am sure I don't know," said the little woman, covering her face with her apron to hide her tears that suddenly gushed out, and sobbing as though her poor heart would break.

"Well, I am sorry I asked," said the estimable Mrs. Spigh, who had the key to the happiness of the whole neighborhood in her possession, and judiciously dashed a sprinkling of discord around it, now and then, in order that people might remember that they were not in heaven, — a thing very likely to occur where her voice was heard. "I am really sorry I asked," continued she, "since it affects you so; but I always think it a favor if anybody 'll tell me when they see Spigh walking with anybody. I think it 's a duty we owe one another, Mrs. Staples, when men is so wicked and so inconstable. Mr. Staples was a walking with a light complected woman; and she was a smiling on to him in a manner that I did n't think becoming, a bit. I even see her squeeze his arm in a manner that no decent woman would another woman's husband. But you are the patientiest woman alive." She went out with a tender and commiserating sigh.

The apron had not been removed from the face, nor the weeping suspended, from the time when Mrs. Spigh went out and Jeremiah came in to his supper, and found it not ready.

"Hallo!" said he, in a boisterously good-natured tone; "what 's the matter, little wife? What 's broke now? What's for supper?" at the same time, playfully trying to remove the apron from her head, evidently deeming it some sort of affectionate bo-peep, where he was to discover a pair of bright eyes laughing out upon him, and a pair of soft, warm lips to bid him welcome, and seal the welcome with a kiss.

No reply but a sob. The poor fellow felt badly, and asked, in a soothing tone, what was the matter.

"Nun-nun-nun-nothing," came at length from beneath the apron, in a tone of the deepest grief; and then he knew that something was the matter, and resolutely took away the apron, and looked at the red, weeping eyes it concealed.

"Now, wife," said he, "I insist on knowing what is the matter. Your sorrow pains me, and I want to elieve it."

"Yes," said she, still sobbing, though speaking now with an emotion of temper mingling with her quiet tones, "yes, you care — very much — for me — I dare say — when you can spend the time — away from me — in waiting upon — other women!" The last two words were uttered with startling energy.

"Ah," said he, smiling, "the wind sets in that quarter, does it? My friend Mrs. Spigh has been here, has she? I saw her, and thought she would come. Now, I have a great mind to torment you and that excellent neighbor into a fever, by not explaining anything; but, little wife, I love you too well to torment you, though you think I do not. *Here*, wifey, is the cause of your trouble: my sister Jenny, from Illinois, the little girl who went away, — the beautiful woman who has come back. I got a despatch from New York, to meet her at the cars, and intended a joyful surprise for you; and now see what a scene you have made of it, — no supper, no welcome!"

"Yes, Jere dear, yes," cried she, springing up, and, in her joy, kissing her husband and his sister over and over again; "yes, yes, a thousand welcomes, a thousand welcomes! I was mad to doubt you, my dear Jere, — very mad. Please, dear sister Jenny, believe me, you are very, very welcome!" She wrung her hand again, and kissed her again, and bustled about, in the cheerfulness of restored confidence, to get her evening meal, for the little wife did not know the luxury of a servant.

"I came in to see," said Mrs. Spigh, opening the door very noiselessly and looking in, "if your husband has got home, Mrs. Staples, because I want to know if he has seen anything of my husband." She was evidently surprised, and appeared somewhat miserable, at finding her little neighbor so cheerful under her wrong; and looked at her in a manner that said, "Well, you 're the most cheerful martyr I ever saw."

"You can ask husband, yourself," said Mrs. Staples, with her face radiant with the fire-light and the smile that played about it; "and you will find him in the next room." She pointed to the little parlor, the door of which was snugly closed, and Mrs. Spigh softly entered, like a cat.

No wonder she at first started back, for there upon the sofa was Jeremiah Staples, — the husband of little Mrs. Staples, the martyr now in the kitchen, — sitting upon the sofa, his arm about her waist, with the identical "light-complected woman" she had seen with him in Washington-street! And so shameless was he, that he did n't change his position on her entrance, and looked up with a brazen effrontery that in the eyes of that excellent neighbor was horrifying. Recovering her speech, at last, she said,

"Mr. Staples, have you seen my husband since dinner?"

"No, ma'am," said he, "I have not; but some prying, spying old woman has, perhaps, and may run in, by and by, to tell you where she has seen him."

Mrs. Spigh passed away; and the slamming of the outside door denoted an energy that was remarkable, which Mr. Staples smiled to hear.

Mrs. Spigh moved from that sorrowing neighborhood with the wrong done her fresh in her mind, and refused to be reconciled; and a whole year had elapsed with nothing transpiring to mar the tranquillity of the Stapleses. Jenny had gone again to Illinois, and little Mrs. Staples was left to her own domestic duties and reflections.

There were no babies in the home of the Stapleses, though they would have been most welcome there; and there were times when a feeling akin to envy would awaken in the breast of the little woman, in her comfortable home, as she thought of the homes of the poor, where the children were counted by pairs and by sevens, with misery and want for an inheritance. To add to this feeling, her husband never saw a pretty child about their door that he did not call it in and pet it; and a visit to their house by any one with a baby,—and little Mrs. Staples had several married cousins, all proprietors of fat, chubby babies, with plump arms and legs, and ball-buttery cheeks, and putty noses, who were delighted to exhibit their pets on the pleasant days,—was a great occasion, and the Stapleses were in their glory, making it a matter of talk for days afterwards.

Mrs. Staples, about this time, read the life of Jose

phine, and she was struck very much with the resemblance between herself and that excellent personage; likewise, the resemblance between Napoleon and her husband, though others might have waited a good while before they saw the likeness. It was all summed up in the fact that neither party had any children. Poor little Mrs. Staples once more began to imagine vain things; again her husband's occasional absence from home looked mysterious; again his clothes were watched for straggling threads; again his pockets turned wrong side out for tell-tale papers; again she became miserably jealous!

Poor Staples saw the change in her, and was unhappy. With no direct complaint from her, he could say nothing, and each day he watched the progress of the insidious disease that was preying upon her peace. One day she was out for a walk, and thought she would call upon her husband at his room in Court-square; for the name of Staples was borne upon a shingle in that locality, he being of the ancient fraternity of lawyers. Approaching his door through an ante-room, she was attracted by her husband's voice, saying,

"I love her as dearly as ever man loved woman, and —" Here his voice fell to a murmur, and she heard no more of the sentence; but heard a man's voice say, as if in reply,

"Does your wife suspect anything about the child?"

Then her husband replied,

"Not one word."

She heard the sound of a subdued laugh, and heard no more; for she left as silently as she had entered, in a state of mind bordering on distraction. She had fallen by accident upon a secret that she would have given the world not to have become the recipient of.

She went through the streets unheeding anything or anybody; until, nearing the street that led to her once happy, but never more to be happy, home, she was arrested by the sound of her name, pronounced by a familiar voice, and her old neighbor, Mrs. Spigh, stood before her.

"Why, I declare," said that estimable woman, without any particular reason for the declaration, "if this is not Miss Staples! I've been a great many times coming to see you, but somehow or other could n't make up my mind to, after —— Well, men are very curious, Miss Staples. I hope you are happy. Are your children well? O, I remember, you never had any. Well, well, some is n't blessed in that way. Rachel mourning for her children that would n't be comfited, you know, and that 's scriptur."

Mrs. Spigh stopped, and poor little Mrs. Staples replied but generally to her, because her little heart was too full to admit of her speaking. Mrs. Spigh continued by her side, like a disagreeable shadow, to her own door, and, as she entered, the dark shadow entered with her.

"I declare," said the shadow, "how natural it seems for me to be setting here! I have n't been here since that night when the young woman — I mean since —— Well, well, 't is n't best to remember everything. Forget and forgive should be our motto, though we have many things to try us."

Little Mrs. Staples fell into a chair, and, unhearing and uncaring for her visitor, went to crying as hard as she could, swinging her body backward and forward, and wringing her hands in the very bitterness of grief.

Mrs. Spigh looked on, with great benevolence in her

expression, as much as if she were exclaiming to herself, "Ah! poor soul, I know just how to pity you."

"Is there anything I can do for you?" said she, at length. On being informed that there was not, she said, in a croaking tone: "Well, well, it is, I suppose, our lot to suffer and obey. Our feelings may be outridged, but we must n't say nothing; our bosoms may be lacerated, but we must n't say nothing; our firesides may be pervaded, but we must n't say nothing; our moral sensibilities may be blasphemed, but we must n't say nothing. I suppose it is all right; and *I* don't want to arrange Providence by calling it wrong."

She folded her hands meekly, and waited for little Mrs. Staples to "revulge" to her the secret woe that bowed her down. At last the salt grief became slightly acidulated by an infusion of Spigh, and an effervescence took place, bubbling up into words and sentences.

"Jere 's found some woman he loves better than me —"

"Of course," said the attendant croaker.

"And he has got a child hid somewheres —"

"Very probable," said the croaker.

"I heard it this day from his own lips. O! that I had died before I heard it!"

The dear little woman! How she sobbed and sobbed, and swayed backward and forward, and wrung her hands as she finished; and how the shadow fell upon her, as Mrs. Spigh, like a huge raven, moved here and there, croaking of the falsehood of man, and exhorting submission to his tyranny, even though he indulged in all imagined departures from the virtuous limits to which they were by law circumscribed, as though it would be different were such restrictions removed! She at last left her victim in a hopeful state, —had got her reduced to the calmness of despair,— with a promise that she would drop in the next day, and see how she did.

It was a fearfully long afternoon to little Mrs. Staples, as she sat waiting for the return of her perfidious husband. So she called him, in her trouble. And there she sat, "nursing her grief," and thinking how she should meet the man who had so wronged her — with what expression she should greet him. She would show him a true specimen of womanly greatness; would reproach him with his baseness, and then give him up to the sting of his own conscience. How calm she would be! *He* should never suspect the bitterness that lay at her heart. She would tell him that she knew his secret, and then forgive him, and win him back by her generous love. Her own heart prompted this. She would keep the secret as an object of terror for him in years to come, when she should *cease to love him*, to reproach him withal, and make his life miserable! How she would taunt him about THE BABY, till he would cower before her glance, and bury his burning face in his hands and cry for mercy. And *would* she grant it?— she, the injured, the slighted, the contemned,— *would* she? How she patted her little foot as she said this in her thoughts!

In the midst of her reflections the door softly opened, and, glancing her eyes upwards from the carpet, they met those of her husband, beaming on her with the light of a serene and sincere affection.

Away with plans of action! away with premeditated feeling! The heart, if true, must act on its immediate impulse. Starting to her feet, little Mrs. Staples threw herself into her husband's arms; but in an instant her wrongs crowded upon her, and, falling back upon the seat she had just left, she swooned away with the pressure of conflicting feelings. When she recovered, she found herself on the bed, by the side of which her husband was tenderly watching.

Poor little Mrs. Staples! How pale she looked! Recognizing her watcher, she took his hand, and told him that she did not think she should live (in a sweet, trembling voice); that she had, that day, become acquainted, by accident, with a momentous secret, and could not die in peace without imparting it to him. She had, she said, been near him when he had told his friend of his secret love, — as dear as ever man bore for woman, — and of the child, that she knew was to crown his life with a joy he so much craved; but she felt that she could give him up, — (particularly as she herself was so soon to have no special need for him), — and begged of him to think of her when she was gone, as one that he had once loved, who would from the spheres still have an eye over him, in an angelic way, and seek for his happiness alone. No jealousy now tormented the dying little Mrs. Staples, so white and pale there amid the pillows.

"And are you strong enough, my love," said he, with a grave smile on his face, that seemed strange at such a time; "and are you able to hear the one named that I love so strongly, of whom I was speaking when you overheard me telling my friend Badger? Are you?"

She assured him she *was* able; and her face assumed a flush with much more of life than death in it, as she spoke. He took her hand and held it a moment to his breast.

"Then listen," said he. "I was telling my friend of a little jealous and unhappy woman, that was tormenting herself to death on my account, at home, whom I loved very dearly, but who would not believe it; and then I told him of a great scheme of mine for winning her to faith in me by a gift, — the most strange that ever entered the heart of man to procure, — and which — (Mr. Badger, please step here a moment) — is ready to be presented to you."

He hid her eyes with his hands as the door opened, and when she could see, the room was lighted, and a woman and a man stood by her bedside, and the woman bore something on her arm, nicely hidden, which, on being uncovered, revealed the features of a plump and beautiful babe.

"Here," said Mr. Badger, "is a present that I was deputized to give you. This is the mother, who freely resigns it, under writing, to your loving care, its father being dead. Take it, my dear madam, and may it long live to bless and comfort you!"

"And my blessing goes with it," said the woman, tenderly kissing it; "and I know my darling Rose is in hands where no mother's care will be missed. God bless you, my dear madam; and if ever I come this way again, may I look upon her sweet face once more? though I 'll never tell her who was her mother, and shall cry to look at her."

There never was such a time about the bedside of a dying woman, and no dying woman ever had interest in life more suddenly renewed. Little Mrs. Staples rose from her bed, and her first duty was to throw her arms around her husband's neck, begging his forgiveness for doubting his truth, and promising him she never would do so again, like a school-girl. Then she took the baby in her arms, and kissed it over and over again, and admired its fingers, and its toes, and its eyes, and its nose, and thought there never was such a sweet baby born, vowing to love it dearly, and hugged it in such a way that the mother was quite affected.

It was quite a young baby; and, as so few were in the secret, it was deemed to be a matter of the quietest and slyest scheming in the world, to have the baby pass as a genuine home production, and so it was resolved. The next day it was announced that Mr. Staples was the possessor of a bran-new baby. A girl was employed, and the mother installed as nurse until such time as little Mrs. Staples should get the hang of the thing. The milkman was surprised to be told that he must not make a noise, because he would disturb the baby. So with the butcher; and an order left for oatmeal at the grocer's was brought over by the grocer himself, who was a family man, and did n't quite believe the obscure hint that Staples had thrown out, about *some* folks having babies as well as *some* folks. So it went on, and every one expressed astonishment that no one had ever suspected anything about it, coming to the conclusion, however, that everything was just as it should be, and they were glad of it.

In the afternoon Mrs. Spigh was surprised to have her summons at the bell responded to by a servant-girl, and was thunderstruck, speaking figuratively, to hear the reply to her inquiry for little Mrs. Staples, that she was up stairs with the baby.

"Whose baby?" said that sympathizing female, in a tone of great wonder.

"Her'n, ma'am; come last night, ma'am," replied the domestic.

"Poor creatur!" cried she; "more sorror, more sorror! Well, our backs are fitted to our burdens. Tell her, young woman, that Mrs. Spigh is here, and would like to sympathize with her."

The domestic went as directed.

"A baby!" said that lady to herself. "I wonder if any accident happened; I hope it isn't deformed, or anything, though it must be a poor unhappy creatur'; I hope it won't be punished for its father's wickedness to the fourth generation —"

Her reflections were cut short by the return of the servant, who assured Mrs. Spigh that her mistress was grateful for her sympathy, but that Mr. Staples, who was up stairs, thought she had better bestow all she had somewhere else.

"Ah, that poor creatur'!" said she, as she went out, "how she must suffer with such a brute of a man!"

In due time little Rose was passed round for inspection, and never in the rounds of Babydom had such another been seen. Some shook their heads, and some remarked, "How old-fashioned!" but it was Staples' baby, and it became an immense favorite. The mother never returned, having married in California.

There was no more jealousy in the home of the Stapleses. The baby was a bond of union between them that never relaxed its power; and though it was but a little plant from another parterre, it was loved none the less.

A COURTING REMINISCENCE

My brow is seamed o'er with the iron of years,
  And the snow-threads are gleaming the dark locks along
My eyes have grown dim in the shadow of tears,
  And the flowers of my soul have died as they sprung;
But Memory bears to me on its broad wings
  Bright images true of my earliest life,
And there, 'mid the fairest of all that she brings,
  Is the little low room where I courted my wife.

That low humble room seemed a palace of light,
  As Love held his torch and illumined the scene,
With glory of state and profusion bedight,
  Where I was a monarch — my darling a queen;
Ourselves were our subjects, pledged loyal to each,
  And which should love best was our heartiest strife;
What tales could it tell, if possessing a speech,
  That little low room where I courted my wife!

Warm vows has it heard — the warmest e'er spoke —
  Where lips have met lips in holy embrace,
Where feelings that never to utterance woke
  It saw oft revealed in a duplicate face!
The sweet hours hastened — how quickly they flew! —
  With fervor, devotion, and ecstasy rife;
Our hearts throbbed the hours — but how I ne'er knew —
  In the little low room where I courted my wife.

The romance of youth lent its rapturous zest,
  And fairy-land knew no delight like our own;
Our words were but few, yet they were the best, —
  A dialect sweet for ourselves all alone;
So anxious to hear what the other might say,
  We scarcely could utter a word, for our life;
Thus the hours unheeded passed fleetly away
  In the little low room where I courted my wife.

Long years have since passed o'er my darling and me,
  And the roses have faded away from her cheek,
But the merciless seasons, as onward they flee,
  Leave love still undimmed in her bosom so meek;
That love is the light to my faltering feet,
  My comfort in moments with sorrowing rife,
My blessing in joy, as with joy 't was replete
  In the little low room where I courted my wife.

FIDGETY PEOPLE

There is a large class of people who, like electrical eels, are always on the jump; who seem so charged with electricity that it appears but necessary to apply the knuckle to one of their elbows to elicit a shock. Indeed, it has been proved, in the experience of many, especially where the battery was a female, that the shock has instantly followed the touch, either in the form of a concussion on the ribs, or a sensation upon the cheek, attended with sparks from the eyes. As a class, fidgety people, enjoying no peace themselves, are unwilling others should experience any, and, through teasing and fretfulness, see their most fidgety disposition gratified. A noisy foot upon a stair, a voice not tuned to the fidgety pitch, a dress a thousandth part of an inch awry, a stray hair escaped from its fastening, and ten thousand other things equally trivial, will excite the battery, and fidgets will ensue, revealing themselves in many unhappy explosions of temper. The fidgety are not confined to the female part of humanity; — the masculine has its share. This need not be told, as so many instances are to be seen. We knew a man change his place of worship from an Orthodox to a Unitarian church, because there was an angle in the wall that was not true, — the fidgets coming upon him every time he looked at it, and he could not enjoy the sermons; and another, too conscientious to change, who kept at home altogether, because the minister tied his neckerchief in a granny-knot. Some cannot remain still a moment, but spend their lives in very busily doing nothing, or undoing what they have done, like poor little Luke West, in his transposition of chairs upon the stage. They are always changing pictures, or clearing up or moving round; coming out, in the end, just about where they started from. This class are unhappy to see a hat hung on a wrong peg, a scrap of paper as big as a pea on the floor, or a door ajar; and fret in most miserable discontent, exciting the same feelings in others, because they are not understood. It takes everybody to make a world; and this doctrine we are growing more and more to believe, every day. Fidgety people are, doubtless, designed, if regarded rightly, to quicken the torpidity of negative people, who otherwise might simply vegetate. They are vitalizers, and should not only be tolerated, but welcomed; and, instead of being unhappy in contact with them, we should note the effect of their fidgeting as we would the effect of a galvanic battery, and cry, admiringly, "What a nice shock that was!" and feel, in our quickened blood, instead of anger, that it had done us good.

THE PHILISTINES BE UPON THEE.

While bound by Pleasure's flowery chains,
  Our souls in guilty dalliance lie,
Listing the enervating strains
  On wanton winds that wander by;
Weakened by dull, luxurious ease,
  Temptation finds us easy prey,
And, some Delilah sin to please,
  We drive our better selves away

'Tis then that Conscience, in our need,
  Cries out, in accents loud and clear,
The foe is on thee — arm with speed! —
  And well if we its warning hear.
The dormant soul shakes off its chains,
  And, once more disenthralled and free,
Over luxurious Sin obtains,
  By Virtue's might, the mastery.

MRS. PARTINGTON ON INTEMPERANCE.

"INTEMPERANCE!" said Mrs. Partington, solemnly, with a rich emotion in her tone, like an after-dinner speech at the samė time bringing her hand, containing the snuff she had just brought from the box, down upon her knee, while Lion, with a violent sneeze, walked away to another part of the room,—"Intemperance is a monster with a good many heads, and creeps into the bosoms of families like any conda or an allegator, and destroys its peace and happiness forever. But, thank Heaven! a new Erie has dawned on the world, and soon the hydrant-headed monster will be overturned. Is n't it strange that men will put enemies into their mouths to steal away their heads?"—"Don't you regard taking snuff a vice?" one asked, innocently.—"If it is," she replied, with the same old argument, "it is so small a one that Providence won't take no notice of it; and, besides, my oil-factories would miss it so." Ah! kind old heart, the drunkard's argument! He who casts stones at his frail brother must first see if there be not something at home to correct, before he presumes upon his own infallibility. Ike all the while was watching Lion, as he lay growling in his sleep, and wondering if he was dreaming about him.

MRS. PARTINGTON AND THE TELEGRAPH

"THE line is down!" shouted Ike, as he swung open the front-door. Mrs. Partington, thinking he meant the clothes-line in the back-yard, darted to the window, but everything was right. The night-caps swung to and fro by their strings, the dresses waved their long arms in the winds, and Ike's galligaskins, inflated by the breeze, seemed struggling to be free.—"You should not tell such wrong stories, dear," said she, "when there is no occasion for it. The line is not down." — "I meant the Atlantic Telegraph line," said he, with a face expressive of the joy of both hemispheres; "and Queen Victoria is going to send it to President Buchanan." — "She is, is she?" said the old lady. "Well, that is very kind in her. I wonder if she will prepay the postage beforehand in advance." — "It is n't a letter," cried he; "it is a cable under the water from one country to the other, over which messages can be sent." — "I don't believe it can be done," said she; "for how can the messages come without getting satiated with water?" — "I guess they'll be wrapped up in gutta-percha," replied Ike. — "Maybe so," said the dame, thoughtfully, "maybe so, but it would be a good deal safer to send 'em by the steamer; for what if they should get stuck half-way?" She pondered on it, and did not see that Ike had tied her ball of yarn to the tongue of the bell, and was even then in a remote position, preparing to send messages of mischief, that would call her repeatedly to the door.

GREAT AND LITTLE STRUGGLES.

We speak of struggles in the field of life,
Where men and women make a rush to win,
And in the bigger ones who urge the strife
We overlook the lesser that "go in."
The gallant Havelock on the Eastern field,
Or Halley tracking comets through the sky,
Or Morse, whose fame in lightning lines is sealed,
Or Webster, whose great name can never die, —
These claim our homage; but those are as great
Who in a smaller way embark their soul,
Who wrestle with the purposes of Fate,
To sink, perhaps, or triumph in the whole.
A mighty instance now occurs to me —
A small boy wrestling with his A, B, C.

DIED OF CRAMP.

It is a fearful thing to be stricken down, alone and unattended, when our last hour comes — without a sigh from loving lips to prove that we will be regretted when we are gone, and to assure us that our life has not been spent in vain, when tender ones can breathe a blessing on our exit. This truth found poor Peasly, in the cholera-time, moving one evening towards home, pondering upon the chances of his being called away in the midst of his usefulness, his young wife a widow, with good prospect of being married again before he had been dead six months. The night was dark, and his mind was as dark as the night was, as he moved along, turning these things over in deep reflection, and wondering if lobster-salad was wholesome in cholera-time; for he had just partaken of a dish of that delicious preparation, and was conscious of an uneasiness in the epigastric region. He had taken the precaution advised by the "Baron," to "soften the hostility" of the salad by a sufficiency of Sauterne, or some other fluid, and was surprised that it affected him so. He felt uneasy in his mind about it. But he remembered the tales he had heard where cheerfulness was a repellant of cholera influences, and of the effects of dismal thoughts inducing the dreaded disease, and he attempted to whistle a cheerful tune. It was a failure. His whistle sounded more like that heard in winter at some cranny in an old barn, at night, when the witches are about, and children hide their heads under the bed-clothes for fear!

Going through Union-street towards the North End, where he resided, he met one of his old friends.

"Lots of cholera down your way, eh, Peasly?" said

the friend. "The Mayor's been a overhauling Spear Place, and found it brim full."

He looked at Peasly by the gas-light, and saw that he was pale and unhappy.

"What's the matter?" asked he.

"I don't feel exactly right," said he; "I — I guess it is n't much, though. I've been eating lobster-salad."

"Bad stuff in cholera-times," said the friend. "You know old Timberly, up by Fort Hill? — well, he eat two lobster-claws, day before yesterday about noon, and next morning he was dead as General Jackson. Good-night."

And the friend was off.

Peasly felt worse: and, whistle as he might, — and he attempted another tune, — the pain increased, as he did his pace.

"Ah, Peasly, my boy, how are ye?" said Styles, the policeman, as he saw him scudding along, with his hand upon his waistcoat.

"Pretty well," replied Peasly, with an effort.

"Glad of it," said Styles, "glad of it. Great times, these. Cholera's all round your neighborhood. Seven carted away this afternoon."

"Anybody that I know?" gasped Peasly.

"Why, there's the Widow Spruce, and Jo Bart, and Uncle Frye, and the rest I did n't know. Don't you think that Frye was fool enough to gorge himself with lobster-salad, and then wash it down with brandy. Confounded fool, was n't he?"

"Perhaps so," said poor Peasly, taking hold of his waistcoat with redoubled force; "but is it generally so bad?"

"Bad!" said Styles, looking earnestly into Peasly's eyes, and, seeing the sweat standing in globules upon his face, and his lips as white as ashes, determining to guy him; "bad! you have n't seen the proclamation about lobsters, made on the recommendation of Doctor Smith, to have every one thrown into the dock, and the men prosecuted for selling of 'em? 'T was sent down to the watch-house to-night. Smith says they 're rank pisen, — red cholerys, every one of 'em."

How the pain took hold of Peasly, as the policeman moved on! Down the street a crowd of people attracted his attention, and for a moment he stopped to ascertain the cause.

"What 's the matter?" asked Peasly of a bystander.

"It 's a feller that was picked up on the wharf, sir," was the reply. "Guess he 's got the cholery; been eating lobster."

Mr. Peasly ran from the scene towards his home, and never had that spot appeared so sacred to his fancy as at that particular juncture. He had got within a few doors of his haven, when he met a man coming down the street with a lobster under each arm, from which he was breaking the claws and sucking them.

"He 's a goner," said Peasly to himself, as an extra pain made him almost cry out with its acuteness; "and I 'm afraid that I am."

Mr. Peasly reached his door, a wretched man; but he was *at home*. Here he could find consolation and peppermint-tea. Here he could have the hand of sympathy held out to soothe his brow, or to drop laudanum for his infirmity. With a strong hand he pulled the door-bell, when, overcome, he sank upon the door-step. No one came at the summons, and, rising up, he gave another pull, and sat down again.

A window in the next house opened, and a female voice was heard telling Mr. Peasly of the fact that his wife had gone to a religious meeting in the Bethel, and would n't be back till ten o'clock, and it was now but half-past eight. Wretched Peasly! An hour and a half betwixt him and peppermint-tea, and he dying of cholera! The reflection broke the back of the little resolution he had left.

He fancied to himself the trouble that would arise in finding out how he had died, — for he knew he was dying, — and, taking a piece of chalk from his pocket, he wrote on the door, in legible characters, "*Died of Cramp*," and became insensible.

His wife arrived home sooner than she anticipated, and found him still lying there. One of the brethren who came home with her helped get him into the house, where he was plied with proper applications, but was not fully restored till the next day, when he found his pain all gone, and a wonderful appetite possessing him.

"What have you got in the house to eat, wife?" said he, putting his right foot out of bed; "I think I could eat a little something — something that 's delicate, you know."

"I have," said she, smiling, "something that will please you. I have bought a nice large lobster, and am going to make a lobster-salad for you."

Poor Peasly! He fell back upon the bed and re lapsed again into forgetfulness. It was three weeks before he recovered, and all the time he was sick people marvelled at the strange inscription upon his door, "*Died of Cramp*." It was only owing to a strong constitution and proper appliances that it was not true.

Peasly, to this day, has n't the courage to look at a lobster. His sensibility is so acute that he can smell lobsters three squares off, and thus is enabled to avoid them. He refused a sergeant's warrant in the Boston Fusileers because they wore red coats, and the mention of lobster gives him the horrors for days thereafter.

COSMETICS.

"THAT 's a new article for beautifying the complexion," said Mr. Bib, holding up a small bottle for Mrs. Partington to look at. She looked up from toeing out a woollen sock for Ike, and took the bottle in her hand. — "Is it, indeed?" said she; "well, they may get up ever so many of these rostrums for beautifying the complexion, but, depend upon it, the less people have to do with bottles for it the better. My neighbor, Mrs. Blotch, has been using a bottle a good many years for her complexion, and her nose looks like a rupture of Mount Vociferous, with the burning lather running all over the contagious territory. You 'd better not try the bottle as a beautifier, Mr. Bib." Mr. Bib, with a smile, informed her that this was simply a cosmetic, harmless in its character, and intended to go upon the face, and not inside it; whereupon she subsided into the toe of Ike's stocking, murmuring something about "leaking in." Ike, in the mean while, was amusing himself by rigging a martingale on Lion's tail, securing that waggish member to his collar, and making him look as if he was scudding before the wind.

A TALE WITH A MORAL

In Thessaly, off in the ages dim,
Apuleius the author, queer in his whim,
Went to board with a female grim,
A sort of a witch,
Considered as sich,
Who in Tophet's necromancy was rich.
Now, she had the power
To change in an hour
A man to a bird, or a beast, or a flower;
And Apuleius he
Took the wild idee
That he a beautiful birdling would be!—
He would sail through ether
As light as a feather,
And sing 'mid the trees in summer weather,
And the finest fruits and flowers would gather!—
O! how he'd revel in exquisite things,
And the dew of the morning should shine on his wings—
He'd be richer than Jews, and prouder than kings!
This mighty change,
That was deemed so strange,
Was wrought by ointments' subtle force,
And, rightly applied
To his outer side,
A man became bird, flower, or horse,
Or anything else that his fancy chose,
To sport in feathers, or hair, or clothes·
But this one care
They in mind must bear,
Who used these wondrous ointments rare,—
To mind from which pot
The salve they got,
And well it was that they *should* beware;
For each was applied to a different use,
And a change might play the particular deuce,
Transforming one,
As sure as a gun,
From a would-be dove, perhaps, to a goose:
Apuleius the author would be a bird,
But how to procure the witch's charm?

A lucky thought his cranium stirred —
He 'd tickle her servant's itching palm;
A proof that wielders of the pen
Were somewhat flush with "the ready" then.
So the servant was sought,
And her services bought,
And the magical charm was straightway brought,
For the servant in such exploits was adept,
And prigged the salve while her mistress slept;
Concerning which, we, in our brighter light,
Should say it was n't *salving* her right!
Apuleius happy now was made,
And scarcely a single moment delayed,
And his heart beat high
As the hour drew nigh
To open to him the doors of the sky,
When he 'd spread his wings and thitherward fly.
So elated his thought,
He the caution forgot,
And did n't even look at the pot;
Till too soon, alas! the unfortunate elf
Discovered he 'd made an ass of himself!
Not much of a wonder, some might say,
When such things happen now every day
The witch discovered the theft, and, alack!
She "played the deuce and turned up Jack," —
She straightway decreed
That he ne'er should be freed
Till he found some rose-leaves on which to feed
And a sad decree
It was for he,
For there were n't any roses in Thessaly,
And therefore the ridiculous ass
Was brought to a very unfortunate pass.
From land to land, and from clime to clime
He wandered on for a weary time,
Braying — but whether in prose or rhyme,
Is not by the history stated; —
And instead of flying in upper air,
He cropped the thistles here and there,
Seeking for roses everywhere,
But was long uncompensated.

At last Apuleius, the long-eared, found
A rose-tree on his sorrowing round,
And, blessed release ! all right and sound,
He stood erect once more on the ground,
A happy fellow, we may be bound,
And from it we draw this moral.
We should always be content with our lot,
Nor wish to be birds and things we are not,
And never with Fortune quarrel,
Lest we prove ourselves to be asses, at best,
By action more than by ears confest,
Braying along, nor knowing rest,
And seeking rose-leaves east and west,
To find but thistles and sorrel.

ELECTRO-CHEMICAL BATHS.

"THIS is a great discovery, to be sure," said Mrs. Partington, with animation; "when a person who has experienced salvation, through calumny and all sorts of pisenous grediences, can have it soaked out of 'em." We asked what she meant, and looked at her as she sat in meditation and the little low chair in the corner, revolving the idea, which pressed upon her brain like a weight of steam two hundred and fifty pounds to the square inch. "Why," said she, smiling like the moon with reflection, "there is a contrivance for soaking a man who has taken calumny and minerals all his life-time, till his joints are stiff as wooden legs in the last war; and when he comes out of the bath, and wipes himself with a hacmetac towl, he has n't a single mineral in him, — he is a perfect vegetable, as limber as an eel!" What a gratified look it was she gave, as an imaginary procession of cripples, the victims of calomel, passed before her mind's eye, like the spirits of Kossuth's countrymen, as she thought of their leaping, all cured, from the bath! though she shut her eyes just then, and Ike stole away during her abstraction, and was seen a moment after peeping round the corner at the ancient priestess of Pomona, who sells apples opposite, thinking what a fine thing it would be if a cart should come down and capsize her table.

TRUE COURAGE.

"SOME men are more courageous than others, and some an't," said Mrs. Partington, as the conversation turned upon heroic deeds. She was the widow of a corporal of the "last war," and her estimate of heroic deeds, as may be supposed, was based upon a thorough knowledge of what those deeds were. "Some will go to the Chimera to exercise feats of arms, and some will exercise their feats of legs by coming away. It needs more courage to face danger in the dark — to be waked up in the night by the howling salvages, with their tommyhawks and scalpel-knives, or to hear midnight buglars breaking into your house, or, like the lady who waked up in the night and found a big nigger man standing right horizontally by the side of her bed. It takes great, great courage to meet such things, depend upon it." The blood mantled to her cheek, like the hue of a damask rose-bush in bloom on the side of a yellow-painted house; heroism sat behind her spectacle-bows, and peeped out of the glasses; while Ike was engaged in putting a clean paper dicky and a black cravat upon a "marble bust of Pallas," just forninst our closet-door, — only this, and nothing more

MY GRANDMOTHER.

THAT old chair, painted black, with the new bottom of some sort of mysterious cloth, provided by the upholsterer, was the property of my grandmother, —

> "Dear old lady, she is dead
> Long ago," —

a gift from her mother, when she was married. It is a queer old straight-backed affair, and I remember it, all my lifetime, as the "Easy-Chair," though a more positive misnomer never could have been applied. It was anything but easy, was the old chair; but when any of the family were sick, they were placed in the "easy-chair," that always sat beside the bed in the best room, and made themselves comfortable, or imagined themselves so, by the appliance of pillows, propped bolt upright as a soldier on parade.

That "best room" — and poor was the best — comes back to me in memory, redolent with odor of pine-boughs, gathered in the woods around Fox Hill, or the denser shades of Chase's Pasture. The little low fire-place was filled with such, while upon the mantel above it sported dried bouquets of wild field-flowers and grasses, that were in keeping with the simplicity of a sanded floor, scoured to half its original thickness by the hard rubs of time, and revealing numerous knots that lay about like hassocks in a meadow, that could *not* be scoured down. There were upon the wall some striking profiles — ancestral effigies — in fly-stained frames, once beaming with the bravery of unsullied gold-leaf. These profiles, cut from lily-white paper, behind which was placed a black back-ground, presented the *tout ensemble* of the family, though why more than one was necessary to emblemize the whole, I never could think; for they were all alike, and all looked "down the corridor of Time," with their peaked noses ever pointing pertinaciously in one direction. Then there was the black old desk in the corner, with its brazen and glaring impudence of finish, thrust out ostentatiously, as if conscious of aristocratic importance, as though saying, "I am the chief article of furniture in this establishment!" I never see it, at this day, without thinking of some portly gentleman standing with his thumbs in the arm-holes of his vest, at a meeting of second-mortgage bond-holders of the Vermont Central Railroad; but I can't, for the life of me, explain the points of resemblance. Then there were in the desk mysterious apartments, from which the ends of antiquated papers protruded; and once I remember seeing distinctly a silver dollar in an old pocket-book in the desk, which book I have now, but the dollar is not. There was an ancient gun that hung over the desk, with which I used to shoot rats, using gravel-stones for shot; and another gun behind the door, with which my brother used to shoot teal, in the mill-pond which flowed past the plantation where the house stood in which I first knew, and first learned to love, my grandmother. The house was a little, dingy, low structure, which seemed then large enough, but which now appears so small that the wonder arises how a huge six-footer, like the writer, could ever have managed to be born there; and it takes very materially from his self-esteem to admit that he could n't very well help it. But he has reason to thank God that he was born; for he has had many a happy time since, and much misery, which last he is equally thankful for, as it has made him, he knows, through suffering, a better man.

The first face which he distinctly remembers among the early home-scenes was one old with years, but radiant with cheerfulness and love. This never changed. The same kind look, and the same kind manner, marked it. By the sick bed or in the social circle, at home or abroad, that face, like the sun, bore comfort and joy in its beams. She had been very handsome in her *youth*, so everybody said; but I saw that she was *then* beautiful. The old face had no trace of age upon it to me. The smile that marked it was always young, and it went to every young heart like a sunbeam. I cannot sit in the ancient arm-chair, nor look at the grim profiles, withbout thinking of her, and recalling the good old face surrounded by a cap-border of ample frills, rendering it an island of benevolence, surrounded by an ocean of spotless purity, reminding one of a sunny isle in some summer sea.

It is the lot of almost everybody to have grandmothers; but it is not always the custom, I believe, for everybody to remember them. I had two, and always thought I had the advantage of other boys in this particular, until I became aware that Providence had planned it so that to each was allotted the same number, as each state is entitled to two senators, to operate as a "check upon the House." Although I had this number, and my respect for both was equally divided, still I *loved* "my grandmother" the best; and the love which then glowed warm in my youthful breast, even now, when the sod has lain upon her gentle form for thirty years, and the silver threads are gleaming among the dark locks about my brow, is stronger and purer than at the beginning. The elements of gentleness, and kindness, and sweet household piety, were so mixed in her that her life was angelic. There was no querulous complaining no Rigglestyish jealousy about inattention, no ascetic dogmatism, too much assumed by the aged, no exaction, about my grandmother. Her life flowed on, like a river through meadow land, eighty years long; and as it deepened towards its close, when about joining the great sea of eternity, it was more quiet and gentle, and made the little green things around it, my self included, better by its unconscious influence There was no gossiping about my grandmother. No neighborhoods were scandalized by brawls enkindled or encouraged by her tongue. Her counsel was ever on the side of peace. She always had a good word for the erring, and the largest charity for the fallen. No bitter denunciation of guilt passed her lips. "We are born, but we are not dead yet," was her remark; and to do unto others as she would they should do to her, her rule of conduct.

My grandmother was a dear lover of children, and she was that marvel, an old person who could tolerate all their wildness, and make the whirlwind of their exuberance subservient to her love. She drew them around her by the magic of her manner. All of them loved her, and found themselves by her side in a sweet but incongruous companionship. She had a fund of stories for them, and took part in all their childish sports. I remember she was great at Cat's-cradle, and at Fox and Geese she was immense — always managing, however, to get beaten, and would be delighted at the exultation with which her juvenile competitors proclaimed their victory; though all the while she would wonder, in a profound manner, how it could be that she was so unlucky. Delight shone in her eyes, all the time, that would have betrayed to older experience the secret of her ill-success. There is not a boy or girl among them who will not, at this late day, recall my grandmother, and avouch for the truth of all that is herein written.

With the aged she was an old woman, talking gravely of the past, and dwelling in cheerful trust on the future. That future was all bright to her. The vicissitudes and cares and sorrows of eighty years had done their work, and she was ready to go. This readiness was based upon no canting pretence of good, and no belief in a prospective crown earned in the discharge of Christian duty. Her duty had been done for the love of it, and had received its reward in the reflection of its own good. She was good because she could n't help it. The close of her life was like the calm glory of an autumn evening, and the mild benignity of its setting sun gave it a softness and beauty that plainly heralded the night of peaceful rest that was to follow, and the glorious resurrection morn beyond.

Such was my grandmother, whose humble history is here attempted. She was entitled to no greater historical prominence. Her life was in a small round of duties well done, her aim limited to the wish to make others happy. This wish sprang from the infinite love that burned within her, and marked all her life; and when she passed away, it was felt that, though her immediate sphere was circumscribed, she had been no inactive liver here, but that the world was better that she had moved in it.

THE MILL-BROOK.

Pleasantly soundeth the old mill-stream,
In the summer time when the air is still;
It steals on my ear like a voice in a dream,
And it moves my heart as it moved the mill.

I drink in its gentle monotone, —
'T is a plaintive ditty it sings to me,
Of an early love that its youth had known,
Of sundered ties, and constancy.

Ah, dearly it loved the sturdy mill,
And day by day, and year by year,
Did the influence sweet of the gentle rill
The oaken heart of the stout mill cheer.

The bright stream gave its life to the task,
And loved the mill as 't were its bride,
And ne'er a higher boon did ask
Than day and night to seek its side;

To do its bid with earnest zeal,
And uncomplaining e'er was found;
Content, e'en though to turn a wheel
Might prove alone its duty's round.

And Time swept o'er the ancient mill,
And wasted it with a cruel touch,
But lovingly still did the little rill
Cling to that it had loved so much,

Till the wheel was stilled, and drear decay
Became enthroned on the corner-stone,
And the dam a shattered ruin lay,
And the race with weeds was overgrown

But constantly the gentle tide,
As if with time it had truer grown,
Alone ran on, with a loving pride,
Amid the scenes its joy had known.

And as gently yet it flows along,
  A beauteous type of a loving heart,
That death, desertion, or cruel wrong,
  Can ne'er make from its course depart.

And this is the story of the stream
  That with a witchery comes to me,
And mingles with my pensive dream
  Beneath the shade of the wide-limbed tree.

DAMAGED GOODS.

"AH!" said Mrs. Partington, as she stood looking at the placards stuck all over the front of a store, advertising *damaged goods* for sale. It was not a big R, like those which doctors begin their prescriptions with, but the simple ejaculation "ah!" and, as she said it, people going along listened to what she had to say. "This," continued she, running on like a wheelbarrow, "is what is meant by Mr. Jaquets, where he says 'sweet are the uses of advertisements;' but," — and here she butted against the word "damaged," making two words of it, with a profane construction on the first, that made her hold her hands up in unqualified horror, — "but, though the goods are aged, I don't see the need of putting it quite so strong, — so much stronger than the goods are, I dare say." Ike here pulled her sleeve, at the same time kicking a big dog on the nose, who was smelling at her "ridicule," and the old lady moved on amid the crowd.

THE SPIRIT OF SEVENTY-SIX

A JULY DREAM.

WHILE sitting alone in my easy-chair,
With my feet on my desk, in abandon of care,
My eyes in a dull and dreamy eclipse
By the cloud of a Yara that rolled from my lips,
My thoughts in a whirl, like the whirl of the smoke,
Part sermon, part poem, part satire, part joke,
Now wrought into romance, now framed to a speech,
All things considered, and but little of each,
I heard a great sound like the flapping of wings,
Or the rushing of waters released from their springs,
And said, with a nod, as the sound hastened near,
"Should that be the comet, now, won't it be queer?"
But, I thought to myself, "If it is, let it come;
I'm exceedingly glad it has found me at home."
I'd scarce entertained this complacent suggestion,
And ere I had time to ponder the question,
Down through the roof by invisible door
A bright form descended, and stood on the floor.
"Halloa," I exclaimed, as I saw the descent,
"You've come in a hurry, now what's your intent?"
I looked at him closely — a queer garb he wore,
Yet noble and grand was the mien that he bore.
A three-cornered hat on his powdered hair rested,
A broad-skirted coat his figure invested,
A waistcoat of buff of capacious degree,
And breeches by buckles secured at the knee;
Long stockings he wore, irreproachably white,
And shoes whose paste buckles gleamed in the light.
His face was as bright as a morning in May,
And my room was lit up, as it seemed, by its ray.
He smiled as I spoke, and, touching my arm,
His power enfolded my soul like a charm.
"I've just dropped in, my friend, as you see,
Abruptly, I own, and may be too free,
But, whether you like it or not, I care nix,
For I am the Spirit of Seventy-Six!
A blustering fellow was I, in my day,
And somewhat disposed to have my own way.
You've heard of me, surely?" I nodded and smiled,
And ventured: "You're known to every child."

"Yes," said the ghost, "for children are true,
And love what is free, and practise it too;
But, when they are older, 't is different then,
And the vim of the boys dies out with the men." —
"Be careful, old Seven-and-Six!" then I cried,
As my breast bubbled over with patriot pride,
"You are off o' the track — miles out of the way —
To cast such reflection on men of our day.
You just tarry here till the Fourth of July!" —
"O, bosh," said he, tartly, "that 's all in your eye
Your Fourth of July is naught but a jest —
A sort of a snap-cracker fizzle, at best; —
Like Sunday devotion, put on for effect,
That Monday's example will show you neglect.
The day comes along, 't is confusion and din,
And feathers and fuss, and fever and sin,
A pebble of fun to a cart-load of 'bricks,'
And *this* is the Spirit of Seventy-Six!
There are noble spirits, though, I will allow,"
He said, as he saw the frown on my brow,
"And present company 's always exempt
From all implications of shame or contempt.
But look at the land; from year's end to end,
What strifes and dissensions on all sides ascend!
No union, no harmony, ever prevails,
And cries of discordance burden the gales.
Here they 'd dissever the bond that I tied,
For whose mighty braid my children have died,
And there they would stab in intestinal strife
The 'parient' thought that breathed them to life, —
Uniting in purpose in only one way:
Consume pig and powder on this common day!"
"*Our* party —" I said, in a tone of dislike. —
"Excuse me," said he, "at no party I strike;
Each pot cannot black the other one call, —
Depend on 't, you 're all of you black enough, all.
The picking of holes in each other's coats
May end at last with knives at your throats.
'T was a watchword of ours, and worthy your ken,
'All for principle — nothing for men;' —
Should you kick to the dogs the political quacks,
And turn upon all false pretenders your backs,

Give heed to sound sense, and steer for the right,
Keeping Freedom's old beacon-fire ever in sight,
Still clinging to UNION, — its symbol the charm
To strengthen each heart, and nerve every arm,
As it floats in its beauty o'er land and o'er sea,
The flag of a land undivided and free, —
Then would the Fourth be no meaningless thing,
But a yearly returning to Liberty's spring,
And the jubilant feeling with which it is crowned
Be woven in action the whole twelvemonth round!"
Just then, a treacherous fly, I suppose,
Tickled the tip of my sensitive nose,
And, swinging my arm with a motion too rash,
I lost my nice balance, and fell with a crash.
I woke with the jar, and wildly did stare,
But nary a seven-and-sixpence was there!
So plain was the vision, I scarcely could deem
That I 'd been essentially hum'd by a dream.

IKE PARTINGTON AND PUGILISM.

MRS. PARTINGTON was much surprised to find Ike, one rainy afternoon, in the spare room, with the rag-bag hung to the bed-post, which he was belaboring very lustily with his fists, as huge as two one-cent apples. "What gymnastiness are you doing here?" said she, as she opened the door. He did not stop, and, merely replying "training," continued to pitch in. She stood looking at him as he danced around the bag, busily punching its rotund sides. "That 's the Morrissey touch," said he, giving one side a dig; "and that"— hitting the other side — "is the Benicia Boy." She said, "Stop," and he immediately stopped, after he had given the last blow for Morrissey. "I 'm afraid the training you are having is n't good," she said; "and I think you had better train in some other company. I thought your going into compound fractures in school

He did not stop, and, merely replying "training," continued to pitch in. P. 1[illegible]

would be dilatorious to you. I don't know who Mr. Morrison is, and don't want to; but I hear that he has been whipping the Pernicious Boy, a poor lad with a sore leg, and I think he should be ashamed of himself." Ike had read the "*Herald* with all about the great prize fight" in it, and had become entirely carried away with it. "How strange it is," said Dr. Spooner, as he was told the above, "that boys take so naturally to cruelty and violence! In the time of boyhood, the reason has not got control, and hence temptations to tyranny and wrong have at this time potent force. We all remember the tale of a child, — not a caudality, but a narrative, — who was seeing a picture of the holy martyrs torn to pieces by lions, in the days of Nero, wherein one, according to perspective, that was in the background, appeared smaller; and, as it appeared to be taking no part, the child, instead of being horror stricken at the scene, remarked, with considerable anxiety, that the little lion would n't get any martyr, if he was n't very quick! So, within our knowledge, urchins in school were punished by their teacher for tying up a cat and whipping it to death. It was on such cases that the doctrine of man's total depravity was based. Boys who thus began, with none to guide them by the dangerous period, kept right on in wickedness, whereas the merest slant of the helm to port might have saved them. The boy is the least understood of anything in the animal kingdom." There 's an opinion as is an opinion.

THE OLD SOUTH BELL.

WITH effluent note and musical swell,
Comes the voice of a friend — the Old South Bell!
It speaks to me with an eloquent tongue,
As for years and years it has spoken and sung.
By night and by day has it served us well,
The faithful, truthful Old South Bell.

Though a hundred years have winged their flight,
And generations have sunk in night,
The bell still rings with a tone as true
As that which its morning hour first knew,
When old Trimountain hill and dell
First heard the sound of the Old South Bell.

We love to think of that olden time
When first outspoke its pleasant chime,
And fancy the ancient matrons and men
In the quaint and queer old garb of then,
As the hour of prayer the tongue did tell
Of the sanctimonious Old South Bell.

How gravely of old on the Sabbath day
Did it bid the people to church away,
And gallants and maidens in silence trod
The paths that led to the house of God —
Though their *hearts* conversed, we know right well,
As talked the musical Old South Bell.

'T was a glorious peal its tongue outspoke
When Freedom's thrill through the land awoke;
And ever since, on each natal day,
We 've felt our pulses the quicker play,
And we 've loved each note on our ear that fell
From the jolly, jubilant Old South Bell.

When fire has threatened the town with harm,
The Old South Bell has waked alarm,
And the firemen rushed, in fleet career,
Its clanging and warning tones to hear,
While the timid trembled at the knell
Of the blatant, garrulous Old South Bell.

And sad the notes the bell has flung
When the loved have passed from the loved among;
And the mournful throb of the funeral strain
Has given the aching heart more pain,
As the frequent and meaning measure fell
From the grieving tongue of the Old South Bell.

And other people will hear its voice,
And with it grieve, or with it rejoice,
When the men now living shall pass away
To join those of the earlier day —
But still, unchanging, the tone will swell
Of the faithful and truthful Old South Bell.

THE FALSES.

THE list would be large, should we attempt to enumerate them, prevailing as they do everywhere. The falses would be found to far exceed the trues. They enter the world with us at our birth, beset every avenue to our education, and stick to us very tenaciously till we are called for, and go. The falses are our pets. We fondle them, and cherish them, and enshrine them, and, through their speciousness, often, the devil becomes transformed to an angel of light. They come in the guise of false appetites, false tastes, false ideas, and false intentions, — the worst of all, where we make falsity a virtue knowingly, leading us to concealments and covert action, which makes the hypocrite, what he is, the most detestable of men. What a hideous spectacle it would be, if we could see each other as we are! If the scales should fall from our eyes, what scaliness would be apparent where we now are assured of goodness! The shrines where we have brought our offerings would be found in ruins, and we should long for our blindness again. But, speaking of falses, awakens a ludicrous conceit — the false making-up of the exterior man: the false eyes, the false legs, the false teeth, the false noses, the false hair, the false lips, the false complexion! Suppose these falses should be removed, what a mumming among the toothless, and what a stumbling among the lame, there would be! How the roses of beauty would wither, and what a lank longitude the human form divine would assume! Almost every other man we meet has some false feature in his external making-up. Timms, with his false teeth from Cummings and Flagg's, — the very climax of dental art, — grins at Toby, who uses Roathe's hair-dye; and Toby revenges himself by pointing at Hardup, whose bald head is covered with one of Bogle's wigs, who, in his turn winks significantly, as Beau Nipchin passes wearing one of Page's mechanical legs! Thank fortune, we say, that we have been preserved from a necessity for any such resorts.

HARD TIMES.

O, THE wild fever of this mad unrest,
  When baffled man, amid his hopes and fears,
Smites in despair his over-anxious breast,
  Not knowing in the dark which way he steers;
With brokers on his lee, and subtle sands,
  That late seemed stones, but now prove naught but stocks
He wrings imploringly his trembling hands,
  And, just like those in Scripture, prays the rocks
May fall upon him — but prefers the sort
  From California; and, howe'er their power,
'T would be to him, just now, delightful sport
  To stand and weather the auriferous shower,
Begging propitious Fortune to let down
Boulders of any size — he 'll risk his crown.

A NIGHT OFF POINT JUDITH.

Dark was the night, and o'er the ocean's breast
  The angry winds went howling on their way,
Vexing the billows into wild unrest,
  Uncheered by e'en a star's descending ray;

When, struggling through the tempest and the gloom,
  Our bark complained like one in bitter woe,
As if in dread of some impending doom,
  That threatened in the strife its overthrow.

But at the darkest, when the shrinking soul
  Was merged in depths of bitterness and fear,
Above the elemental din there stole
  A bell's sweet tone, — glad music to our ear!

And broad before us beamed the beacon-light,
  The twin-star trembling upon Judith's breast,
That put at once all brooding fear to flight,
  And gave our hearts an augury of rest.

Light out of darkness! — so amid the shade
  Of sorrow's night a light supernal breaks,
And from the dream of grief that late dismayed
  The soul to peaceful consciousness awakes.

LETTER WRITING.

There is no accomplishment that any one can possess superior to the gift of letter writing. It is unquestionably a gift; and those possessing it make no effort to acquire it, but simply lay their pen to paper, and thoughts flow from its point with the fluency that words drop from the tongue of a conversationalist. Letter writers are not necessarily talkers; their forte lies in the *scribendi* rather than the *loquendi*. It is painful to read the labored efforts of many very sensible people, in an epistolary direction; and it almost militates against the pleasure of hearing from them, so great a labor is evident in the construction of their missives. The easy letter writer is one who writes from a full heart; who knows just what to say, and how to say it; and the spontaneous flow with which it gushes makes us forget, wherever they occur, lapses in grammar or orthography. We feel the spirit of the writer in every word. The dryest details are illuminated by it, and the homeliest matters assume an almost poetical interest under the touch of genius. The most charming letter writer of this description, who poured his soul most apparently into his epistles, whether in relation to the correction of a proof-sheet, or to a matter affecting the tenderest of human relations, was Robert Burns. His letters are models. They speak with the simplicity and pathos and strength of his great nature, and everybody is as interested in their subject-matter, after the lapse of three quarters of a century, as those probably were to whom they were addressed. Though a gift, practice will overcome many natural impediments in the way of success, and the encouragement of correspondence among the young will be found advantageous in after life.

SYMPATHY.

"WERE you ever at Lake Winnipiseogee?" a friend asked. We assured him that felicity was in reserve. "Well," said he, with animation, "I should like to go up there with you, next summer, and show you the greatest sights you ever saw; such beautiful hills, such magnificent distances, such delightful sheets of water, such splendid sunrises! Why, a sail across the lake would reveal to you more delights than you ever dreamt of after witnessing a fairy spectacle. You must go." And we resolved to go, but not with him. Such a companion, with so much enthusiasm, would be insufferable. Companionship is only desirable where silence, not voice, expresses sympathy with nature and with ourselves. The utterance of delightful adjectives is a bore, the human voice is a bore, the officious proffering of opinion is a worse than bore. We know the annoyance of the concert-room when the soul is at its acme of appreciative bliss, to have a vein of small talk permeating the melody. The nerves, stretched on the tuneful rack, are more susceptible then, and the chit-chat, untimely carried on, is sadly provocative of violence. We feel that it cannot be tolerated, and a counteracting bitterness is excited in proportion to the effluence of the sweet. So by the sea-shore, or on a mountain, or a lake, or a prairie, or in a wood, the same feeling prevails, the delights we realize fixing the measure of the annoyance. We feel sometimes that it *is* good for a man to be alone, when he lends himself to enjoyments like those afforded by communion with nature.

The voice of friendship sounds harsh when it disturbs the silence of the fields; and the kindest words would fain be dispensed with, or deferred till a more convenient season, if uttered when the soul is filled with its devotion. But infinitely worse is it when the garrulous drive of ordinary companionship chatters about one's ears, obtruding itself upon the sacredness, like a parrot in a church. This fastidiousness is not peculiar to ourselves, and, though it may not be expressed, it is very generally felt.

SEA-AIR.

"ARE there many people masticating at the sea-side?" asked Mrs. Partington of one who had returned from there, bearing evident marks of being used up. He informed her that there were, but that the wet weather had had a tendency to keep them in-doors, and that rusticating by the sea, if she meant that, had been attended with some mastication likewise. "How pleasant it must have been," said she, smiling like the distant sunshine, "when denied the pleasure of imbibing the air out doors, that you could imbibe within! It has had a very beneficious effect on your health; for your countenance is as blooming as a peony." — "The sea-air is very salubrious," replied he, "and the constitution soon begins to show its effects." — "Yes," said the dame, taking a pinch of snuff, "so I should jedge; and not only the constitution, but all of the revised statues, besides. I have no doubt the sea is slewbrious, very —" — "And a great slew of people go to see it," said Ike, breaking in. — "But depend upon it," continued she, "there 's some thing at the bottom of it." — "What is that?" inquired the young man, raising his eyes from a page of Chitty's Pleadings. — "The telegraph cable, perhaps," replied she, concluding her pinch. The young man whistled faintly, and Ike at the instant knocked over an ink-bottle with a feather-duster, in an attempt to kill a fly.

AN ODD FELLOW'S FUNERAL.

BENDING sadly o'er thy form,
Late with Love and Friendship warm,
Brother, in our night of grief,
What shall give our hearts relief?

Shrined within this mortal clay,
Such a loving spirit lay,
That we shrink, with half distrust,
Ere we give it back to dust.

Charity's unfading light,
Honor's lustre, pure and bright,
Truth's effulgent radiance blest,
Ever filled that faithful breast.

Generous manliness and grace
Found a constant 'biding-place
In the fane here closed and dark,
Quenched its late illuming spark.

Brother, from thy heavenly rest,
From thy home amid the blest,
Come, in angel guise, to cheer
Those who sorrow for thee here.

From that radiant "Lodge on High,"
Comes to us this glad reply:
Mourn not, for the path he 's trod
One degree is nearer God.

THE COURTS.

The courts are great institutions. We always take our hats off in a court-room, partly from reverence for the law, partly from respect for the custom of the place, and partly from fear of having it knocked from our own poll by the pole of a constable. What a dignity — awful and sublime — seems embodied in the justice, who figures in the reports as the alphabetical and familiar "J." We hear him addressed as "yer honor," and the spirit prostrates itself before the exponent of stern justice, while fancy draws an imaginary sword and a pair of huge scales in his hand — the latter of which are to be used in weighing the exactest awards, and the former to cut off from the side on which the surplusage remains, as a butcher would divide a piece of beef, or a grocer would divide a cheese. We cannot divest ourselves of the idea that we have seen his honor eating a hearty dinner at Parker's, and laughing like he 'd die at a funny joke, and telling many himself with infinite gusto, and "dipping his nose in the Gascon wine" with stupendous relish, as though he were an excellent judge of such things. The judicial ermine becomes, in the light of reality, a genteel black coat, made by Armington, and the sword and scales fade away like mystic things seen in dreams. What a subject for contemplation is the jury,—that "palladium of our liberty," as some one has called it,—which stands between the law and trembling rascality, in dignified impartiality, to listen to the evidence, the pleadings, and the charge, and remember enough of the combined stupidity — if they are capable of remembering it — to say which side shall win. We love to look upon those devoted conscripts of the state, with their minds made up to one point before they begin — that they are *bored.* The sheriff's wand and the sword, that fearful implement, ready to impale any one who may transgress, are fearful things to contemplate; and we turn to listen to the oath so solemnly administered to the trembling witnesses, who hold up their right hands and bow when the sound of the clerk's voice has ceased, just as if they had understood what he said. But a spectacle sublime as is to be met with in court is the examination of witnesses in order to arrive at the truth of a case. Had this not been so faithfully described in the report of the case of Bardell *vs.* Pickwick, it would be well to speak of it at this time. Of course, every one who goes on the stand is a conspirator on one side or the other, and is disposed — so great is the depravity of the human heart— to lie; hence it is necessary for counsellors, who are dear lovers of the truth, to browbeat and harass them by a thousand impertinent questions, in order to worry the scoundrels into truthfulness by making what they say sound as little like the truth as possible. A man goes upon the stand with an idea that he is, like Hamlet, indifferent honest, but leaves it with a strong impression that he combines in himself the qualities of all the great liars that ever lived, from Ananias to Munchausen, has robbed a grave-yard, passed counterfeit money, spent ten years in state-prison, and deserves to go there again! Great is justice, and her courts are sacred. We take our shoes off, figuratively, in reverence, and move out, shutting the door quickly, lest any of the atmosphere of the precinct be displaced by the obtrusion of unsanctified air.

SICK OF IT

THERE is a vaulting ambition that o'erleaps itself, and falls on the other side — a biting-the-nose-off operation, to manifest a contempt for the face — a performance of very hard work, to avoid a very simple job. This was illustrated, during the skating season, very capitally, by Ike. He had asked permission to remain at home, but Mrs. Partington told him, if he ever expected to be an 'iminent man, he must be acidulous in his studies;" and he went to school with a feeling something akin — perhaps a second cousin — to disappointment. His new skates were aching to be tried, and the dim, hazy atmosphere had in it a foreboding of snow. Temptation beset him from within and without. All the Bill Joneses and Tom Smiths seemed to be going skating. He met them as he went along to school, and they all pulled him by the sleeve, and asked him to join them. "I'll tell you what you can do," said one of them: "eat a piece of this when you get to school, and it'll make you sick enough to go home." He gave him a small piece of a dark substance, and Ike went to school. — "Please, ma'am," said one of the scholars, "Ike Partington's sick." He sat with his head bowed down on his hands, and his teacher spoke to him. He looked up, as she spoke, and his paleness startled her. "You had better go home," said she, in a tone of alarm; "perhaps the air will make you feel better." He went out, but the earth seemed sick to him. It appeared to heave at every step. The Bill Joneses and Tom Smiths were watching for him round the corner; but they seemed to him to be diseased — they looked jaundiced and yellow. They took him by the arms to lead him to the creek, but he longed to throw himself beside every fence.

The skates looked hateful to him, and the ice was a big mirror in which a naughty boy had to see himself magnified. The whirling of the skaters made his head swim. He never felt so before, and he thought he was going to die. The thought of his duplicity made him feel worse, and he resolved to go home, as Mrs. Partington told us, "like the Probable Son," and "make a clean breast of it," which was accomplished by confession and a draught of warm water. We publish this story for the benefit of little people who are interested in Ike, who might be induced, like him, to eat tobacco in order to get out of school.

LOOK UP.

Look up, and let your ravished eyes unfold
  In purer airs than these terrestrial mists;
Embrace the firmament above unrolled,
  And sun and stars, God's bright evangelists;—
Look upward, and the heavenly light will pour
  Down in your soul, and cheer it with its ray,
As, through the sun's sweet effluence, the flower
  Unfolds to beautify and bless the day.
Look up, and thus the earth-environed soul
  May get a glimpse of the pellucid stars,
As prisoners held by outraged law's control
  Catch day's bright glories through their dungeon bar
But where those masons make the mortar fly,
'T were best then to "look out," and "mind your eye."

A DOMESTIC STORY.

MRS. CLEMENT declared that she was not jealous. She had affirmed this so often that she believed it, as fully as she believed that Tom Clement, her husband, was the handsomest fellow in the world. The Clements had been married for several years, and it had been fair weather with them all the time. It was a standing joke with them that nothing inclement could occur where both parties were Clement, and all went on smoothly enough. Children were born to them, — beautifully harmonious children, — born under pleasant auspices, and were models for the world's imitation. Such babies rarely were to be seen, and they were tall feathers in the family cap, and added greatly to the happiness of the worthy couple who boasted their paternity.

Nothing like jealousy ever entered that happy household. Clement regarded his wife as an angel, and when any visiting friend would joke with him concerning the wickedness of the times, and about standing on slippery places, he would snap his fingers, as much as to say he did n't care a snap, not he, for the suggestion, feeling so confident in her integrity.

While this feeling was at its height, a new family moved into the Clement neighborhood. They were young people, and genteel according to the orthodox standard of gentility. Their name was Seville. They had moved into Hopetown from abroad, and brought with them letters to the best families in town; among the rest to the Clements, who took an early occasion to call upon their new neighbors, and proffer them the courtesies usually bestowed upon new comers by old settlers. They found the Sevilles very fine people; the one a gentlemanly and pleasant man, the other a lady of rare beauty and winning address, and the visit afforded great satisfaction to the Clements. It was renewed afterwards, and a very agreeable sociality sprang up between the families, and mutual and frequent visitations were exchanged.

At these visitations, Mrs. Clement noticed how attentive her husband was to Mrs. Seville, and Clement remarked that his wife seemed very happy at the attentions of Mr. Seville. Still, there was no jealousy mingling with the feeling.

"Mrs. Seville is a charming woman," said Clement, as he was proceeding home, with his wife on his arm, "a charming woman."

He looked up at fiery Arcturus as he spoke, as if he were informing that luminary of the fact; and the star seemed to wink at him in return.

"Don't you think Mr. Seville a very splendid man?" asked Mrs. Clement. "Such a noble bearing, such a tenderness of manner, such whiskers!"

She spoke earnestly, and bore down heavily upon Clement's arm, looking at a distant gas-light, which seemed to glare upon her like a burning eye. And thus they walked home, without exchanging another word.

It occurred to Tom Clement, the next day, that his wife was strangely intimate with Seville, the night before, and he remembered her eulogistic remark concerning him with a feeling akin to pain. But he was not jealous. The feeling was simply a dread lest she should be deemed imprudent.

"How strangely infatuated Thomas is with Mrs.

Seville!" said Mrs. Clement to herself, the next day, as she sat alone. "What attention he pays her! How he lolls over her chair, and turns over the leaves of her music-book! It is years since he has been so attentive to me." There was a tear in her eye as she said or thought this, and something like a sigh escaped her lips. But she was not jealous. That was an admission that she would never make, even to herself.

And thus things went on. Weeks passed away, and harmony was unbroken in the home of the Clements.

"Are not Seville's attentions to you rather annoying?" asked Clement, one morning, at breakfast. He asked it carelessly, as though he were indifferent about it himself, and only spoke on her account. She colored up very warmly, before she replied,

"I asked Mrs. Seville the same question concerning your attentions to her. I guess, if she can endure her affliction, I can mine."

There was a little mustard in the reply, — about as much as is found in a lobster-salad, rendering it slightly acrid.

Clement was surprised at the reply. He — *he* — the model husband, whose irreproachable constancy had long been a subject of admiration — to *himself* — to be thus assailed, by implication even, was not to be borne without suitable notice. He laid down his knife in order to give due effect to what he was to say, as a rebuke or a moral lesson, given with a mouthful of food for mastication, loses in its effect as food for reflection, — a fact duly enforced by a recent decision of the Retro-Progressive Unity.

"Do you say, Jane," said he, severely, "that I pay more attention to Mrs. Seville than is called for by the rules of courtesy?"

"And do you think, Thomas," replied she, "that Mr. Seville pays more attention to me than gentlemanly politeness might warrant?"

"I do," said he, rapping his knife-handle on the table.

"Ditto I do," said she, spilling her coffee, in her agitation.

Clement pushed his chair away from the table, and, with his breakfast unfinished, left the house. It was the first domestic squall that had ever swept over their home, and, like the received opinion of the effect of the fall of man upon the earth, sorrow followed it. At home, the children were cross, the cat had a fit, the clothes-horse fell over upon the stove, the maid burst a fluid-lamp, and general confusion prevailed. At the store, Clement quarrelled with his partner, offended a customer, could n't raise money to pay a note, took a counterfeit bill, was drawn on a jury, and had his pocket picked.

It was with a sad heart that he proceeded homeward at night, where he had found so much peace and happiness. He dreaded to go home, *dreaded* to meet the wife he had so long loved; and yet he felt angry that she should treat him thus. *He* had done nothing wrong, and *she* alone was responsible for all the darkness that he felt was lowering around his house. And then there arose in his mind dark images of separation and disgrace, that haunted him like devils, and the picture of a ruined home and banished peace; and he shut his eyes and groaned in the bitterness of his spirit. He entered his door with a moody brow, and, like the shadow of his own, his wife's brow was troubled, and she acted as if she felt, for the first time, the *duty* of house-keeping. There was no cheerfulness in it.

"I have business that will keep me late this evening," said he, dryly.

"Very well," she replied, in a tone of indifference; "I shall not sit up for you, then."

And thus they parted for a second time. I am a believer in the utility of these little acidities. The mild reäctions of temper have an effect to break up the crust that environs a life possessed of too much peace. The iron lying unused dies of corrosion. Gentle rubs are needed to keep us bright. Love glows diviner when emerging from the little clouds which for the moment obscure it. But this quarrel was more serious; it sprung, not from matters inherent in the parties,—little pettishness, or wilfulness, that has but a momentary existence, which, like Cassio's temper, emits a hasty spark, and then is straightway cold again. It had its rise in extraneous ground, and jealousy, that snake in the grass, lay coiled at its root. They were not jealous, however, if one were to believe them.

Clement was away every night for a week, on *business*, of course, as he told his wife, in the brief conversation that occurred between them; and she expressed no concern about it at all, though when she was alone she cried as if her heart would break with her sorrow. She would not let him know she felt so badly, for the world, so stubborn is the womanly nature; and he, though he felt penitent, would not make advances towards a reconciliation, so obstinate is the manly nature. As some one has said, there is a good deal of human nature in men and women.

Neither had visited the Sevilles all the while the quarrel had lasted. They had thought so much of each other that they had no room for any other thought.

"I saw your wife, last night, Tom," said a neighbor,

coming out of Seville's gate. You did n't know his wife had gone out of town, did you?"

If he had received a pretty hard knock on the head, he could not have been more astonished. But he tried to assume the old confident tone.

"You did, eh? well, what of it?"

"Why, it 's all well enough, I suppose," said the tormentor, giving a wink to a bystander, which Clement did not see; "but I thought it was rather a queer time to visit a house, at ten o'clock at night, when the mistress of the house was away. She went three days ago."

"I 'll risk it," said he, with an attempt at a smile that was a positive failure, and turned away to conceal his emotion.

He was as crazy as a spirit-rapper, all the rest of the day. He made entries in the ledger, and attempted to strike a balance in the day-book. He drew a check payable to Seville, and put his wife's name to it. He addressed his partner as Seville, and drew up a promise to pay, payable at "ten o'clock at night," instead of ninety days. But amidst it all he came to a great conclusion — he would *watch* his wife. What a step this was, where distrust resolved to tip-toe it through the dark, and watch the movements of one his heart told him he loved! Though it has been a madness of mine that jealousy and love were incompatible; that true love expended itself irrespective of its object, and would lead to sorrow and death, but not to hate; that jealousy is a selfish feeling, springing from passion unrequited, but passion is not love, though the dictionary says so. This may be only a craze, so let it pass that he loved her. It was a mean thing to watch her, at any rate.

He informed her, when he went home, that business would keep him out; but the tone of his voice was so different from what it had been when he had previously made her the same grave announcement, that she was struck by it. At that moment, from some quarter, a little suspicion dropped down into her mind, just as she dropped a lump of sugar into her tea, though the suspicion was not as sweet, and the figure of Mrs. Seville became revealed to her gaze plainly in the lump of butter on the table. She had heard, that very afternoon, that Mr. Seville had been called out of town on business, and her little head at once assumed it to be certain that the treacherous Tom was to spend the evening in the society of the lonesome wife. Harrowing reflection! But she said nothing.

Clement went out, like a lamp filled with bad oil, and, after a little while, Mrs. Clement came down stairs dressed in a perfect disguise, she having drawn largely upon the servant's wardrobe, and her own mother would n't have known her from the Milesian Biddy whose dress she wore. She opened the door softly, and went out.

"There she comes," said Clement; "I know her through all her disguises."

He stood just across the street, leaning upon a post. His heart beat a quick measure against his ribs, and his knees knocked together as he thought of the perfidy he was about to detect. He moved down the street, with his eye upon the little figure flitting along before him in the gloom of night, with which his own gloom was in perfect sympathy. She stopped, at last. His suspicion was too true. She entered the gate leading to the Seville mansion. He waited long enough to give her a chance to enter before he ventured to follow.

A bright light burned in a lower corner room, in which room were two windows, one looking towards the front of the house, and the other towards the end. He hesitated a moment, and then, with "Tarquin's ravishing strides," he stole into the enclosure, and took position beside the end window. There was an indistinct sound of voices inside, — masculine and feminine, — but whose he could not determine. The curtain, too, was obstinately close, admitting not a single convenient eye-hole, so essential in cases where a criminal thing is to be proved. He listened painfully, but the voices were provokingly indistinct. He thought he would go round to the other window, and see if he could see better. As he stealthily neared the corner, feeling his way along in the dark, he came in contact with another form, that appeared to be groping in the direction which he came. He grasped the form in his arms. A shriek rang out on the night-air. The door opened, and Mr. Seville and his wife were revealed, by the light of a lamp, standing on the door-step.

"Hallo, Clement!" said he, in a tone of surprise; "why don't you come in? Who screamed?"

"'T was — 't was — 't was my wife," replied he, rather confused. "She struck against something, and was much alarmed."

"Well, come in," said Seville; and they stepped inside the door.

"I declare," said Mrs. Seville, "I should think you were coming to surprise us, you look so strangely. Why, how queerly you are dressed, Mrs. Clement!"

"'T was a whim of mine," said that little woman, with a faint attempt to laugh; "please excuse it, do."

She did not dare give the reason for her strange disguise, but held her head down, and seemed rather ashamed of it, or of herself. As she glanced up into her husband's face, and saw the troubled expression it wore, she wished to throw herself upon his breast and explain the mystery to him, and beg to be forgiven, and to forgive him, whether he begged it or not, for the pain he had caused her, but was restrained by the presence of the Sevilles. She saw the necessity of keeping from them the secret; and so, overcoming the embarrassment of her manner, she became the vivacious and sparkling little creature, to all appearances, that she ever had been. She laughed at her bonnet, and laughed at her dress, and made fun of herself in every way; but there was a terrible choking in her throat, all the time, and she would much rather have cried.

Somehow or other, her husband's attentions to Mrs. Seville did not seem half so pointed to Mrs. Clement, and the assiduity of Seville to please his wife did not seem any way offensive to Tom Clement. His thoughts were all with his wife, as hers were with him; and they mutually longed to be together, that they might have the mystery cleared up. The feeling became insupportable, at length, and, bidding good-by, they brought all the hypocrisy and lying of dissembled pleasure to a close, and went home — home, that had not been home for a week, that had seemed as long as four common sunless weeks; for the sun of their love was under a cloud.

As soon as they arrived, even before she had taken off her disguise, she threw herself upon his neck, and asked his forgiveness.

"Forgive me! — forgive me!" said she, sobbing; "will you forgive me?"

"Yes, yes," said he; "anything, everything. But what particular thing shall I forgive first?"

"Forgive my doubting your love; and for believing that you cared more for Mrs. Seville than you did for me; and for watching, in this disguise, for two nights, to see if you was n't there, while her husband was away, as Mrs. Screed said he was."

Poor Tom caved in, on hearing this, and he could n't trust his voice to answer her, but gave her a hug that had a very long sentence of meaning in it, while a tear or two fell on the upturned beautiful brow before him, as their lips met in a forgiving embrace. The sensitive reader will forgive me — as forgiveness is here the theme — if I am a little warm in my description. My old blood fires up, at the portrayal of such a scene, and my words smack a little of the enthusiasm of the moment.

"And will you forgive my doubt of you?" said he, at length; "I, who had so little cause? who was at Seville's house for the purpose of watching you, when we met, set on by that sneak of a Screed, who has been for two years trying to make me jealous?"

"Then you *were* jealous?" said she, archly.

"A little," replied he; "were n't you?"

"A little," she confessed.

"Well, here I record my vow," said he, kissing her lips, "that I will be no more jealous of you, and may heaven keep me loyal to it!"

"And here I register my vow," kissing him back again, "and reverently ask for the same strength."

And the vows were religiously kept; and, though Clement was attentive, and courteous, and friendly, and loving, to others, she was not jealous; and, though she was admired, and courted, and beloved, by others, he was not jealous; for they both knew that, however the whole world might worship in the outer temple of their hearts, there was a holy of holies within where none but themselves might enter.

AN INNER SHRINE.

EVERY man, who has a home as big as an ordinary kennel, should take some corner of it for himself, and hold it in possession sacred from the profaning foot of any save whom he shall choose to admit. This is as necessary as that he should wear his own clothes. It should be a spot to which he may retire and commune with himself, which he cannot do when agitated and harassed by out-door influences; and a half-hour thus spent would be better for him, humanly speaking, than many dollars, if it may be measured by dollars. This self-communion is not enough practised, and ourselves are the least acquainted with ourselves of any that we profess to know. Such little *sanctum sanctorum* is a constant incentive to thought. Do you smoke? Yes? Then here is just the place for you. Enter, lock your door, light your meerschaum or cigar, throw yourself on your easy-chair or lounge, and there *think*, as the smoke curls gracefully over your head. There is a luxury in thought at such time. The demons that came in with you, which all day long may have haunted you with insidious, or tantalizing, or perplexing shadows, holding them before you like stereoscopic pictures, fly out with the gracefully curling smoke. At such time your mind, stormy previously, perhaps, has subsided to a calm, having nobody to quarrel with, and gentle fancies come in as Memory summons them, and delightful reverie, the fairy-ground of the intellectual realm, is entered upon through the avenue of silence. This is luxury. Dream, now, with your eyes open. You see and do not see the uncertain forms and scenes that lead a mystic dance before you. Eyes long lost, that the mould has claimed for years, look once more lov ingly upon you. Smiles, that faded into thin air, as the rose-blush exhales, to form deathless roses in the upper sphere, beam again upon you. Voices, that bore love in their tones, and remained not long enough to give love expression, again are heard! All fancy, but yet real — impalpable, but more substantial than the coarse world about you. The half-hour's thought or reverie is worth a day, to your spirit, of the harsh encounter of life. "Enter into thy closet," and prayer becomes a natural effluence, flowing out of the very holiness of repose. *But shut the door.* White arms and pouting lips are inveterate enemies of solitude, and they are very obtrusive.

CONSTANT DROPPING WEARS.

THERE'S an old saying — very old and trite —
  That constant dropping wears away a stone;
But this conclusion of accretive might
  Is not confined to rugged stones alone.
The stoutest spirit sinks beneath the word
  That constantly in peevish cadence swells,
And, worn and weary, it is wildly stirred,
  Or, banished peace, in recklessness rebels.
Indifference blunts the force of captious flings,
  Which all innocuous fail the heart to move;
But, O, how sharp the cruel barb that wings,
  Thrown by the hand of those we fondly love!
Such drops as those, the world has ever shown,
May, by their dropping, turn the heart to stone.

EMULATION.

Emulation — a healthy emulation — should be encouraged. Generosity should characterize it always, and prevent the mingling with it of any bitter rivalry, to which it is too liable when undirected. "Never do anything enviable or malicious, Isaac," said Mrs. Partington, with a grave expression upon her face, and an iron-spoon in her hand. "Immolation should be encouraged; but, then, we should be always willing to make sacraments of ourselves, sometimes, for others; for the world is wide enough for everybody, as the little boy said, when he let the bumblebee go." — "What did he let him go, for?" said Ike, who was rather interested in natural history. — "Because he did n't want to nurt the inseck, and might have got hurt himself, if he 'd ha' tried to. This should be a sample for you, Isaac. Hurtin' others, through a wrong spirit of immolation and riflery, depend upon it, will never help yourself. 'Fair play for all' is the mortar for you to sail under, which you should always nail to your kilson as a guide." She brought the spoon down with emphasis, as she concluded, seeing that her young auditor had left her, and was playing ball with Lion in the yard. The old lady was right. Among the variety of things that awaken emulation among men, it were curious to know how much accident has to do with its quickening. The best-laid schemes of parents become as naught when striving to direct their children businessward, when accident fires some latent train, the will is magnetized into action, and a noble ambition fixes the purpose. Of all the incentives, however, to emulation, of which we have heard, that which brought out the great Newton was the queerest. He was dull at school, and gave no evidence of superiority until a boy above him in the class kicked him in the stomach. Newton could n't flog him, so he determined to surpass him in study, and beat him in this way, which was done; and Sir Isaac became great, and made that discovery about the apple, which has been such a blessing to the world, because, if it had never been discovered that apples were attracted towards the earth, we should have naturally supposed that they fell from their own weight, and could n't help it, like the water over Niagara Falls

---

PARTINGTONIAN WISDOM.

Ike is remarkably fond of turkey; and the hug-me-close and the merry-thought he is as much attached to, almost, as if they were a part of himself. "Bless me!" said Mrs. Partington, at table, on Thanksgiving Day, looking at the boy, whose face was as greasy as that of a New Zealander, "why, you look like a gravy-image, dear, and your face shines like the rory-boralius."—"With this difference," said old Roger, winking at the Brahmin: "the aurora-borealis appears in fair weather, but this in fowl." The Brahmin, by a motion of his long beard, was supposed to smile, and a sound resembling "travels in Turkey and Grease" came from his lips. But Mrs. Partington saw not the point. "You should learn, dear, to bemean yourself before folks; because, without good behavior, a man may be ever so imminent for debility, but will never be inspected." She ceased here, and baled a spoonful of the stuffing upon the juvenile's plate, which he took very kindly.

A CUP OF TEA.

A CUP of tea! There is nothing like the gentle excitation of tea. We quaff the delectable decoction, and grow happy amid its genial vapors. The cloud that erewhile, perhaps, had brooded over us, and that had hung like an incubus upon us, takes wing and vanishes in the silvery steam, as from the Hibernian's mud edifice,

——— "the blue devils and all other evils
Flew off with the smoke through a hole in the roof."

Tea is the best inspirer that ever exerted an influence upon men. The inspiration of strong fluids is madness. The brain is fired through their infernal agency, and the glow of its evolved genius is like the glare of the baleful fire of the pit, that flashes a while, brilliant and sparkling, to go down and leave darkness behind it. There is no such evil in Souchong, and in Young Hyson is the excess of poetical fancy. It leads to music naturally, and the voice, the scene, the lights, run directly to immortal song. The brain dances with jollity, the curtain of the universal stage draws up, and the Beyond reveals itself by rose-fire from the wings. Ecstasy is installed. Such is its effect upon the true tea-drinker — the connoisseur. There be bunglers, however, who should never touch a drop better than Bohea, and even raspberry-leaves are good enough for them. They guzzle down everything that is tea with the same appetite. They don't know Orange Pecco from Gunpowder. They drink unappreciatively. Your true connoisseur regales all his senses in his cup of tea. He *sees* the golden sparkle of the fluid as it is decanted from the urn; he *hears* the laughing gurgle that attends its passage to the cup; he *tastes* the pleasant beverage with a gout made more susceptible by cultivation; he *inhales* the delectable aroma with infinite delight, and *feels* exquisitely the sweet distillation as it trickles towards its destination, and most sensitively when he spills it over into his lap. It is a pity that the first discoverer of tea were not known. The world should unite in a monument to him. Tea has found eulogists in all languages, and it would be a very curious matter to embody the many things that have been said; but we shall do no such thing, contenting ourselves with a few extracts from the works of some of the best in the English vernacular. First, we have the testimony of him who spoke of tea as the draught which cheered without inebriating, and who again says,

There is no charm commended to our sense
Like that which meets us by the evening board,
Where the celestial herb distils in balm,
And falls in tinkling cadence on the ear
A fount delectable — a rill sublime!
Its vapor in a steamy volume rolls,
Kindly and gently, like a halo, round
Each waiting head, and gratefully inhaled
It steals like magic through the brain,
Lulling to dreamy bliss our wild unrest.
We sip and sip, oblivious though the winds
In wild confusion rage without, or snows
In fearful hurly fill the air, or sleet
Like fairy needles prick the tender skin,
Content with tea — our true felicity!
The voice grows rich in unctuous mellowness,
As brisk Young Hyson lubricates the tongue,
Or Old Souchong exerts its balmy power
To move the heart to gentleness; and Pecco!
Orange Pec! thy fragrant name we speak,
And memories most genial in us rise:
We see the table spread, with doughnuts crowned,
As erst it tempting sat, while beaming eyes

Shine round it, fraught with olden kindnesses,
And rosy hues of youth, and smiles of age;
We hear the cheerful word, the tender sigh,—
All floating by as vapory as the cloud
That folds us round in aromatic bliss,
And in the plenitude of present joy
We snap contemptuous fingers at old Care,
Bidding him, figuratively — go to grass.

The following, by Pope, is doubtless familiar to all:

"Here, my St. John, where Hyson's fumes arise,
And Souchong's vapors dance before my eyes,
The fancy soars in a voluptuous dream,
As sweet as sugar, and as rich as cream —
Roaming through rose-fields of ecstatic scope,
Tinging anew the golden clouds of hope,
Urging the stagnant blood through swollen veins,
And waking melody to bolder strains,
But, misdirected, leaves life's wholesome side,
To mix in scandal's darkly-flowing tide.
There be who claim for wine a potent power
To soothe the sorrows of the dreary hour,
While some, again, would fain exalt the praise
Of stronger fluids lagging life to raise;
But o'er them all my task it e'er shall be
To sing the praises of a cup of tea"

Dr. Johnson's love of tea is proverbial, and his wisest and wittiest sayings, as recorded by the faithful Boswell, proceeded from the inspiration of the herb.

CHRISTMAS HEARTHS AND HEARTS

A TALE FOR THE HOLIDAYS.

CHAPTER I.

ALL well remember the disastrous period when the Eastern Land Bubble exploded; when many who thought themselves wealthy discovered their mistake, and became plunged in irremediable ruin, either as principals or as endorsers. It was a fearful time, and in the change which occurred in the fortunes of such as had been living in luxury was a depth of misery that knew no relief. Families that had been reared in affluence were reduced to poverty, and many fair eyes became familiar with tears that had seldom known them before, and many hearts ached as clouds of doubt fell upon a future before bright and joyous.

It was on a fair morning, in the summer of 1836, that Mr. Milling, the merchant, entered his counting-room, and sat down to read the morning papers. His brow was unruffled, and his spirit was calm. The money-market was tight, but he had no notes to mature that he could not meet, and there was paper due the concern which was well endorsed, that could be counted on at any moment. He did not notice that it was long beyond the time when Mr. Upshur, his partner and confidential clerk, was usually at his post, — Upshur, the careful and prudent man, whose advice was always taken, and whose shrewd business tact had done much to secure the position which the house of J. Milling & Co. had attained, at home and abroad; Upshur, whose assiduity, never tiring, had won the praise of all the commercial community, and whose opinion was sought by all in intricate matters of trade; Upshur, whose honesty was as well established as his shrewdness, and whose word alone had, in severe times, carried the house he represented through monetary crises.

At length Mr. Milling looked up, and, missing his partner from his accustomed desk, asked,

"Is Mr. Upshur ill to-day?"

"I don't know, sir," replied one of the porters; "he spoke, last night, about going down to ship the Manchesters on board the Baltimore packet, this morning, and he has n't been here yet."

Mr. Milling read on, until, growing impatient, he said,

"Jones, go down to the packet, and see if you can learn anything of Mr. Upshur. Something may have happened to him."

The young man did as he was directed, and returned, soon after, bringing the intelligence that Mr. Upshur had not been at the wharf all the morning, and that, calling at his boarding-house on the way back to the store, he had been informed that Mr. Upshur had not been home during the entire night.

Mr. Milling was alarmed, and looked at his watch. Eleven o'clock! He walked the floor, and appeared troubled. There was a cloud on his heart that he could not dispel, which reflected upon his brow, and flitted across it like a shadow above a meadow. A vague and undefined sense of impending trouble took possession of him, and a boding of gloom, as if a dark spirit breathed in his ear, made him thrill to his inmost core.

"Mr. Milling seems troubled," said Mr. Partelot, the clerk who stood next in the rank of promotion, in the event of Upshur's disappearance; "wonder what 's become of Upshur?"

"Don't know, and don't care," was the response from the surly-spoken and rough-looking Mr. Savage, who occupied a position by his side.

Mr. Partelot gave his companion a reproachful look, and kept on with his writing and his secret thoughts, occasionally glancing from the corner of his eyes at Mr. Milling, who was seen, through the glass-door of the little back counting-room, pacing backwards and forwards with an anxious step.

"Mr. Partelot," said Mr. Milling, opening the door, "will you step in here for a moment?"

Mr. Partelot obeyed, and when the door was closed behind him, Mr. Milling said,

"What do you think of Mr. Upshur's disappearance?"

"I trust he may be detained by something which can be accounted for satisfactorily," said Mr. Partelot.

"I hope he may; but I want you to examine his books, and see that everything is right. I fear that he has left us clandestinely, though it is but a suspicion as yet. Read this note. It was received a year ago, and has lain in my desk ever since."

Mr. Partelot read:

"MR. MILLING: Be wary of Upshur. A pitcher that goes too often to the well may come back broken.

"Yours, COMMERCE.'

"Well, sir," said Mr. Partelot, "did you pay any attention to the note? Did you detect any irregularity in Mr. Upshur?"

"Not the least," was the reply; "I have ever observed the same prudence and care, and never have wavered in my confidence in his integrity. And even now I scarcely know what leads me to suspect, but wish you to run over his books, and satisfy me that all is right."

Mr. Partelot promised so to do, and subsequently reported that he could detect nothing which betokened any carelessness on the part of Mr. Upshur; that all appeared fair, straight, and methodical; and the mystery was left to be unravelled by time.

"The old man seems queer enough," said Partelot to Savage, on his return to his desk, "about Upshur; and it is rather strange his disappearing so, is n't it?"

"Don't bother," said Savage, who was engaged in casting up a column of figures.

"Do you know, Savage," continued Partelot, "that the old man suspects Upshur?"

"Of what?" asked Savage, abruptly, looking up.

"Twenty, and five are twenty-five, and seven are thirty-two," repeated Partelot, as if engaged in reckoning, on seeing Mr. Milling close by his side.

"Partelot," said his employer, in a whisper, "I shall trust to your prudence. Make no talk about what has transpired. It may be that Mr. Upshur will return, and give satisfactory reasons for his absence. Say nothing about the suspicion I have expressed."

Mr. Milling left his counting-room, and his two posting clerks at their books, while the great business of selling was going on in the outer store, and went out upon 'change. Change! a spot where the sensitive spirit can detect a metallic ring in the contact of sharpened wits, and in the whisper of "exchange" the rustle of bank-bills. Change! where a man coins his blood for money, and becomes mammoned in the godless whirl of speculation. Change! through whose mutations the lord of wealth to-day becomes the slave of wealth to-morrow. And here, for a while, Mr. Milling partially forgot his anxiety, although occasionally the thought of his missing partner, and the uneasy sensation before experienced, would obtrude themselves, in despite of all he could do. Even the excitement of a rise in flour failed to move him, though he had thousands of barrels upon his hands; even the failure of a firm that owed his house thousands of dollars agitated him not. The one idea at last took entire possession of him. He walked the pave with an abstracted air, and men pointed at him and spoke in whispers as they passed him.

He was at last aroused by one of his clerks, who touched his arm, and said his attendance was immediately wanted at the store.

"Has Mr. Upshur returned?" he inquired of the messenger.

"No, sir."

"Any tidings of him?"

"Can't say, sir, but Mr. Partelot is in trouble about something."

Mr. Milling left the pave hastily, and walked by the shortest path to his store. He saw through the window, before he entered, that Mr. Partelot looked much disturbed, and that a stranger was conversing with him.

"Glad you have come, sir," said Mr. Partelot, as he entered the counting-room door; "we have trace of Upshur, sir." There was, however, no joy in his tone, even though he said he was glad.

"What is it?" said Mr. Milling, his voice betraying the deepest anxiety; "what trace?"

"Here, sir," said the clerk, placing in his hands a number of papers; "this, I think, explains his absence."

Mr. Milling glanced at their purport. His brain whirled with the intensity of his feeling, as he read. He seized the back of a chair to support himself, the while his form trembled with agitation.

"What is this?" said he; "obligations — J. Milling & Co. — eastern lands! The firm never had a dollar in that infernal bubble. What means this?"

"This gentleman can tell you," said Mr. Partelot, turning to the stranger. "The papers are made out in his name. Mr. Barrus."

"The same, at your service, sir," said the stranger, stepping forward. "Barrus, of the firm of Barrus & Emms, Bangor, commissioners. These notes are the first of a series made by J. Upshur, for Milling & Co., in consideration of certain lands lying in Maine, purchased by him. These for twenty thousand dollars have matured. The balance to be paid monthly."

"Perfidious! damnable!" cried Mr. Milling, grinding his teeth with rage. "This explains the absence of Upshur!" He fell into his chair, as he spoke, and groaned in spirit. Starting to his feet, he demanded of the stranger the full amount of the notes he held.

"One hundred and twenty thousand dollars," was the reply, "by our concern. There are other notes held by other parties."

"Ruined! ruined!" said Mr. Milling, "irredeemably ruined by that rascal, whose friend I have been — whose baseness has been returned for my constant kindness! But I deserve it for not regarding the caution I received."

"Here is a letter, sir," said the porter, handing a paper to Mr. Milling. He took it in his trembling fingers, and recognized the hand-writing of Upshur. He read it to himself, and then handed it to Mr. Partelot. The letter ran as follows:

"MR. MILLING. — Sir: You may deem me a scoundrel; but I am to be pitied. I have been led into the temptation of speculation, have compromised our firm in its prosecution, and have fled, like Cain, with the brand of disgrace on my name. But, while thus leaving like a thief, I solemnly promise that my future shall be devoted to a reparation of the trouble I have caused. You shall not hear from me until I am able to wipe the stain from the name of yours, most ungratefully,

"JOHN UPSHUR."

"A dark affair, sir," said Mr. Partelot, handing back the letter.

"Well," said Mr. Barrus, as he found attention diverted from himself, "as we understand each other, I will leave you, and hope this affair will all be settled satisfactorily. There 's no use in worrying about it, anyhow, and I guess it 'll all come out bright."

With this sublimely philosophical remark, Mr. Barrus left the counting-room of Milling & Co., his mind full of visions of islands of dollars rising from submerged lands, while all around them swam drowning men, with haggard looks, grasping at straws as they sank beneath the waves.

Mr. Milling sat late conferring with Mr. Partelot with regard to the course to be pursued in the strait, and the shadows of evening fell upon the street before the merchant left his counting-room for home.

20

CHAPTER II.

THE MERCHANT'S HOME.

MR. MILLING occupied the finest house in Chestnut square. It was built at a time when land was plenty, and men had expansive ideas of room and comfort. The rooms were spacious and magnificent. Large staircases led from broad entries to broad galleries above, upon which a twilight gloom was shed from a Gothic window over the entrance. Heavily corniced and massively finished in all particulars, the house was a fitting residence for a merchant prince. Herein luxury had expended its utmost art, aided by good taste and abundant means. The grounds without were in keeping with the elegance within, and everything bespoke the abode of wealth and ease.

Mr. Milling was happy in his domestic relations. He had married his wife when he was a clerk with a salary, and had arisen to his present eminence in the commercial world with much of the freshness of feeling which had marked his beginning. He was a domestic man, and delighted in the society of his wife and two daughters. The eldest, Matilda, was a tall, imperial-looking, and elegant girl, of some twenty years — handsome, but proud; the youngest was a fair and gentle creature of ten, delicate as a snowdrop, and almost as frail. A sickly infancy had left her an object of deep solicitude, and care was taken that naught but the most tender attention should be paid her. She was kept free from the restraints of study, and at the age of ten was as artless and undeveloped a little creature, intellectually, as ever was made the subject of culture. But she had grown in spirit. The angelic wealth of her nature had developed in flowers of soul and made her life one constant joy. There was none of the waywardness of childhood in her seeming, and her blue eyes were ever lustrous with tender womanly light. There was a marked contrast between Lily and her sister—as wide a difference as between their ages. The one was admired for her beauty of person and accomplishments, the other was loved for her sweetness of disposition and unselfishness. There was but little external sympathy between the sisters, but deep in their natures was a bond which knit them closely together, exhibited outwardly in gentle authority on the one part, and passive obedience on the other.

Mr. Milling had always acted upon the belief that the best way to make sure of the moral worth of his clerks was to encourage intimacy between them and himself, and, through a close acquaintance with them, obtain an insight into their characters, and learn the motives that operated to control their conduct. He had thus opened his doors to them on all occasions, made them welcome to his fireside, and given them the assurance that he was their friend.

John Upshur had been specially favored. Possessed of a very prepossessing appearance, from the first Mr. Milling had been struck by him. Acquaintance had proved him intelligent, high-minded, and faithful. From a boy in the store, he had risen, step by step, through the encouragement of his employer, until he had become confidential clerk and junior partner in the house of Milling & Co., with an irreproachable reputation as regarded honesty, and a character for business capacity and shrewdness that was not to be excelled.

Eugene Partelot and George Savage, the two clerks previously introduced to the reader, had likewise enjoyed the almost parental regard of Mr. Milling. Mr.

Upshur, however, had come before them. His light was at its zenith, and the beams of their small lanterns were ineffectual in its superior blaze, in the eyes of Miss Matilda, who was from the first specially significant in her attentions to the polite and handsome clerk, until, as his position enlarged in the firm of J. Milling, and enabled him to be known as the Co. that was added to the sign on the first of January previous, he became the accepted lover of the young lady, and the particular friend of the family.

There was a wide difference between Eugene Partelot and George Savage. The former possessed great suavity of manner, paid much regard to personal appearance, was punctilious in all his habits, and possessed a full consciousness of his own transcendent merits. He was called by all a good fellow, and his society was sought on all occasions. His presence gave life to a party, his figure in a ball-room was indispensable, and there was not a wedding or a party in the neighborhood to which he was not invited. With George Savage it was entirely the reverse. His appearance was uncouth and careless, his voice rough and uncourteous, his manner abrupt and startling. A thorough conviction of his honesty alone made him tolerable to Mr. Milling, who never received him at his house with the cordiality that he extended to the other, it being evident, although he used him well, that his companion was the favorite. He would often find himself left alone by his employer and more favored associate, to amuse himself as best he might. It was on one of these occasions, while sitting in moody discontent in Mr. Milling's library, that the door opened, and little Lily came tripping in. He had seen her frequently before, but had never spoken to her, deeming that she avoided him. Now she broke upon his darkness of spirit like a light from the spheres. She approached where he sat, and reached out her hand to him, with a smile, saying,

"You are all alone, Mr. Savage?" The tone was so kind, that the Savage was melted. He took her hand, saying, as gently as he could,

"No, Miss, they have all left me for more agreeable company."

"Well, then," said she, "I will take their place, and amuse you the best I can. Shall I sing for you?"

Savage replied that he should be delighted to hear her, and she sang for him several little airs that she had learned, in a voice so sweet and tender, and prattled on so prettily, that an hour passed unheeded away, and the absence of all the rest of the household was forgotten. When they returned they found the little prattler engaged in her task of amusing. Her sister informed her that she must not come down when company was in the house unless she was invited, and George Savage saw her no more on any of his visits. At last he discontinued them altogether, and no question was asked why he did so.

Mr. Milling's family were very uneasy concerning him on the day named at the outset of our story. The dinner was left untasted, as hour after hour passed. He had often staid away, detained by important business, but had always sent a message to inform his family, in order to remove their uneasiness. His present omission to do so was inexplicable. At last, at the hour when night struggles with day, his step was heard upon the pavement, but it seemed weary and slow, his hand upon the door was less active than usual, and the lock gave not the energetic click as was wont, denoting by its sound the happiness of the master at returning. His care-marked brow was seen as he entered, and loving voices inquired if he were ill. Lily's arms clasped his neck in a fond embrace, and her head bowed upon his breast in the mute expression of her heart's full love.

"I am not ill," he replied to their inquiries; "but I am sad. I may tell you at once my trouble. Treachery and fraud have done their worst with me, and I am ruined!"

"Ruined!" said Mrs. Milling, in a voice of extreme dismay, which was echoed by Miss Matilda. "Ruined!"

Lily trembled, and nestled closer to her father's heart. She felt his arms tighten about her, and a fervent kiss impressed upon her curls.

"By whom?" was the question that followed.

"By one whom we have all trusted too much, and who has proved a villain."

"Savage?"—"Partelot?" were the inquiries that broke upon him from the astonished women.

"No!" said he, with a groan, "Upshur!"

Miss Matilda, who was watching his lips for the name, with eager curiosity, with a shriek fell upon the floor, as he uttered the word that crushed her hopes; and Mrs. Milling, seemingly struck speechless with astonishment, turned her attention to her fallen daughter, who, by the aid of a servant, was carried to her chamber, insensible.

Mr. Milling and Lily sat alone. She had started from his arms at the fall of her sister, but had turned to her father again, as the rest left the room. She got upon his knee, took his hands from his face, and gazed long and earnestly into his eyes.

"Father!" said she, at last, with startling energy for her, "love is left us. God gives it to the poor, instead of wealth; and, O, how they love one another who are bound together by the ties of a common necessity!"

He started, while a feeling of awe crept over him, as he looked upon her pale face, and her large, spiritual eyes, beaming with a lustre he had seldom before noticed.

"And who told you this?" he asked, as he held her from him, and continued his gaze upon her.

"There is something that comes from there," replied she, pointing upward, solemnly, "that tells me many things I never dare speak to mortal ears — that I dream of and think of when others are at rest. It tells me of happiness beyond the present, and that, though all earthly hopes may perish, and fortune fade away, the true source of happiness is yet left us in our loving hearts — away down below, where the storms of the world cannot come."

Mr. Milling bowed down his head before his child, and caught from her words a new hope, as if an angel had spoken.

His wife returned to his side; and, at her approach, Lily kissed her father's heated brow and retired, turning upon him her deep, intense glance, full of love and pity, as she disappeared.

They sat long together in conference, the merchant and his wife; for she was a woman who mingled no reproaches or invidious reflections in her counsel, and was an intelligent adviser in matters requiring prudence of judgment, and wisdom of forethought. She was a jewel to her husband, fully realizing the scriptural standard — a crown! The result of their deliberation was that, if the matter should terminate as badly as was feared, everything should be given up to the creditors; that, as honesty had been the corner-stone of the business of J. Milling & Co., it should not be disgraced by a dishonest termination.

The next day the creditors of the firm were summoned to a meeting, and its affairs laid before them. Mr. Barrus, of the house of Barrus & Emms, Bangor, was present with his claims, the large amount of which it was found impossible to meet; and, as there were claims supposed to be held by other parties, as Mr. Barrus had suggested, the result was that the house of J. Milling & Co. failed, and the property was placed in the hands of assignees for settlement. Before Christmas the names of Partelot & Savage occupied the position of the once familiar name, they having purchased the business of the assignees, by the advice of Mr. Milling.

It was a town talk for many days; but, after a while, the waters of silence closed over the affair, as the waves enfold themselves over the scene where some gallant bark has gone down.

CHAPTER III.

THE GLOOMY CHRISTMAS.

THE large house that had been the home of Mr. Milling was now the home of another, and its former occupants, who had passed so many pleasant years beneath its roof, whose hearts were woven with it, as though it were a part of themselves, had removed to other quarters, more in keeping with their present circumstances. But a small remnant of his former wealth remained to Mr. Milling. His fortune had crumbled beneath him like a shelf of sand, and he had gone down to a depth of ruin corresponding with his former exaltation. His integrity was unimpaired in the estimation of those who best knew him; but the story gained circulation that he had been a party in the transaction that had ruined his house, and his presence on 'change was marked by a coldness on the part of many with whom he had formerly been on the most intimate terms. His heart had sunk with the first blow; but the discovery of his waning credit gave him the most pain. Where the stories originated, it was not known. They could not be traced to any reliable source, and worked with subtle and secret influence, until, unable to withstand the look of suspicion that was cast upon him, he left the scene of his former labors, a broken man. His mind was gloomy, almost morose, and even his family failed to awaken him to anything like his former cheerfulness. The feeling that was gnawing at his heart wore upon his frame, and it was evident that he was sinking beneath the sorrow that was preying upon him.

His wife endeavored by every means in her power to cheer him. Her words, however, were mechanical and worldly-wise, and had little effect. His oldest daughter said nothing. Her high spirit and pride sustained her in her new position. She had withdrawn from a society she still could have graced, from a sense of her fallen fortunes, and a determination to avoid all association that would remind her of them. She made no complaint; but her heart was deeply touched by her father's distress, surpassing even the keen sensibility felt at her lover's desertion — for that was subdued by the pride that filled her and gave her strength.

Much talk to a grieving heart is an addition to its affliction. Even words of kindness are of non-effect. A tear, shed in sympathy, is better to the one who grieves than a whole vocabulary of terms. So felt Mr. Milling. The words his wife spoke were addressed to his ambition, mixed, occasionally, with half reproaches, that added bitterness to his despondency. There was but one comfort for him. His little Lily was ever by his side, by her attentions endeavoring to soothe him;

her face not gloomy with the clouds of disappointment, but radiant with love and faith. Her young eye saw beyond the present of earthly trial, and knew that through affliction alone could be won the crown of the faithful. Her voice was music to him, and when by her side his heart beat with a lighter pulsation. He was stricken so deeply, however, that even her ministrations could not bear him wholly up. He felt that he was done for earth, and that the world would be better to be rid of him — the hallucination of a morbid fancy. The feeling at length, by insidious advances, gained entire hold upon him; his body gave way before it, and he was brought at last to a condition compelling him to take to his bed. The kindness of old friends—among whom were his successors, Partelot and Savage — failed to revive him, the assiduity of those around him was ineffective, and Lily's face and Lily's voice alone gave him pleasure. It seemed now to his distempered fancy like the voice of one long gone before — a sister of his early years — and her eyes appeared to reflect the glories of the world to which he was hastening. There were no tears wetting the face he saw, — the little face that bent over him, — but there was a sublime expression resting there, as though she were an angel waiting patiently by the gates of time, to bear his soul to its immortal home — seeing the end of human woe from the beginning, and its need in the scheme of man's progression.

It was Christmas, and the usual hilarity attending the day was observed. Parties were given in all directions, and the fires of the genial season burned brightly. But there was one home, that was wont to observe its festivities, now silent. Mr. Milling was dying! The angel had entered his abode, and waited for a little while ere he should clip the slender thread that bound him to life. His family ranged around his bed — Lily, with her solemn eyes, gazing upon him with an almost superhuman earnestness and tenderness. Suddenly, the dying man revived from a stupor in which he had long lain. He turned his gaze with a meaningless expression upon those who surrounded his bed, until it rested upon Lily. His face brightened, and, seizing her hand with sudden ecstasy, he cried, "Welcome, sister! I am ready." His hand fell upon the coverlet, and Mr. Milling was no more.

The wife and eldest daughter were borne from the chamber. The earthly tie — the whole that they knew — was sundered, and the mortal mourned for mortality, the earth for the earthly. Lily, the delicate and beautiful, stood gazing calmly upon the wreck before her. The brightness of heaven was around her brow, and her face assumed the soft expression of an angel. Serene and calm she stood gazing down upon the immovable features; there was to her no division of the tender chord that had bound them—soul had been knit to soul, and in the mortal dissolution she felt that the sweet compact had not been interrupted. In this consciousness there was no room for terror or despair. Something like a tear trembled in her eye; but there was a joy in it that gave it a glory like a star, as passed before her young vision the remembered kindness and devotion of the one who lay there still and cold. But the triumph that burned in her expression dried up the tear, as the sun dries up the dew that the night, in its darkness, has wept.

She passed from the chamber to make way for those whose duty it was to prepare the body for sepulture, and proceeded to her mother's room to endeavor, by her attentions, to soothe her grief. This was an impossible task. Outward comfort in such a crisis is unavailing, and, though ministerial consolation was tendered, the blackness of darkness rested over the tomb, unpenetrated by a hopeful ray. They had been of the world's people, and their spiritual light was obscured by the mist of materialism; and the ministers, themselves as spiritually dull, knew no solace beyond the mere word of hope — no living faith, no sweet trust in the future of life and love.

Mr. Milling was buried with becoming honors. Many of his old friends attended his funeral, and paid him the respect, as they rode to his grave, of talking over again the transaction by which he was ruined, the slanders that had followed it, the credit of his successors, and the probable condition of his family, ending with profound expressions of regret for the unpleasant affair, and the melancholy circumstances in which his family had been left. The cheap sympathy was all expended, and the price of stocks mingled with the regretful words awakened by the demise of the unfortunate merchant.

When the melancholy cortège returned to the house, Mr. Partelot stood by the door of the carriage containing the family, and handed them out. His eyes were red with weeping, and his hand trembled as he took the hand of Matilda Milling within his own. Following them into the house, he proffered his condolence with them in their loss, and assured them of his life-long devotion to their interest, from a sense of gratitude to Mr. Milling, and a personal regard for themselves. All that he knew of prosperity, he said, had been attained through his beloved employer, and he could not do enough in return for such kindness. His words were full of sweetness, and fell upon the stricken hearts of the family like the small rain upon thirsty ground, and grief broke out anew as he spoke. When he left, it seemed to the mother and eldest daughter that some exalted being from another sphere had paid them a visit with the special object of comforting them. Lily had heard him not. Her eyes were directed towards the western sky, glowing with the brightness of wintry sunset, and were drinking in the inspiration of the glory that rested there, filling her with peace and joy.

Turning to her mother, she threw her arms about her neck, and pressed a kiss upon her forehead.

"Mother!" said she, "is it not selfish to cry for those who have left us? Does n't my father still live — more loving and more beautiful than before?"

"I hope so," was the reply.

"Then, why mourn? We are told to rejoice with those that rejoice; and, if my father is living, should we not rejoice that it is so? His cares and pains are all over for earth, unless, seeing the grief which enshrouds us, he feels sad at our weakness. O, mother, I am but a simple child, and can teach you nothing; but my spirit feels much. It goes with yonder sinking sun to its resting-place, and sees a glorious to-morrow following the night that intervenes; so the resurrection follows the darkness of the grave, as you have told me. Be comforted, my mother."

"Child, you do not know what you have lost!" said the poor woman. "It does me good to nurse my grief." She indulged in a fresh paroxysm, and Lily left her to time and self-pride to work the peace that she had failed to implant.

Thus was the dreary Christmas passed, and the hearth and hearts of the household of the late Mr. Milling were desolate and wretched, with scarce a hope to flash its light forward upon the darkness that lay beyond.

CHAPTER IV.

BUSINESS — AID — EFFORT — MYSTERY.

MR. MILLING had been dead a year, and had he been a dozen beneath the sod he could scarcely have been more effectually forgotten than he was in the little twelvemonth by those who had formerly associated with him, and shared his friendship and confidence. Not a word had been heard of Mr. Upshur, and the house of Partelot & Savage enjoyed the reputation of being worthy successors of the late house. But little change had taken place in the business. The old clerks were employed, as formerly, at their long-accustomed places. Even the two heads of the house, as formerly, spent many hours by the desks at which they had commenced.

"The Millings have become much reduced," said Mr. Partelot, one afternoon, pausing from his writing.

"Indeed!" said Savage, gruffly, not stopping to utter the word.

"Yes; I called upon them, the other day, to offer them assistance, and found Matilda teaching music."

"She shows her sense, then," said Savage, "better than half of those who are circumstanced as she is. I like her for it."

"Why don't you ever go and see them, Savage?" asked his partner. "They are wondering at your strangeness. You have n't been to see them since the funeral. We should try and do all the good we can."

"Small good I can do them!" was the caustic reply. "They don't want to see *me* — they never did. Or at least only one — the youngest."

"Ah, yes, Lily," said Mr. Partelot. "She is a strange girl — a perfect marvel; and the manner in which she improves in her education is astonishing."

"Ah!"

"Yes; and it has never yet been discovered at whose expense she is being educated. There is a perfect mystery about it. Did you ever hear about it?"

"Never."

"Well, the manner of it was this: Mr. Milling had not been dead more than a month, before his wife received an anonymous letter, professing to be from an old friend of Mr. Milling, generously offering to pay for the education of little Lily, besides the other expenses of her maintenance, the only condition being that no inquiry should be made concerning the writer, and that all sense of obligation should be banished, as it was but a mere return for favor received. At first they were reluctant to accept, but friends persuaded them to regard the delicacy of the proffer, and an answer was returned to the post-office address given in the note, thanking the liberal friend for his kindness, and consenting to his proposition. For nearly a year teachers have visited her constantly, — coming mysteriously as the slaves of the lamp and ring. No questions are asked them, as it would violate the condition, and thus it goes on. Strange, is n't it?"

"Humph! The same old story of romantic folly," said Savage. "Some fellow, probably, is doing it, who has more money than brains. Were Lily not a child, one might fancy there was an ulterior motive beside the one of mere education. Can you not guess who this benefactor is?"

Mr. Savage looked at his partner steadily, and that worthy young man said, laughingly,

"'Nay, never shake thy gory locks on me!
Thou canst not say I did it.'

My province extends no further than to be a friend of the family, and all I can do for them is simply to advise. I wish you would go up and see them."

"I tell you, Partelot, they don't want to see me. It is you, the smooth-tongued and light-footed, that is wanted. My croaking notes would set their teeth on edge. Leave me with the merchandise; bale-goods are not so sensitive."

Mr. Savage turned away as he spoke, to attend to some other business, and an expression very like "churl" trembled on Mr. Partelot's lips. That gentleman felt satisfied at that moment that he was very unfortunate in having so unsympathetic a partner, and drew some self-gratulatory comparisons betwixt himself and Mr. Savage, that were in no wise flattering to the junior member of the firm.

The death of Mr. Milling had, indeed, left his family very poor. Everything but what the law strictly allowed them had gone to the creditors, and they found themselves reduced to the alternative of working for a living. The proud Matilda — her pride lifting her above the degradation of dependence — brought the resources of a cultivated mind to the business of life, and, through the assistance of the few friends who remained true to them, procured pupils for the piano, and work for her needle, that gave a moderate income. The greatest care was on account of Lily. She was likely to be a burden because of her helplessness. There was small sympathy between her and her mother and sister, who deemed her a dreamer; and she moved about the house in listless inactivity, her large eyes full of angelic significance, and her heart full of loving impulses. It was at this time that her mother received the following note:

"MY DEAR MADAM: I am a man of few words — a friend of your late husband — with means sufficient to carry out what I propose. I wish to return a portion of the benefit he conferred upon me, a poor boy. I am aware of your family circumstances, and would relieve a portion of your burden. Your youngest daughter should receive an education. I have the ability to secure it, and would deem it a favor to be allowed to incur the expense attending it. The only condition I propose is that no sense of obligation may be allowed to overpower you, and no effort be made to discover the writer. Your obedient servant,

"MEMORY.

"P. S. Address me through the post-office, and keep my cognomen a secret from all."

"Well, this is a mystery!" said Mrs. Milling, as she read the note, and handed it to her oldest daughter. "Who can it be?"

The daughter scrutinized the letter for a long time in silence, in an endeavor, if possible, to detect the writing. At last she said,

"I strongly suspect it is Mr. Partelot, who takes this delicate way of doing us a kindness. Shall you accept the proposition?"

"Not without advice. We should be particular about these things. The world is very censorious."

"The world!" said the daughter, bitterly; "what is the world to us, if it cares nothing for us but to find fault with us? If it be Mr. Partelot, his kindness deserves a corresponding return."

"But if it be *not* his?" replied Mrs. Milling. "I declare I do not know what to do. I must ask advice. Shall I of Mr. Partelot?"

"By no means," was the reply; "anybody but him. Ask Mr. Urbin, father's old friend. He will advise for the best. I will endeavor to learn from Mr. Partelot if he wrote the letter."

Accordingly, on Mr. Partelot's next visit, the daughter mentioned the fact of the letter, — reserving the secret of the cognomen, — concluding with the remark, significantly made,

"Tax your *memory*, my dear sir, and see if you recall none who would be likely to do this thing."

She bent her eyes on him with an expression implying that she suspected his participation in the transaction, which he read at a glance. He lowered his eyes beneath her look, and asked her if she suspected him.

She confessed that she did.

"Then," said he, "it places me in a position where I shall claim the privilege of the doubt. I shall not confess, and shall claim that you intimate your suspicions of me to no one, for a very particular reason."

He took her hand in his as he spoke, and kissed it very respectfully. She withdrew her hand, but a flush of pleasure passed over her features. Her love for Upshur had been but a superficial feeling, with which temper and pride had more to do than the softer emotion of the heart. This pride was wounded by his desertion, this temper was aroused by his perfidy; and she had banished him from her heart with no regret, or even reluctance. The supposed discovery of a benefactor had excited her gratitude, — a kindred feeling with love, — and she felt a glow of happiness that had not been known to her for months. Partelot became a constant visitor at the house of Mrs. Milling, and his attentions to the fair Matilda were of the most assiduous character. People talked of it as a fixed thing that it was to be "a match."

It was about this time that the conversation occurred above recorded. Mr. Savage knew nothing of his partner's affair with the daughter of his old employer, and Mr. Partelot had reserved it as a surprise for him, just as Savage was called away by business. After a while he returned, when Mr. P., resting a moment from his writing, said,

"By the way, Savage, I 've got a secret for you."

"Well?" said his partner.

"What should you think if I was to tell you that I was going to be married?"

"I should say very little about it. It 's no business of mine. Your wife would n't become a member of the firm, nor a part of the stock."

"Very good! That 's true, Savage; and yet she is one that you may be interested in. Suppose I should tell you that it was Mr. Milling's daughter, eh?"

"What, Lily?" was asked in a tone of excitement, Mr. Savage starting up as he uttered the words.

"No, no; Lily 's but a child. 'T is the beautiful Matilda, man. Ha! I see the savage is moved. She has given me encouragement to hope that she will become Mrs. Partelot. Fine woman, Savage."

"But do you love her, Partelot?"

"What a question to a man who has been dancing attendance upon a woman for a year, studying how to love her!"

"Love is a lesson, however, not to be learnt. It is

imparted, and few breasts are warmed by it through education."

"Bah, Savage!" said Partelot; "you are a croaker. Men learn to love as they learn to eat olives. 'T is unpalatable, perhaps, at first, but after a while one gets used to it."

"Humph!" said the imperturbable partner, and turned to his ledger.

Time moved on, and brought again the cheerful season of Christmas, with its pleasant associations and reünions, and delightful surprises; and the house of Partelot & Savage still maintained its integrity.

CHAPTER V.

CHRISTMAS PRESENTS — A DISCOVERY.

"WHAT can this be?" said Mrs. Milling, as she returned from the door on Christmas morning, bearing a small square package in her hand. "For you, Matilda, I dare say."

The package was unrolled, and was found to contain a little rosewood casket of rare beauty, upon opening which a beautiful necklace of oriental pearls was discovered, pendent from which was a cross of the same, arched by a golden ray, on which was wrought in delicate letters the word "*Memory!*" On a card in the box was the simple name, "Lily."

"It is for Lily," said her sister, with a tone of marked disappointment. "Why did *he* send it to *her?* It must be a mistake."

She threw the bracelet into the box, with a petulant gesture, and handed it to her mother. Lily was called, and, to her great surprise, was presented with the beautiful gift. The fair girl stood as if spell-bound a moment, when, kneeling by her sister's side, she laid the box upon her lap, and bowed her head before her, saying,

"Sister, it is for you. You alone are worthy to wear it. My heart accords it to you."

The proud girl threw it from her, with a disdainful motion, and said, sharply,

"Never will I accept it, nor wear it! Such trifling I will not endure!"

She rose from her seat as she spoke, and left the room. Lily continued to kneel by the chair she had just left, and when she arose she found herself alone. The box was at her feet, opened, and the necklace lay upon the carpet. She looked upon it with a feeling of sorrow, half regarding it as the means of a new misery, when the card on which her name was written attracted her attention. She examined it minutely, and then proceeded to where the letter was kept that had proposed to pay for her education, and compared the writing. It was the same, beyond a doubt. But, though one wrote them both, who the one was was a matter still of impenetrable mystery.

Mr. Savage had never been at the home of the Millings since the death of his old patron. His diffident and abrupt nature made him withdraw himself from other besides business association, and, though he entertained as far as he could a friendly feeling for the family, he did not dare to intrude himself upon their time. His partner's confession had awakened in him, apparently, a new interest for them; and, one day, in response to the question why he never visited them, he promised to join his partner there in a visit on Christmas night.

The night came, and found Mr. Partelot at Mrs. Mil

ling's house. The little parlor was neat and bright. A wood-fire burnt briskly upon the andirons, and flashed a ruddy light around the room. An air of comfort prevailed, that mocked the inclemency of the night outside. Presently the door opened, and Matilda entered. Her brow was gloomy and dark, and the welcome she extended was very stately.

"I 'm sorry," said he, "that Savage is n't coming. I don't see what is the matter. He has just sent me a note, saying he is unavoidably called away to Mulberry-street on business."

Some brief expression of regret alone was uttered in response. He resumed:

"A strange man that — the most singular man I ever knew."

"I hope he is *sincere*," said she, with a significant tone.

"I think he is," said he.

"Is he accustomed to pretend an attachment for one person, and then to insult her by bestowing gifts upon her sister and slighting her?"

"Upon my word, I think not; I never had the least idea he was such a person. By the way, I have brought you a small token for the festive season."

He took a small paper from his pocket, and handed it to her. She unrolled the package, and a pair of lady's gloves met her view.

"Thank you," said she, with seeming delight. "Do you present these to me at the invoice price, or retail?"

"We have them invoiced to us; but why do you ask?"

"Only to know how to compare your present to me with that of yours to my sister."

"To your sister!" said he, with a tone of alarm. "I have made none."

"Then you did not make the generous proposition with regard to Lily's education?"

"I never said that I did," replied he, nervously twisting Savage's note around his finger.

"No," said she, "but you allowed me to infer that you did; and the man who can meanly take to himself the credit that belongs to another is below contempt."

"Well, madam," said he, "then, as I am below contempt, I am below your graciousness, and hence am not worthy of you. Good-evening."

He took his hat and passed out, as a butterfly vanishes at the approach of a chill, leaving the fair being that he was to have soon claimed as his own to a new mortification. Her mother and sister soon after found her in tears, and another dreary Christmas folded its wings over the home of the Millings.

The next morning Lily was alone in the parlor, engaged in her studies, when she saw a paper upon the floor. A thrill passed over her frame as she took it in her hand, — an indefinable commingling of fear and joy. She opened it, and read:

"DEAR PARTELOT: Please excuse me to the family. I am suddenly called to Mulberry-street. My sister has arrived from the country. My regards to Mrs. M., and Misses Matilda and Lily. Yours, SAVAGE."

"It is the same writing as the letter and the card," said she; "there is no mistaking the word 'Lily.' But shall I betray the secret thus confided to me, though unsought? I will regard the delicacy that prompted it, and keep the secret hidden. And this is the nature that has been looked upon as base, uncouth; this is he who has been treated by those he has so much benefited as a clown!"

The fair girl had forgotten the little seed of kindness sown in his heart a long time before,—sown as unconsciously as the birds spread luxuriousness and beauty in their flight, and make hitherto barren and inaccessible places pleasant and fruitful. She had forgotten —so unconscious was she—the words of kindness addressed to him in the library of their old home; but acts and words of kindness, springing from the God in man, partake of the eternal nature of God, and cannot die.

Mr. Partelot came no more, and his name was not mentioned in the circle where he had formerly been so constant a visitor. But bitter tears were shed for him, as men bend over a grave and weep, by eyes that had once beamed for him so brightly. It was worse than the grave, for the grave is honest; there is no treachery there to add poignancy to grief,—and there is a resurrection beyond, but none to buried friendship.

And Lily kept her secret locked within her breast, nourishing a gratitude, approaching to idolatry, for the noble being who was doing good secretly, expecting and hoping for no return, and even incurring the suspicion of churlishness from those around him. She grew in grace of mind and body, and her eyes lost none of the spiritual power that seemed to enter within the veil.

CHAPTER VI.

THE CONCLUSION, IN WHICH HAPPENS:

THE house of Partelot & Savage was the best house upon the street. Their paper was as good as gold, and both members of the firm were esteemed rich. But the repulse of Mr. Partelot at the hands of Miss Milling could not be healed by time or business, and, after enduring it for a time, he thought he would try a European tour. It was not that his heart was touched, — that could not be reached, — but his ambition was thwarted. Men talked about it, and his quiet partner looked, in his disordered eyes, very knowing. So much did these things prey upon him that he concluded to sell out. He made Mr. Savage an offer to place the business in his hands for a consideration, which was accepted, and Mr. Partelot left for the Old World.

Mr. Milling had been dead six years, and his family remained the same as at the beginning of their desolation, save that time had done its work with them. But time had been gracious with Lily. Her beautiful form was a marvel of grace, her face was as bright as an angel's, and her mind endowed with qualities that placed her far before those of her own age and condition. All loved her for her virtues; but there was one, of all the rest, whom she sighed to reach, — to throw herself at his feet and confess her indebtedness, and devote her life to his service. He had been prompt, year by year, in his strange benevolence, and year by year she had received some elegant token of his care, all bearing the same motto, "*Memory*," and all addressed simply "Lily." Safely had she kept that secret so strangely gained, amid the often-expressed wonder concerning it from those near to her. While her whole nature was as transparent as the day to loving eyes, she kept this little thought enshrined in a holy of holies, within which none might enter but Him who readeth all secrets

The singularity that had characterized her earlier years marked her growth. There were few who understood her, few that she recognized with the endearment of friendship; and, although her companions loved her, it was with a feeling allied to awe, so different was she from them. Of those who knew her the least were her own mother and sister. They ascribed to indolence the listlessness which at times seemed to mark her conduct, and to fanaticism the lifting up of spirit, which they comprehended not. Her words fell like music about her path, and, though she had no wealth to give, her " God bless you " thrilled the heart of those who received it like a heavenly benison.

Among her *friends* was one, with whom she had but recently become acquainted, a little older than herself. Endowed with more positiveness of character, she was a desirable companion for Lily; and, drawn together by sympathetic proclivities, their companionship was of the most agreeable description. Agnes resided in a distant part of the city, and Lily had never visited her in her home, although they frequently met at the houses of mutual friends. She had frequently spoken of her brother, of whom she was very fond; but Lily had never met with him.

It was again the Christmas time of year, and Agnes Loyle was going to give a select party on Christmas night. Cards were despatched, and preparations made suited to the occasion. Music and conversation and social pleasure were to form its essential features. Its ulterior object, however, was a deeply-conceived and womanly scheme of bringing Lily Milling and her brother together, though this was hidden from all but herself. Lily, retiring and reserved, would have been better content to have enjoyed her friend's society alone, but she gave her assent to the arrangement. She was to be accompanied by her sister.

The night was pleasant. The moon and stars glittered in the frosty atmosphere, and the merry sleigh-bells made music as the fleet steeds dashed on over the flinty snow. The vehicle which bore Lily and Matilda Milling stopped before a small but elegant house, brilliantly lighted, and seemingly the abode of comfort and taste. Entering, they were met by Agnes herself, who conducted her guests into the parlor, where several of the company had assembled, and where the rest soon after joined them.

"Miss Matilda, shall I make you acquainted with my brother, Mr. Savage? Lily, my brother, Mr. Savage," was said in the pleasant voice of Agnes Loyle. But with far different feelings was the name heard. In one heart it was associated with crushed hopes and buried pride; in the other, with veneration, and love, and gratitude; but by both it was received with evident emotion. It was an incomprehensible mystery that George Savage should be the brother of Agnes Loyle, and yet so it was; she was a sister by a second marriage. She was his only sister, and he loved her devotedly. When their mother died, some years before, he sent for her to come and live with him; and she arrived in town on a *Christmas day*, and had been installed mistress of the little house in Mulberry-street.

"The Misses Milling will remember in me an old acquaintance," said he, with a smile; "and," he added, to Lily, with a softened tone "my memory recalls a sweet child, who was as much of an angel in character as she is now angelic as a woman."

He took her hand and kissed it, as he spoke.

Bravo, Mr. Savage! The ice has melted suddenly the ungentle and uncourtly man has bowed before a little girl. What would Mr. Partelot say to see it? He once called you a churl. What would the world say to see it? It has called you a churl for years. Mr. Savage cared not for Partelot, — for the world, — but he cared for Lily, the sweetest flower that ever blossomed in a human garden.

"You are confused at finding me the brother of Agnes," said he; "she is my half-sister, and I need not praise her goodness to those who know her so well. She had advantages of cultivation that I never knew, and is the redeeming feature of my home, and gives it its refinement."

How gentlemanly he spoke, the uncouth and churlish Mr. Savage! The visitors scarcely spoke, all busied with their thoughts, when the voice of Agnes broke the spell.

"Come, come, there are sports going on here that rival those of the Olympiad, and are as rich with forfeits as an argosy. Come and help us."

The Christmas games had commenced, and fun and frolic ruled the hour. Young men and young women vied in their playful zeal; but, soon wearied with the excitement, the noisy games broke up, and charades and enigmas were personated.

"Let us try fortune-telling," said one of the party; some rare sport comes out of it sometimes."

Fortune-telling was at once decided upon; but who would be the fortune-teller? Several refused to personate the eldritch dame, when Lily was asked to assume the wand of inspiration, to which she assented. It was deemed strange that she should; but the very singularity of her consenting accounted for it. She accordingly was installed in a large old-fashioned chair, and before her came those whose fate she was to determine. And wise were her words, and momentous the matters of advice or prophecy that crossed her lips. With intuitive keenness she enlarged on matrimonial probabilities and collateral contingencies. The gentle Lily's witchery was perfect and irresistible, and crowned by an applause that knew no bound.

"And what has the prophetess to say for me?" said George Savage, standing before the Power.

She gazed upon him with an emotion imperfectly concealed, before she trusted her voice to speak; and then she spoke low, in a manner that those around could not hear.

"I have to say for you," said she, "that the hidden charity of a life, and its unselfish devotion to others' good, has a reward beyond that waiting upon its gratification."

He started, as she spoke.

"What means the enchantress?" said he, endeavoring to assume his former light-hearted and indifferent tone.

"I mean," continued she, "that the flowers one plants by the way of life do not die in meaningless beauty, but yield a fragrant adoration for the kindness that planted them; that a mind, enkindled by the loving and secret care that sought to hide its own benevolence, would be unworthy of its development, did it not show by its gratitude that it treasured the act in *memory!*"

She whispered the words in his ear, her face glowing with the fulness of her delighted heart, and, lifting a little cross that lay upon her breast, suspended from a string of pearls about her neck, she pointed significantly to the word "*memory!*"

Mr. Savage turned as pale as death, for a moment, and then a burning flush passed over his features.

"What did she say?" said many voices, eagerly.

"Nothing," said he; "that is, nothing which need be spoken of. I make way for any one, and truly believe in the sibylline character of the one you have installed."

The Christmas evening sped merrily, and joyful hearts throbbed in delightful harmony with the pulsing moments. Mr. Savage was silent and gravely pleasant; but there was a satisfaction on his face that dispelled all idea that pain made him grave. He sought constantly the side of the graceful Lily, who seemed imbued with life scarce her own. At last, when away from the gay revellers, he asked her to explain the discovery of his secret. She did so, and told him her own feelings upon becoming its recipient; and, as she dwelt upon her perception of his delicacy in the affair, and her warm appreciation, he clasped her hand, and, dropping upon his knee by her side, said:

"The sweet budding Lily of my boyhood I have long worn in my heart secretly. O, could I but hope to wear the flower, in its expanded beauty, there!"

Her hand, not withdrawn, trembled in his, as he spoke, and he accepted the emotion as an answer to his prayer.

"My secret has been my bane," said he, with her hand still in his. "I have avoided meeting you, for fear of betraying it — watching you, however, as you have grown in grace and beauty, and loving you at a distance, until my angelic sister, who guessed my feeling, though she did not the secret, has brought us together."

Lily was happy, and true enough to tell him that she loved him, and had long done so, but without knowing him, save as one true heart knows another; and was true enough, also, to tell him she would be his wife when a year or two more should better fit her for the honorable station, so little understood, even with six thousand scriptural years resting on it.

And thus ended the Christmas, with mirth, and love, and hope, to sanctify it. *Memory* became present joy, and an augury of future happiness. The years rolled on, and Lily lived the angel, rather than the wife, of Savage, — the synonym of the true woman who truly loves, — whose love is divine, and allows no grosser element to mingle with it. Based on respect and gratitude, it was a lifetime wave of devotion and trustfulness, bearing their bark of happiness on to the heaven of rest.

Mr. Partelot returned home, after an absence of some years, bringing with him a foreign wife. He became again engaged in business, and is now regarded as an excellent man, — oily and profuse, — though he is as hollow-hearted as ever. Matilda married a seafaring gentleman, and wears the largest crinoline on the street. Mrs. Milling, as if having nothing else worth living for after she had seen her daughters disposed of, died and was buried. Mr. Upshur was never heard of, and it was supposed that he was devoured by the Fejee Islanders, as it was ascertained, from a returned missionary, that one answering his description had been served up about that time.

Our story has no thrilling interest; but this may be gathered from it — that scenes are enacted at our doors, which, could we but see them, would be found to be great dramas, where the heart plays its part, performing its role with painfulness or joy. But few spectators are allowed to enter the portals, where no passport but human sympathy can find admittance, and the curtain often shuts down in darkness on a tragedy of ruined hopes.

HIGHER.

Pleased with our loves and low desires,
We sit like children midst the flowers,
No thought our listless soul inspires,
Or wakes to life its nobler powers;
We feel the sunshine round us glow,
And smile in imbecile content,
Letting the golden moments go
That heaven for ripe fruition meant.

As one by one our idols fade,
We moping sit and weakly sigh
That earthly loves so frail are made,
That earthly hopes should ever die!
Amid the beauteous wreck we mourn
Our altars prostrate in the dust,
And to the opening future turn
With heart of doubting and distrust.

Captive we lie in flowery chains,
By enervating pleasure bound,
Forgetting life's broad battle-plains,
Where work and its reward are found
Forgetting for the grovelling toys,
Around our feet as meshes spread,
E'er to look upward for the joys
That hang in clusters o'er our head

How idle we to strive to hold
The shadows that our joys eclipse,
Or eat the fruit of seeming gold
That breaks in ashes on our lips,
When ready to our outstretched hand
Celestial fruits their claims commend,
The product of that promised land
To which all manly strivings tend!

REVERIES

RIGHT before the window yonder is a wall, left bare and naked by the removal of a building torn down to make way for modern improvements. Upon the wall, clambering up over its surface in tortuous winding, is the mark of an old chimney-flue, black and sooty with the accumulative smoke of years. It is not a very beautiful object to contemplate, but it thrusts itself upon the vision, and will not down at our bid, because, probably, it can't get down. There 's a desolateness about the wall, and we count the places where the beams, that supported the floor, entered it, and extended along in tiers like the port-holes in the side of a ship-of-war; and we sit looking out upon it, while fancy reconstructs the old edifice, and peoples it again, and makes it all full of bustle and life. Piece by piece the old structure goes up, and we move among its living occupants — old fashioned, maybe, and quaint in dress, but with the same heart underneath all — and sit with them in the low-studded rooms by the side of the old fireplace, of which yonder is the flue. They burnt wood-fires then, that crackled and blazed upon the hearth, and sent their cheerful warmth out into the rooms, and flashed in ruddy light upon as pleasant faces as one could desire to see — illuminating the wainscot, and the ancient furniture, and the plate that shone upon the side-board. We hear again the pleasant joke, followed by the laugh that circles the band, and the repartee that sparkles like the fire-light, or the bright eyes that reflect its beams. That is punch — a jolly and generous bowl of it — that stands upon the table, sending up its steamy and savory breath; and the silver ladle above its brim is a quaint old thing that has been in the family for many years, and stands up with a consciousness of importance that is delightful to see. All partake — the old and the young — and beautiful lips press the goblet's brim, nor think shame of it, though modern usage might condemn it; but those were rum days. That old hearth was, doubtless, the scene of many tender episodes — shut out, however, from gaze by the roseate screen which delicacy wove in the days of their enactment. But fancy enters the veil, and the sigh and the tear, the kiss and the vow, are things of *now*, redolent with the sweetness of yesterday's love. The voices of children sound around the old dark hearth, and the gentle tones of age in wise counsel give serenity and sanctity to the whole. And grief obtrudes its pictures, thrusting the bier and the pall amid the roses and the myrtles, and a skeleton hand writes "*Death*" upon the wall opposite where the wood-fire brightens and flashes. What a queer train of fancies has the old wall conjured up! But, as we gaze, the fabric falls piece by piece away; the scene fades out; the murmur of voices becomes again the familiar sounds of trade; the fire is quenched by the snow that drips upon it; positive bricks take the place of unsubstantial fancies, and the flue, black and repulsive, stares us again in the face, a cold and cheerless presentment of desolation.

OLD AND YOUNG.

THE term young is used in contradistinction with old, and, as applied to young people, refers only to the condition of juvenility. There be, however, some young people who never are young, and old ones who never are old, where the two states appear to have been transposed. We often meet with such strangely old children that they seem from their cradles to have stepped right over the sunny land of youth into maturity. We are startled at their wisdom, and listen to their old words as to the teachings of an oracle, deeming them influenced by some mysterious power. We cannot treat them as children, nor pet them, as we think that Socrates or Plato may have hid themselves in the infantile organism, and stand ready to launch upon us some abstruse question in metaphysics. The young-old people are those who have, all their lives, kept their feelings young by active sympathy, and love, and kindness; and it is very beautiful to witness such as in this very latest season of life enjoy this Indian summer of the soul. The tenderest and the most mature do homage to such, and we draw towards them as we draw towards a shrine full of beautiful relics. This condition of youth in age is too rarely met with. The world comes soon between the soul and its better self, and the fermentation of care, and strife, and toil, sours the milk of kindness in the nature, and men grow crabbed and miserable as they grow old, when they should, in tranquil pleasure, be like the going down of the sun, calm and undisturbed.

THE VALLEY OF THE SHADOW

Down the dark valley, alone, alone,
Has our white-winged dove in her beauty flown;
Her tender eyes that shone so bright
Have closed forever to earthly light;
She has left the love that was round her thrown,
And down the valley has fled, alone.

There were bitter tears when she passed away —
A sad, sad cloud obscured our day!

She had twined herself round each loving heart,
Till she seemed of its very self a part;
O, *how* we loved her!—but she has flown
Down the dark valley—alone, alone.

She was but a fragile and beautiful thing,
A blossom to bloom in the lap of Spring;
The noonday heat with its feverish glow,
And the chilly breath of the wintry snow,
She could not abide, and thus has flown
Down the dark valley—alone, alone.

O, dark to us doth the valley appear,
And we shrink aghast from its shadows drear:
The earthly sense is chilled by the gloom
Of the sombre midnight of the tomb;—
Thus we gave her up, while our hearts made moan,
As she went down the valley—alone, alone.

Alone, all alone! but beyond the night
Of the darkened vale is a radiant light,
That breaks from above with diviner ray
Than shines the glory of solar day,
Which springs from God's eternal throne,
And lights the valley she trod alone!

And seraph hands in joyfulness hold
The little wanderer from our fold;
Her gentle feet shall feel no harm,
Sustained by the angelic arm,
And brighter than the sun e'er shone
Is she who passed down the valley alone.

THE MODEL HUSBAND.

Mr. Blifkins is a social and genial man. He belongs to a number of associations, that require his absence from home occasionally, and there are times when he chooses to indulge in a little sit-down with his friends, and enjoy for a time an abandon of care, whether of a business or of a domestic nature. Mr. Blifkins has one of the best of wives. She is exemplary in all the walks of life, and fully up to the Solomon standard of domestic excellence, as set forth in the thirty-first chapter of Proverbs. There is but one thing in the way of Mr. Blifkins' entire felicity, and that is her disposition to measure Mr. B.'s grain by her own bushel, so to speak, and because she is perfect, and feels no drawing towards the pursuits of her amiable husband. Preferring her own home to everything else in the world, and knowing no desire or wish beyond it, she expects Blifkins to be the duplicate of herself. Hence, without meaning anything unkind, she presumes occasionally to lecture her spouse, and wonders that he should go and sleep with the children rather than hear lessons so well intended. These lessons afflict poor Blifkins, who loves his wife and loves his children, but he has a love for friends likewise, and does not believe in the crucifixion of all affection outside the domestic ring. He even believes that integrity to his manhood *requires* that he should cultivate such affection, and that to crush it down would be to make his other affection diseased, as the entire physical system may be thrown out of bias by a felonious finger or a gouty toe. This is heresy to good Mrs. Blifkins, for the reason that she don't understand it, and continually persists in making herself unhappy by the unhappiness she reflects from the audience to which she lectures — Blifkins.

"Mrs. Blifkins," said he, one day, "will you condescend to give me your idea of a perfect husband?"

"Certainly, Mr. B.," said that most excellent lady, "and I hope the model I shall draw will be followed by you, and, heaven knows, there is need of improvement; for, what with lodge-meetings and such things as I don't know about, you don't act as a married man should, with a lovely family, that need a head to look after them."

"Well," said Blifkins, lighting a cigar, and putting his feet upon the table, "now fire away."

"Well, then," said she, "my model husband would not address his wife in that way; he would have said, 'Proceed, my dear.' It all comes of keeping company with masons and odd fellows, and fellows that, perhaps, — I can say *perhaps*, Mr. Blifkins, — are not so respectable. My model husband has none of the small vices of *some* husbands that I could name; of *one*, at least. He does n't spit in the house, nor put his feet on the table, nor smoke when his wife is speaking to him. He is too respectable for that. He stays at home every night, and finds his lodge at that shrine of the true heart, the domestic fireside. He never comes home with excuses that nobody knows if they are true or not. He never has people come to see him, to be shut up with him for an hour, in conversation that his wife is not allowed to hear. He never goes out without he takes her with him. He never spends money that he cannot account for if she asks him, and never doubts the wisdom or the expediency of purchases that she may make. He is just where he is wanted when he is wanted. He never contradicts his wife, nor treats her like a brute, as some husbands do, nor makes her cup a bitterness, when he should strive to make it pleasant. In short —"

"In short," said Blifkins, starting up, and throwing his cigar into the grate, with startling violence, "in short, you want a miserable, spiritless, senseless, contemptible *thing*, — brainless and heartless, — that will throw himself under the wheels of the matrimonial juggernaut, and allow it to crush him, without turning; and then, when you have found such a being, and the world points at him as the 'hen-pecked,' the 'spoon,' the 'automaton,' you would love him better, would you, than you do the gallant, handsome, and spirited Blifkins, who has the delight to acknowledge you as his wife, but not his tyrant nor overseer?"

Mrs. Blifkins brightened up at this a very little, but she does n't know where it will end.

SONNET TO PAN.

O Pan! once held the Deity of woods,
Now changed thy place, — thy former state forgot, —
We see thee ranked amongst our household goods —
Not gods — thy sacredness all "gone to pot."
Thy ministers are cooks, an unctuous crew,
Who all thy old austerities ignore;
The grateful incense of the morning dew
Goes up from off thine altar never more;
But odorous fries wake gustatory qualms,
And simmering compounds scent the ambient air,
The "siss" of sausages ascends like psalms,
The fume of mutton rises like a prayer.
Thus do we change; O Pan! with heathen man;
Thou wast a god — now thou 'rt a dripping Pan.

ILLUSTRATIVE PANTOMIME.

THIS is excellent in its way; a good sentence is helped materially by an appropriate gesture in the right place, and even a dull one is saved from absolute stupidity by a timely illustrative motion of the hand. But we deprecate the practice of some, who, when telling a story involving an account of their conversation or conduct with others, particularly of a quarrelsome nature, go through the motions again in public, as if we were the party in difficulty, leaving people passing to infer that we are the victim of their deadly hate. How terrible it is to have one of the bellicose sort back us to the wall and force us to listen to the account of his trouble with another like himself, maugre our protestations of business and haste! "Only a minute," he says, and then, taking us by the collar, while we endeavor to give a smiling lie to our real feelings, he commences to say that he called on his antagonist, and, says he to him, "*What do you mean by such conduct?*" This, of course, is yelled at the top of the voice, and people look round to see what the row is about. He then goes on: "He had no explanation to make." This is said in a moderate tone. "Then, says I," he continues, in a loud voice, "*you are an infernal rascal,*" — doubling his fist in our face, and holding our collar by the other hand, — "*and deserve to have your nose pulled!*" We try, with a very severe effort, to look good-natured; but people stare at us, and policemen stand on the opposite side, watching for the moment of actual strife, to pitch in. "I told him," — still brandishing his fist, and speaking loud, — "*you are a scamp, sir*, and when I meet you on 'Change *I'll kick you!* He tried to go into the house, but I took him by the collar with both hands,"—suiting the action to the word, —"and, says I, *No, you don't go so easy.*" We are in despair. Another policeman has come along, and everybody who has passed has reported the row. Even the newsboys come and thrust their inquisitive and unwashed mugs in between us, evidently estimating how much they are going to make out of the disturbance in a fair retail of its detail, while the reporters stand waiting at the corners to secure the item that seems impending. Thus all seems to our disturbed fancy, as we stand back to the wall, with the fist coming up before our eyes, and the loud and violent tones in our ears. It is fearful to fall into the hands of such people, and we rush from their presence as if we were the ones on whom the real violence, and not the delineated, had been practised. Were we a teacher of elocution, we should recommend that this species of illustrative gesticulation be omitted.

ON THE MISSISSIPPI.

FATHER of waters!—here upon thy breast
  I lay my head in trusting confidence;
Too long a prey to terror and unrest,
  I may, thank heaven, banish them from hence.
How proudly scattereth our prow aside
  The turbid tides, as vainly on they sweep;
And the good steamer, with a seeming pride,
  Laughs in huge billows to the conquered deep!
But stealing o'er me like a misty cloud
  Come dreams of sawyers and perfidious snags,
And many scenes upon my memory crowd,
  At thought of which my resolution flags,—
And, as fears trench on confidence and trust,
I quake to think, what if the biler bust,

MRS. PARTINGTON AT SARATOGA

"EVERY back is fitted for its burden," said Mrs. Partington, as she stood by the Congress Spring, from which one had just emptied the eighth tumbler down his spacious gullet, "and every stomach for its portion. Heaven, that tempers the wind to the shorn lamb, I dare say will likewise also temper the water to their compassity to bear it; for we read that Apollos shall water, and that the increase will be given, which must mean Saratoga water, and the increase the debility to hold it, though how folks can make a mill-race of their elementary canal is more than I can see into." Roger stood looking at the victim, as tumbler after tumbler disappeared, when he turned round to Mrs. Partington, and asked her if she remembered what Macbeth said to the Fifer, in the play. She could n't recall the name of Macbeth, but remembered having heard the name of Macaboy somewhere mentioned. He told her that the remark alluded to applied to the scene then enacting; for the hard drinkers seemed to be saying, by their acts, "Damned be he who first cries, Hold enough." — "I think they all hold too much," remarked the dame. Roger nodded, and smiled, saying, "And need damming, too." Ike stood watching the boy who drew up the water, pocketing the half-dimes so coolly, and wondered what he was going to buy with all his money, thinking how he could make it fly, if he had it. He had invested all his available funds in red crackers, and had n't a cent to bless himself with.

A PICTURE.

THERE 's a little low hut by the river's side,
Within the sound of its rippling tide ;
Its walls are gray with the mosses of years,
And its roof all crumbly and old appears ;
But fairer to me than a castle's pride
Is the little low hut by the river's side.

The little low hut was my natal nest,
Where my childhood passed — life's spring-time blest ;
Where the hopes of ardent youth were formed,
And the sun of promise my young heart warmed,
Ere I threw myself on life's swift tide,
And left the dear hut by the river's side.

That little old hut, in lowly guise,
Was lofty and grand to my youthful eyes ;
And fairer trees were ne'er known before
Than the apple-trees by the humble door,
That my father loved for their thrifty pride,
Which shadowed the hut by the river's side.

That little low hut had a glad hearth-stone,
That echoed of old with a pleasant tone,
And brothers and sisters, a merry crew,
Filled the hours with pleasure as on they flew.
But one by one have the loved ones died
That dwelt in the hut by the river's side.

The father revered and the children gay
The grave and the world have called away,
But quietly all alone there sits
By the pleasant window, in summer, and knits,
An aged woman, long years allied
With the little low hut by the river's side.

That little old hut to the lonely wife
Is the cherished stage of her active life ;
Each scene is recalled in memory's beam,
As she sits by the window in pensive dream,
And joys and woes roll back like a tide,
In that little old hut by the river's side.

My mother! — alone by the river's side,
She waits for the flood of the heavenly tide,
And the voice that shall thrill her heart with its call.
To meet once more with the dear ones all,
And form in a region beatified
The band that once met by the river's side.

That dear old hut by the river's side
With the warmest pulse of my heart is allied,
And a glory is over its dark walls thrown
That statelier fabrics have never known;
And I still shall love, with a fonder pride,
That little old hut by the river's side.

Nov., 1857.

JOB A DRUMMER.

There was a lecture preached in the little brick school-house, when Mrs. Partington lived in Beanville, upon the natural and practical application of the Gospel. The old lady, who all her life long had attended at the Old North Church, looked upon the discourse with suspicion, and watched the preacher with much jealousy, in hopes of catching him tripping. At last he spoke of the book of Job, commending its grandeur and great beauty of thought, but saying that he regarded Job as simply a drama. The old lady was near the door, and as she heard this she immediately arose and left the house, saying, with a warmth scarcely in keeping with her character,— but religious prejudice, even in the best, will induce a queer feeling, and we would throw this pen into the fire rather than pretend that Mrs. Partington was perfect,— "Well, well, I wonder what he 'll say next? What a presentiment from a pulpit where the Gospel has been so long dispensed with!"— "What 's the matter, mem?" asked old Mr. Jones, who ran against the dame as he was going in, reminding one of the concussion of the irresistible and immovable bodies, — "what's the matter? what's broke?" — feeling round on the ground for his specs, which had been knocked off by the collision. — "Why," said she, pulling down her cap-border, which had been, like her temper, a little disturbed, "why, he has just said that Job was n't nothing but a drummer; and if that is n't blastphemy, I should like to know what is." — "Did you judge, from the tenor of his remark, that Job was a bass drummer?" said Jones, at the same moment. — "No," replied she, "but the remark was very base." Mr. Jones laughed, and the dame greatly wondered thereat, deeming that he was yet, as she said to herself, "in the intents of wickedness."

A SLIGHT MISCONCEPTION.

"THERE 's where the boys fit for college," said the Professor to Mrs. Partington, pointing to the High-School house. — "Did they?" said the old lady, with animation; "and, if they fit for college before they went there, did n't they fight afterwards?" — "Yes," said he, smiling, and favoring the conceit; "yes, but the fight was with the head, and not with the hands." — "Butted, did they?" said the old lady, persistently. — "I mean," continued he, "that they wrestled with their studies, and went out of college to be our ministers and doctors." "Ah!" said she, "I never knew that people had to rastle to be ministers and doctors before." They moved on, Mrs. Partington pondering the new idea, and Ike and Lion striving for the possession of the old lady's umbrella.

STORY OF FRAZER'S RIVER:

REVEALING THE FATE OF A MAN WHO INDULGED IN FLUIDS TO WHICH HE WAS NOT ACCUSTOMED.

[The story was told in the California papers, on the authority of a German Doctor, that a man at Frazer's River drank some water that he found in the quartz rock, and was urned to stone.]

I feel a shiver
Come over my frame at the very name
Of auriferous Frazer's River,
Where gold in lumps as big as a biggin
Is lying all round awaiting the digging;
Where they pick the locks
Of crystalline rocks,
Such fabulous riches showing,
That men to-day in seedy sorrow
May homeward go, elate, to-morrow
With pockets overflowing;
And this is the reason why I shiver
At tidings brought from Frazer's River:
Onesimus Guile
Had made his pile
In a very inconsiderable while,
But the weather was good,
And the nuggets were whoppers,
And Guile always stood
To look after the coppers;
And so, his greed growing stronger and stronger,
He said to himself,
As I 'm in for the pelf,
I might as well tarry a little while longer;—
A little more rhino
Will not hurt me, *I* know,
And while Fortune is kind I 'll engage her,
Men's favor I 'll win
With my surplus of tin,
And though I 'm a miner — he gave a grin —
I can hold up my head like a major.

Then he went to his raking
And rocking and shaking,
With weary brain and body aching,
Toiling on, if sleeping or waking,

Not a moment of comfort taking,
His hope of home for the time forsaking,
In wet weather soaking, in hot weather baking,
    To add to his earthly riches ;
Digging and delving early and late,
Scratching the soil with an anxious pate,
Running a muck with a golden fate,
    Wearing out body and — boots.
Just the same as your millionaire,
Who asks at first but a moderate share,
And takes for his motto old Agar's prayer,
    But, as his wealth increases,
He cannot fix on a quantum suf.,
And never knows when he has enough,
His greed being made of elastic stuff,
    That in its stretch ne'er ceases.

    As he picked his way,
    On a subsequent day,
    A boulder of quartz before him lay,
His greedy eyes making richer ;
    One sturdy blow
    He gave it, when, lo !
    A stream of water from it did flow,
As though poured out from a pitcher.
As clear as crystal, and icy cold,
'T was a very charming stream to behold,
    And Guile stood still, enchanted ;
For sparkling water, clear and bright,
Is ever a source of true delight ;
It comes to us in dreams of night,
When our lips are dry and parched and white,
And fever, like a hideous sprite,
    Our sleeping hours has haunted ; —
Though many there be who are better suited
To have the water a little diluted !
Guile bowed his head to the mystical pool,
And tasted its waters pure and cool,
    Then drank till he felt satiety ;
Saying that, though from *quartz* it came,
There was n't in it the baleful flame,
The burning and abiding shame,
That flowed from a source with a similar name,

That tripped the heels of sobriety,
A wild, agrarian, levelling thing,
A jet from an infernal spring,
That flowed to plague society!
But soon he felt he had drunk too deep:
A cold chill over his frame did creep,
His eyelids drooped with a sense of sleep,
And he yielded to its action;
He slept, but over his sleep there stole
A spirit power of dread and dole,
That quenched the flame of his being's coal,
And changed poor Guile from a living soul
To a thing of petrifaction!
To rouse him his mates tried all their devices
But vain did they strive
And drive and contrive,
He was stiff as a saint in the temple of Isis.

* * * * *

They carved him up
In goblet and cup,
In pipes and folders and handles,
In bracelets rare,
And combs for the hair,
And sticks for holding candles;
His wife wore his chin
As a cameo pin,
And earrings wrought from his toes;
His fingers were sought,
Into chess-men wrought,
And a paper-weight made of his nose!
Till never was known in the world before
A case where a man went into more
Extensive distribution,
Or where, if he should claim his own,
The chances would be fainter shown
Of getting restitution;
And this is why I always shiver
To hear the name of Frazer's River.

HABITS.

THE force of habit is very great. It becomes, after a while, our second nature; and it is very unfortunate that the habits are so often wrong, leading us, almost in our own despite, to believe the dogma of man's innate depravity. We are bigots from habit, inebriates from habit, gluttons from habit, swearers from habit, — there is no need of extending the list. How subtly habit steals upon us! We laugh at the caution which would save us, and take the first step in sin, that leads to the plunge down the abyss from which there is scarcely an escape. How we pet our habits, and palliate them, and justify them! They get their hold upon us through an inefficient will, which in itself is a habit. The will should be cultivated and strengthened, as much as the body and mind; but habit, at the very outset, says the will of the child must be crushed out. It should be encouraged, rather, and directed to its proper end. With stout will and resolution, we may throw off or resist habit; but without, it holds us with hooks of steel. It is unfortunate to know that more than half of our time is spent in repenting of habits contracted during the other and better half; and more unfortunate to think that our own habits have, by example, involved others in the same habits. In vain we say, "Get thee behind me, Satan!" if we have not the back-bone to command it. Satan laughs at us, and treats us contemptuously every way; for we are weak, and Satan is strong. We may make loud protestations at high twelve in prayer-meeting, for we are courageous with the multitude; but when left to ourselves, and our own weakness, like Peter on the water, we sink.

CHECKERS.

We often hear about life's "checkered scenes,"
And every man's experience owns the same,
And this is what the trite expression means:
The world 's a checker-board and life 's the game.
The men are placed when we sit down to play,
The rows unbroken, and we boldly move,
But oft disaster marks the first essay,
And, pushing blindly on, we losers prove.
Let us be wary, watching close the board,
Looking for traps that may on us be sprung —
For fate propitious cannot be restored,
If lost the vantage when the game is young.
Through vigilance alone we ever win
O'er those shrewd players, Appetite and Sin.

GRAMMAR.

"People may say as much as they please about the excellence of the schools," said Mrs. Partington, very terribly, "but, for my part, I think they are no better than they ought to be. Why, do you know," continued she, in a big whisper, "that Isaac's teacher has actually been giving him instruction in vulgar fractions?" She took off her spectacles and rubbed the glasses, in her excitement putting them on bottom side up. The charge, we admitted, was a just one. "Yes," continued she, brightening up for a new charge, like a slate beneath the action of a wet sponge, "yes, and see what other things they learn, about moods and pretences and all sorts of nonsense. Gracious knows we learn moods enough without going to school, and as for pretences we find enough of them outside. There are too many pretenders in the schools and out of 'em, without trying to make any more." She was provoked because Ike did n't get the medal for his splendid composition on the "American Eagle."

FEELING.

A LECTURER once claimed for feeling the whole of the qualities that characterized all the senses as they are distinguished by the old dogma. He argued that through the eyes, ears, palate, nose, all arrived at the sensorium, and hence were feeling. And there was truth and beauty in it; for what were all those open doors to consciousness, if the feeling were wanting to give the glow to beauty, or the melody to song, or the perfection to art? We see many living illustrations of the truth of this in the world, in whom feeling lies an uncultivated thing, withering in the air of frigid indifference. They are called heartless people, which is very expressive; and we feel chilled by contact with them, as though, in our summerish feeling, a breeze from over an iceberg had fanned us.

AN IMPOSTOR.

"TRUTH is stranger than friction," said Mrs. Partington, as she listened to one who came to her with a fearful story of incredible calamity. "I 'm not nat'rally incredible; but, if you had n't told the story yourself, I should n't have given credulity to it. You 'd better go to the society for the prevention of porpoises; for they are very malevolent, and might give you something to do." How thankful the individual seemed to feel at her kindness; and he went off invoking blessings upon her, though she marvelled very much to see him go in an opposite direction from that she had indicated. The something to do had evidently staggered him.

MESMERISM AND MATRIMONY.

OR, SCIENCE VERSUS WIDOW.

MARTIN SPEED was a bachelor. He had backed and filled, and hesitated and doubted about entering upon the "blissful estate" of matrimony, until the fire of youthful passion was all spent, and matrimony had become a problem to him as dry and formal as one in old Walsh's arithmetic; to be ciphered out for an answer, as much as that proposition about carrying the fox, goose, and bag of corn, across the creek, that everybody "problemly" remembers. Being a phrenologist, he left the province of hearts altogether, and went to examining heads, to ascertain by craniological developments a woman's fitness for the position of a wife to Martin Speed, Esq., as letters came addressed to him at the Speedwell post-office. The town of Speedwell was named for an ancestor of his, and boasted of several thousands of inhabitants; and, as it was a factory place, it had a goodly share of good-looking marriageable girls.

Martin studied Combe and Spurzheim and Gall, and grew bitter as disappointment saw him enter his forty-first year a bachelor. He looked back on the past, and saw the chances he had neglected, and the happiness of those who had started with him, and were now portly people, the heads and fronts of families; and the delicate damsels he had slighted, respected mothers in Israel, and exemplary and amiable wives. He sought every opportunity for examining the heads of such as would submit themselves to his hand with a hope of catching the bachelor; for they knew his weakness, and he was well-to-do and an eligible match. But in vain he looked for perfection. The bumps would not be arranged as he wished them. If he took a liking to a pretty face, phrenology impertinently gave it the lie straight, and he at once avoided it.

It was at this juncture that a biological lecturer — a grave professor in that science — came to Speedwell and gave a series of exhibitions. These Martin attended, and biology at once became an "intensity" with him,—a "new emotion." He attended all the exhibitions;—saw men personate roosters and crow; hens and scratch; shiver with cold or burn with heat, at the will of the operator; saw a miser endeavor to clutch an eagle held out to him while under the influence of the wonderful spell, and the tongue of a woman stilled who for twenty years had been the pest of Speedwell by her loquacity.

This put the mind of Martin on a new track. He sold his old phrenological works, and devoted himself to the study of the wonderful science through which such marvels were performed. The professor was a fine teacher, and Martin placed himself under his tuition. He succeeded admirably. In a short time he surpassed his instructor, and had more than his powers in influencing the susceptible among his weak brethren and sisters.

He formed a resolution to himself, that through this means he would gain a wife. Could he find one that his science could control, — one that at a glance he could transfix, like the man who was stopped by the mesmerizer half-way down, as he was falling from the roof of a house, — he would marry her; for the reason, dear reader, that Martin had not married, was that he had heard of wives wearing the —— authority over their lords, and he was a timid man. In this new science he saw security, and sedulously sought for one of the right description. At every party where he was invited, at every sewing-circle, at every knot of factory girls in which he mingled in the summer evenings, he tried his art, but without success. At last, when on the point of despairing, accident gave what he had failed of obtaining by earnest seeking. A widow — dangerous to bacheloric peace, as edged tools are to the careless hands of the inexperienced — came to the village on a visit. The weeds had not been removed that marked her bereavement, and the merest touch of melancholy rested on her brow; but her eye was laughing, and a sweet curl strayed away and lay like a chiselled eddy upon the marble of her cheek. She had a jewel on her hand, and the black dress she wore was cut judiciously, — the milliner that cut it had been a widow herself, and knew how to manage such matters, — showing a beautiful white shoulder, and revealing a bust of rare loveliness.

Martin met the widow at the residence of a friend, and liked her. He had never seen so prepossessing a woman, he thought. But she had buried one husband, and that was rather a drawback. One visit led to another, the liking still increasing, until he broached the subject of biology, with a wish fervently felt that this might be the woman he sought. She was fully acquainted with it, and, in answer to his question if she was susceptible to its influence, she replied that she did n't know, but was willing to have the fact tested. What a position for Martin! Seated by her side on a sofa, with her hand laid in his, her rich dark eyes resting upon his with a look equal to that which the widow Wadman poured into those of the unsuspecting Toby, in the stillness of a summer evening! But science held him secure and his nerves were calm as the summer day of that evening. By and by the beautiful lids drooped, the head bent gently forward, and the widow, with a sweet smile upon her lips, lay fast asleep. Martin could have shouted "Eureka," in his delight at the discovery. Now his pulse quickened, and he stooped to kiss the lips that lay unresisting before him; but he did n't. By the exercise of his power he awakened her, and she was much surprised at being caught napping, and blushed at the strangeness of it; and blushed more when Martin told her how he had been tempted, and how gloriously he had resisted; and laughed a little when she slapped his cheek with her fingers as he took pay from the widow's lips for his self-denial, and went home half crazy with joy at his new-found treasure, more like a boy of nineteen than a matured gentleman of forty.

Every night found him a visitor at the widow's, and every night the success of the science was proved, until by a mere look or a wave of the hand the beautiful widow became a subject to his will, and he became at the same time a subject to hers. She was such a splendid creature, too! You would not find in a long journey another fairer, or more intelligent, or more virtuous. The question might be asked, which magnetism was the most pleasant or most powerful, his or hers. But he thought only of his own, not deeming that he was in a spell more powerful, that was irrevocably binding him. What could an old bachelor know of such a thing?

This state of things grew to a crisis, at last, and Martin formally proposed to the widow that the two should be made one, by the transmutation of the church. To this she assented; and it was announced soon after, to the astonishment of all, that Martin Speed had married the widow Goode. The punster of the village made a notable pun about Good-Speed, at which people laughed very much; and the editor of one of the papers, who was a very funny man, put it in print.

It happened, shortly after the marriage, that they had a famous party, and some of the guests bantered Martin about his marriage, upon which he told them of the manner it came about. They were a little incredulous, and he volunteered to give them some specimens of his remarkable power over his wife. She was in another room attending to some female friends, when he called her to him. She came obediently, and he asked her to sit down, which she did. He took her hand and looked into her eyes, to put her to sleep. Her eyes were wide open, and a lurking spirit of mischief looked out of them broadly into his. He waved his hands before them, but they remained persistently open. He bent the force of his will to their subjugation, but it was of no use.

"Mr. Speed," said she, laughing, "I don't believe the magnetism of the husband is equal to that of the lover; or, perhaps, science and matrimony are at war."

She said this in a manner to awaken a strong suspicion in his mind that she had humbugged him, and had never been put to sleep at all. His friends, as friends will when they fancy a poor fellow has got into a hobble, laughed at him, and told the story all round the village. For months he was an object of sport to everybody. People would make passes over each other as he passed, and women would shut their eyes and look knowing. But, whether *his* power had gone or not, *hers* remained; and he cared not a fig for their laughing, for he was happy in the beautiful spell of affection which she threw over him, that bound him as a chain of flowers. The attempt to close her eyes was never repeated, for he was too glad to see them open to wish to lose sight of them. Life with Speed sped well, and Martin became a father in time. He never regretted the expedient he adopted to get his wife, though he never could make out exactly whether she humbugged him or not.

THE OLD NORTH MILL-POND.

RIPPLING, rippling on memory's shore,
Comes the sound of waters evermore,
Comes in the dreams of quiet night,
Comes in the day's effulgent light,
Comes with the thoughts of years bygone,
Thrilling my heart with its monotone, —
Thrilling my heart with emotions fond,
As I think of the dear old North Mill-Pond.

There are lakes which glow 'neath warmer skies,
There are waves which shine in grander guise,
There are mightier seas and loftier streams
Than this meandering through my dreams;
But none with me have a stronger claim
Than the humble one with its humble name,
That has drawn my muse from its flight beyond,
To bathe its wings in the North Mill-Pond.

I 've passed far on life's devious track, —
Onward, still onward, but, looking back,
O'er a weary landscape of cares and tears,
A boy by a silvery stream appears,
Who smiles as he stands in the sun's bright ray
As *I* smiled in glad boyhood's day,
Ere the bitter lesson of life I conned,
And left the side of the North Mill-Pond.

O, blessed alchemy of youth,
That holdest the mirror up to truth,
Bnd all that makes the young heart blest
Is on the polished plate impressed;
Each scene by young affection traced
Is vivid still and undefaced,
Drawing me back with a loving bond
Again to the bank of the North Mill-Pond.

The grave-yard lies o'er the water blue,
The old grave-yard which my boyhood knew;
The white stones gleam by the hillock green,
And nameless mounds strew the space between;
And sweetly they rest in their dreamless sleep
Whom the graves in their motherly bosoms keep,
Recalled and held in affection fond
As they rest by the side of the North Mill-Pond.

'T was beautiful, when the eve was still,
To list to the drone of the distant mill,
As it rose and fell on the summer air,
In the dewy darkness resting there;
Its tones were words to my youthful ear,
My heart was soothed with their better cheer,
And was borne away to scenes beyond
The margin green of the North Mill-Pond.

And when in the north the lightning shone
From out the gathering tempest's throne,
In the hush of the winds ere they woke from rest,
To foam o'er the water's placid breast,
I loved to stand mid the shadows dark,
The muttering thunder's voice to hark,
And my soul to its music did respond,
As I sat by the side of the North Mill-Pond

'T is here again with its early note,
Again on its beauteous tide I float;
I bathe once more in its crystal bright,
And sport with the skaters in rapid flight;
And fish for minnows beneath its waves
From the broad flat stone which the water laves;—
All, all are here in remembrance fond,
And my heart is glad for the North Mill-Pond.

Thus rippling, rippling on memory's shore,
Comes the sound of waters evermore!
O, sounds of delight, my spirit hears
And treasures the words of those distant years,
Ere care had deadened or sorrow pressed,
To ruffle my buoyant bosom's rest, —
When hope was bright nor knew despond,
By the smiling and beautiful North Mill-Pond.

THE TRUE PHILOSOPHY.

UNCLE HOPEFUL, as we must call him, because he is everything that is cheerful and happy, was talking with us on the occasion of his seventieth birth-day, and the conversation naturally led to life and its uses. We could not avoid asking the question how it was that, while other men were soured by the cares of the world, and bent over with their weight, he had retained his elasticity of temper and body. He assured us that he had no patent for his remedy, there was no secret involved in it. He had begun life with a determination to do right, and as, in order to do right, it was essential that he should feel right, his prayer had been for grace, a cheerful heart, and a broader nature. He had gone out into the world with this feeling, and the result had been peace. He had never quarrelled, never wronged a man, never joined a church, loved God and men, and was now ready to step from this bank and shoal of time to the destiny beyond, unwavering in his faith that it was well with him. Uncle Hopeful had not been a perfect man, as the world understands the word perfect. He had had his buffetings with Satan in the form of various temptations, from some of which encounters he had come out badly hurt; but the smart had done him good. He had seen in each temptation a new lesson, enjoining upon him the duty of loving the tempted and the fallen, and the uses of adversity likewise had a deep and abiding belief in him. He thanked God for his temptation, for it had made him stronger; and for his adversity, for it had made him better — had softened his heart, and brought him more into sympathy with the sorrowful. "Uncle Hopeful," then we said, "what is your recipe, in brief, for a happy life?" The old man lifted his face, as bright as though he were transfigured, and uttered the words, "Purpose and work — an object and the struggle for its attainment."—"Suppose the object is money?" we queried. —"That is disease," he eplied, thoughtfully; "the object should be the honor of. God and the improvement of man — everything else should be subordinate." We separated, but the lesson went with us. How few there are who live according to Uncle Hopeful's idea of happiness! How many are there now standing on the verge of a life, that can look back along its path with the same satisfaction as Uncle Hopeful? Measuring life by its usefulness, he has lived more than seventy years. When such a person dies, it seems to us that tears are the selfish begrudgings of our nature of the rest he so much needs after his long and faithful toil. A little of his own cheerful philosophy should give us joy at his transit, rather than sorrow.

A CLASSIC.

[The story of Menippus and the Empusa has run together in the following craze of rhyme. Though slightly modernized in its present construction, it retains the peculiarities of the fable.]

I WILL tell you the tale of Menippus the Lycian,
A jolly young fellow, but far from a rich 'un,
Who was just twenty-five
And the fairest alive,
Who fell mad in love with a charming Phœnician.
On the road to Cenchrea
He first chanced to see her,
And rich as a Jew did the damsel appear —
All covered with jewels and elegant laces,
With rings and such things to add to her graces,
And smiles like the Hours'
In heavenly bowers,
That Mahomet held out for Moslem " devours
Then she gave Menippus an invitation
To visit her as he 'd inclination,
At her suburban habitation,
Near beautiful Corinth village;
She promised him wines that beat creation,
And fruit from every clime and nation,
Besides a hint at sly flirtation,
And other delectable pillage.
And then Menippus gave her his card,
And swore by his gods, and swore very hard,
That she was a trump,
And he was a gump
If he did n't at such opportunity jump.
His amorous flame
Had n't given her name,
But this to Menippus was all the same,
For he was in love, and lovers we know
Are the stupidest people the world can show.
So he went straightway to see her as bid,
And she vowed she loved but him, she did,
And she gave him money and gave him wine,
And the path of life seemed all divine,
A precious dream that would ne'er grow dim,
And the world was a jolly old world for him,

Until Apollonius, the mighty magician,
Came down like a sluice on the fair Phœnician.
Says he, "My sonny,
There 's gall in your honey —
Look out for breakers and bogus money!
This lady, whose charms you delightedly howl
Is — this in your ear — a condemnible ghoul.
Empusa hight,
Whose appetite
In things forbidden of men takes delight;
Of a kind who entrap in their infamous mesh
The nice young fellows with tender flesh,
And, pepperless, saltless, eat them fresh!
And this, my friend,
Will be your end,
If you don't to my present words attend:
She only waits for the wedding-day
To dish you up in an epicure way.
She 's a serpent, a toad,
And you take up a load,
If you travel with her the marital road."
Then young Menippus, scratching his head,
Thus to the sage Apollonius said:
"To-morrow, old fellow, I 'm to be wed.
I 'll not be wrecked with the port in sight,
You need n't try me thus to fright;
And, did n't I think
That you never drink,
I 'd certainly say you were rather tight!
Not one word you 've said is true, man,
For I assure you she 's no such woman;
So, as sure as a gun,
By to-morrow's sun
She and your humble servant are one,
And if you 're there you may see the fun

The day shone bright,
And the bride, all in white,
Like a being of light,
In accustomed garb of the bride bedight,
Was called by all a delectable sight.
And the men and maids of Corinth were there,
To see that the nuptials were put through fair,

But just as the Corinthian minister
    Had opened his head,
    And only said,
    " You twain I wed,"
A voice cried out, " Yes, over the sinister ! "
When, as all wondered what it could mean,
Old Apollonius stepped on the scene.
He forbade the marriage, and told them to stay,
For the bride was n't one in a marrying way —
    That she was a ghoul,
    A being most foul,
And tying this knot there 'd be Dickens to pay.
    Then all may see
    What a row there must be —
    The lady raved like none but she ;
And she vowed that in Tophet's gulf *she 'd* toss over
Every one that was called a philosopher.
But old Apollonius, quite up to trap,
For all of her violence cared not a snap.
He told her he 'd soon cut her off root and branch,
If she did n't instantly vamose the ranch ;
    She cried and took on,
    And was loth to be gone,
    But, charged with her crime, she admitted the corn ;
    Then passed from their view,
    And the riches all flew,
    And the jewels crumbled to ashes, too ;
And poor Menippus, as we are told,
Scratched his head in wonder, and muttered, " sold "

MORAL.

Youths, don't at hasty marriages jump,
For every woman may not be a trump.
Remember Menippus's lucky escape,
And use all care to avoid a bad scrape,
Or else you may find yourself, maugre your groans,
Wife-eaten — *wife-eaten* — body and bones.

BE CONTENTED.

"Do you know what the people of Cape Ann do when it rains?" one asked of another. Upon confessing his ignorance, he was informed that they let it rain. This is the true philosophy. It is best not to fret at evils that we cannot help, or even for those that we might help; for fretting does not better a thing any. We always admired the example of the venerable negro in the song, "whose name was Uncle Ned." Of him it is narrated that when his teeth failed him, because of his declining years, and he could no longer eat the corn bread, he "let the corn-bread be," with charming resignation. There is an old saying, that has come down to us from very remote antiquity, that "it is of no use to cry for spilled milk." Fretting shortens life, and makes it miserable while it lasts, tiring sympathy and wearing out surrounding patience. Fretting wrinkles the skin like a baked apple, turns the aspect to a glum sourness, makes the finest eyes look wicked, and places personal beauty at a risk. The Sage of Thorndike was one hundred and ten years old when he died, and at that age his face was as fair as an infant's. When asked the secret of this, his reply was, "I never allowed my face to pucker with the wrinkles of fretfulness and ill-temper." The saying of this herbaceous and venerable sage should be remembered. Paterfamilias, in the midst of his family of discordant elements,— his antagonistic children quarrelling and making a particular hurricane about his house,— never frets. He looks upon them complacently, counsels the noisiest,— that will hear him, — and makes up his mind that if they don't heed him they can let it alone. Some people spend much breath in fretting about the weather. They go about blowing and blurting like porpoises. They see danger to the corn in the cold weather, and fret in anticipation of short crops before the bloom comes. We had better take things as they come, and not fret about them, whatever they may prove, always remembering Mr. Tenny, who ne'er fretted any, who expressed himself so indifferent as to his fate when sick, — not caring whether he lived or got well.

WHIST.

It is pleasant, on the winter evenings, when the wind is whistling by our doors and rattling our windows, as though striving to get in, and howling down chimney at us as we sit by the fire, to draw pleasantly around the table and read amusing tales from books, or indulge in a pleasant conversation, or, if a neighbor comes in, form a cheerful party at whist, and in the healthful interest of the game make the wintry hours pass away on rosy wings. Whist is a great invention — fashionable, interesting, and harmless. It forms a salutary exercise for the reflective powers and the memory, through the study of how to play and the constant tax upon the mind to recall what has been played, involving the nice matters of "finesse" and judicious "third-in-hand." But it should be played in silence, in accordance with its name — *whist!* It is very annoying to have one or more of the select four buzzing and chattering along through the intricacy of the game, where attention is wanted, and memory, to secure a triumph — when the honors do not count, and the odd trick is indispensable to going out. How vexing it is, when the whole turning of the contest hangs upon your partner's third-hand-high, to have some remark induce forgetfulness, and down goes the deuce, maybe, and to the deuce goes the game Whist! it is beautiful, when four sit down to a feast of the intellectual, cut and shuffle calmly, and coolly, and contemplatively, without the intermingling of scandal or souchong-tea remark. We light our cigar, we assort the cards, we deliberate on a lead; we judge by the hand we hold where the strength of the battle lies, and whether to draw out trumps or not. We do nothing rashly. It is science against science. Charge and repel — mine and countermine — plot and counterplot, until the strife is over, to subside into reminiscences of the game, contestants proving on the ends of the fingers that, if so and so had been done, thus and so would have been the result. Ah, happy the hours, in the years gone by, spent in this delightful way — and so sinless, so peaceful, so grateful! The memory, busy with the past, recalls scenes in which we participated, many years ago, before this mould accrued upon our beard, and when the hair bore no traces of accumulating silver — when the band was large that met with us in gladness and joy, now, alas! thinned by the changes of time and the vicissitudes of circumstance, involving separation, and worse alienation, through worldly selfishness and the hard-heartedness that money brings with it. Some may say, like the "detestable Jones," that such memories are vain; that the enjoyments they recall were frivolities better forgotten; that sin found an entrance to the soul through the portals of easy friendship, and the better man was lulled to sleep by the insidious influences of pleasure; but it is pleasant to recall them, nevertheless, and in dreams of joy enact the scenes anew that gave delight then. Whist thus has, like Moses' rod, struck the rock, and memory has poured out like a flood;

the table is vacant; the guests have flown; not a pasteboard is to be seen; the wind howls by the win dow and the chimney; and we sit alone by the fire crooning o'er thoughts of lang syne.

TO A HEEL-TAP.

I SING a heel-tap. Not the like of what,
When midnight wrapt the earth, did erst
Wake maddened echoes in the throngless streets,
And Charleys twirled their rattles all in vain,
That dissonance did make 'mongst walls reverberate;
Nor like to those which made familiar paths
Most labyrinthine in their winding way,
And key-holes mystical and treacherous,
Evading all approach from midnight keys;
Nor like to those which laid the malty knight
Among the porcine tenants of the sty,
Who, when assailed by snout inquisitive,
Did cry, "Leave tucking up, and come to bed!"
  Not such as these—ah, greater bootee mine;
A heel-tap it, of most unquestioned shape,
That lately bore upon the happy pave
The fairer half of man's duality,
Tapping sweet music on the insensate bricks!
O, blissful heel-tap, such a weight to bear!
O, blissful bricks, did ye but know your bliss!
O, muse of mine, which this fair tap hath tapped,
And made to trickle in harmonious streams,
Giving, in fairest measure, soul for sole!
I found thee pronely resting on the pave,
A lacerated sole—and many feet did tread
Unheeding by thee, nor did deign a glance
Of pity on thy upturned pleading pegs.
No Levite I to go the other side,
But sympathizing I essay to heel.
I clasp thee to my heart, e'en though thy pegs
Should gnaw my flesh with their protruding teeth.
  What wert thou? Say, did some slight girlish step
Patter its leathery tattoo by thy aid,

Till sensitiveness ached to hear its note?
Or did some matron press thee with a weight
That made thy lot a burden hard to bear?
Wert thou a-shopping bent, or churchward bound,
Or aiding charity along her way,
Or bearing scholarhood to learning's halls?
No answer — well, my heart gives the reply,
And pictures all your silence would conceal.
  Ah! she was lovely as the month of May —
The glorious month of melody and bloom —
That poets prate about, with noses red,
Sitting by furnaces of Lehigh coal;
Her eyes were blue as heaven's cerulean deeps;
Her hair the sort with which Dan Cupid weaves
The sweetest, strongest, prettiest true-love knots;
Her mouth like strawberries, though by far more sweet
Her teeth more pearly than those patent ones
That Cummings shows up there in Tremont Row;
Her neck, than swan's more graceful (not the Swan
Who makes new school-books for the growing age,
And forms the firm of Hickling, Swan and Brewer);
Her form the embodied type of human grace,
That it were madness e'er to wish to clasp,
But which I 'd worship, like a far-off star,
And bow in adoration 'neath its beams!
  No more! Imagination faints to draw,
And reason whispers in the other ear —
The sinister — through whose weak portals pass
All words of ill, and all vile slanderous things —
"*What if this goddess you have drawn were* BLACK?"

OYSTERS.

Regarding oysters, these delightful esculents enter so largely into the comforts and happinesses of life, that a word in their praise may not be amiss. No entertainment is complete without oysters. Men bet oysters; women dote upon oysters; children cry for oysters. Before the softening influence of oysters, human austerty bends, and kindness irradiates features before dark with clouds. Their odor is grateful to the nostrils as the odor of virtue is to the inward sense; we inhale the steamy and savory effluence from the kitchen as a harbinger of pleasant tastes; fancy burns in anticipation of fancy roasts, or indulges in stupendous imaginings of stews, and poesy winds its shell — an oyster shell — in sounding the praise of oysters. Ruddy Margaret, as she bears the tureen to the table, the epicurean censer, steaming with holy incense to the deity of appetite, becomes invested with new interest. She looks, maugre her "Cork-red" cheeks, angelic amid the misty vapors of an oyster-stew. We draw around the board, happy in gustatory anticipations, never to be disappointed, and uncover (the oyster-dish) in reverence for the occasion, a meet grace before oysters. And participation does not pall, like other pleasures; — we ponder, and dream, and poetize, over our bowl, as the ancients did over their bowl of wine, and are as loth to leave it. But there is no poison in this bowl; no fiend lurking therein to set the brain on fire; no brawls waiting upon it, or frenzy, or headache. Wordsworth's love of oysters was remarkable; and all who are familiar with his writings will recall the following:

Thy history, my oyster, who may tell —
Thy antecedents, and thy hopes and loves?
In oozy mud thou mak'st thy humble bed,
Subject to rakes that dare its fold invade,
To drag thee from thy home, a sacrifice
Unto the predatory maw of man,
Long thirsting for the blood of all thy kind.
Delicious bivalve! how my heart expands
As I thy many beauties contemplate!
The cruel knife has rent thee from thy shell
— Ah! what shall pay such most inhuman rent?—
Not unresisting, and, as on the plate

Thou liest, quivering, drowned in saline tears,
Thou seem'st a fitting subject for the muse.
The throb of pity tuggeth at my heart,
As thus I view thee hapless, hopeless, lie ·
A love beyond all words absorbs my soul.
Yes, thou art lovely, and for thee e'en now
May some lone oyster pine in lands afar,
Where Old Virginia hides its teeming beds
Beneath the Chesapeake's translucent tides.
'Tis thus I 'll hide thee, O my tender one,
And, plunging thee beneath this acid wave,
With pepper intermixed, and salt preädded,
I poise thee gently on my waiting fork,
Gaze for an instant on thy pleasing shape,
Then ope my mouth awaiting for the prize—
And then a gulp—a sigh—and all is done.

CALIFORNIA TAN.

"So you 've been to Californy," said Mrs. Partington, with animation, as Smith the younger returned from the land of gold, with a new suit of clothes on his back, and enough hair on his face to stuff a mattress with; "so you 've been to Californy, and they say you have amazed a fortin." He assured her, with a twist of his long beard, and a half-smile, that was a half-affirmative, that there was not a grain of truth in it; but that he had picked up a little. "Well, I 'm glad of it, and, if you 've amazed anything, it is more than I thought you ever would; but you have paid terrible dear for it, if you have got to look all your lifetime as bad as you do now. Dear soul! How terribly you are tanned!" She said this without her specs, the dark hair having deceived her, while Ike, more observing, sat watching his opening mouth as he spoke, wondering if he ever attempted to eat anything with that arrangemen about it.

A GOUTY MAN'S REVERIE.

Is this rheumatic twinge, so industrious at my knee-pan, kinking nerve and mind with its intensified, irradiating misery, a devil to torment me before my time? The milk of human kindness, that erewhile has found an abiding place in me, has become dried up by the fever of insidious disease, or soured like dairy-milk by summer thunder. And there is that precious fallacy of Shakespeare's staring me in the face, about the uses of adversity being sweet. I can fancy that this may be the case in many instances, but never in the adversity that comes in the form of rheumatic racks and thumb-screws. The current of my nature is all turned back from its usual course. Do I love my neighbor? No. Do I love society? No. Do I wish to make people happy? No. I would have a cloud as black and opaque as my hat envelop everything at this present moment, with no hope of brightness to-morrow. Who said, Patience? It's hackneyed, and infernally unkind, let me tell you, to sit there with your wholesome limbs encased in boots, and tell me to be patient. How everything is discolored by the gangrene of one's feelings! The sun is darkened by the shawl of my own unhappy spirit pinned up against the windows of day; and then sweeps by a long train of funereal fancies—the forms of rheumatic martyrs pass before me, and of ancestors who have died of the rheumatism, till I shriek for respite. O, for the spirit of the past, I cry, that could, by laying on of hands, impart healthiness, sparing to the sufferer the added afflictions of bolus and embrocation! O, sweet Hygeia, on one knee I am able to invoke thy aid! Tell me not, O man of strange fancies, that my distemper partakes of Parnassian qualities; for I can now reveal my genius in limpéd feet. I'd brain thee did I deem thou didst meditate a joke at such a time. A man not very long since published a book to prove that everything is right in the providence of God, and not a wrong or an evil can be left out of our lives without impairing their perfectness. Then may there not be a use in it, after all? and, if it be necessary that I endure a few paroxysms of pain for the sake of a great principle, and be a martyr, — though, indeed, *ne martyr*, a paradox that I leave the learned to construe, — should I not be running counter to Providence in condemning and deprecating it? I'll think of it in meditative calmness and red flannel. May not the rheumatism be sent to teach us how to rightly prize the home qualities of woman, whose assiduous kindness never wearies with doing for us, — who bears with the petulance of our peevish nature, and smooths our pillow with a tenderness that commends even distemper as a blessing; and, as she bends over us, with consolation in her eyes and liniment in her hands, we hail her as our good angel, and learn to say, with tolerable grace, "sweet are the uses of adversity," — alluding, of course, to the rheumatism.

IKE AND LION.

"WELL, what upon earth are you doing now?" said Mrs. Partington, with a tone of anxiety in her voice, and a large iron spoon in her hand, as Lion rushed into the kitchen, followed by Ike. The dog was almost covered up with a thick, coarse coffee-bag, and, in perfect sympathy with Ike, who was laughing tremendously, he wagged his caudality as if he liked the fun. "What upon earth are you doing now?" was a question that called for an answer; and Lion looked up in the old lady's face, with his mouth open and his eyes glistening, as much as to say, "Look at me, Mistress P., for I am all dressed up, you see." But he did n't say anything. "That 's a crinoline, aunt," said Ike; "don't you think it 's very overcoming?"—"Yes; I declare," said she, "I think it comes over him a good deal; but you had better take it off, for it makes him look very ridiculous."—"It 's all the fashion," said Ike.—"All the fiddlestick!" replied she; "and how should I look in the fashion, all hooped up like a mash-tub? Should n't I look well? No, dear, no. I don 't want to portend to be more than I really am; and, if I have n't been made so unanimous as some, I don't want to cast no reflections on heaven for not making me no larger, by rigging on artificial purportions. It used to be the remark of Elder Stick that every tub should stand on its own bottom; and, though this may n't have nothing to do with it, I want to see folks jest as they are. And *now* what are you at?" cried she, breaking off in her subject shorter than pie-crust; and well she might, for Lion was parading the floor in great glee, with one of the dame's night-caps upon his head, tied snugly under the chin, while Ike stood looking on, with great complacency. "Dear me," said she, dropping into a chair, "I am afraid your predestination will not be a good one, if you go on so; and little boys who tease their aunts don't go to heaven, by a great sight." Ike was much subdued by this, and, taking advantage of her momentary abstraction and three doughnuts, he whistled for Lion, and went out to play.

ON A CHILD'S PICTURE.

SWEET memory of one now named as dead!
  A beauteous ray from life's effulgent light,
That but a moment its glad brightness shed,
  Then vanished, heavenward to wing its flight!

That smile still beams, which late made glad the heart, —
  Like a fair ripple frozen in its course;
That eye as then its burning glance doth dart,
  Lit by a love high heaven alone its source.

One only glimpse thou givest of the face
  Whereon a thousand graces ever shone;
We turn from thee, and in our sadness trace
  Those faded charms in memory's light alone.

Thou 'rt but one line of a fair-printed page. —
  A sweet abstraction, wanting all the rest, —
One drop of water, that cannot assuage
  The longing thirst that burns within our breast.

That brow is but a shadow to our gaze,
  Those cheeks but semblances in pictured stone,
Those beaming eyes emit but frozen rays,
  Those lips give back no warmth to greet our own.

O! mockery of life, in loveless frost!
  All that thou art is but a tiny grain
Of the great treasure that our heart has lost,
  And small thy power to ease our bitter pain.

Yet how we prize thee! soulless though thou art, —
  The ghost of loveliness that once was ours, —
Thou quickenest drooping faith within our heart,
  And liftest up the cloud that o'er us lowers, —

Letting God's holy light upon the scene,
  And drawing our sad spirits up to His! —
Art gives sweet evidence of what *has been*,
  And faith assurance that what has been *is*.

WEARING ORNAMENTS.

An immense business is done merely in preparing ornaments for the person, and many people make up dismal faces as they mention personal ornaments among the frivolities of life. Used according to the dictates of taste and judgment, they greatly enhance personal attraction; but, when used merely for the sake of display, they take from the effect of the personal, and become merely a pecuniary consideration, — a glittering bait to tempt some covetous gudgeon, or to drive to despair some rival, whose diamond mine has not yielded so prolifically. A correct taste sees in the simpler adornment more grace than in the profuse, and never exceeds the propriety of decoration; and, though her jewel-box sparkle as richly as Golconda with diamonds, she who possesses this taste will never endanger the effect of beauty, if simplicity is its best adornment, to display a fortune in gems that a princess might covet. The vulgar shine in the ostentation of decoration, — they blaze in the quantity of magnificence, like a decoration of a temple for a fête-day by one who believes that in the amount of bunting and Chinese lanterns is the *summum bonum* of decorative art.

OPERATIC.

"What a strain that is!" said Mrs. Partington, as she heard an aria from Lucia, sung in the highest style, by a young lady where she was visiting. — "Yes," was the reply, "it is operatic." — "Upper attic, is it?" said she; "I should think it was high enough to be on top of the house." Mrs. Partington does not believe that mere screaming constitutes melody.

A NARROW ESCAPE.

SOME people come very near matrimony and miss it, as we have read of those who fell asleep, in their wanderings in the dark, upon the edge of fearful precipices, and waked in the morning very thankful for their escape. We wish to be distinctly understood that the last clause in the simile only applies to the unpleasant nap alluded to. We heard a reason given by a bachelor to his son for never getting married, — we believe, however, that it was his nephew that the reason was given to, but it is of small consequence, — where the individual came nigh marriage, and escaped, that we think worth stating. When young Plume became of age, he was very good-looking, and possessed a fortune in more substantial goods, besides. He was a subject for ten thousand, more or less, direct matrimonial attacks, but resisted them all like a man. Many were after him, and, as he plumed himself upon his good looks, he deemed that Plume was what they sought, and never once imagined that a mercenary idea regarding him and his money could enter into the fair heads that contrived to attract him, or the hearts that beat for him. He was one day speaking of the general homage that was accorded him, and manifested considerable delight thereat. "Ah, my young friend," said Mr. Oldbird, "this is very fine, but do not deem that all this homage proceeds from personal consideration. If you had n't money, it would n't be thus, depend upon it." — "You are mistaken," replied Plume, warmly; "I know you are mistaken." — "Well," said Oldbird, patting his cane, "I 'll tell you what I 'll do: I 'll wager that the one you value the most would jilt you, if she thought you had n't the tin" — "It is a —" he checked himself, and concluded the sentence with — "a very preposterous idea." They separated, and as he recalled that *one* whom he valued the most, he felt that he had done her nothing but justice in defending her against the attack of Oldbird. That night he resolved that he would test the fact. He would glean the delicious truth, that she loved him for himself alone, from her own ruby lips. He had been long regarded as an eligible match by her anxious parents, and a crisis was momentarily looked for by them. "Julia," said Plume, as they sat in the arbor, "if I were as poor as that chap, there now engaged in the miserable business of unloading potatoes, you would not love me." — "O, how can you wound me by so unjust a suspicion? You should know that nothing mercenary mingles with my love; that, were you reduced to not more than two or three thousand dollars a year, you would be just as dear to me." Plume kissed her, and, whispering that he wished to confer with her paternal, he left her. He turned to where he knew that tender parent was to be found at that hour, enjoying a nap in his easy-chair. Suddenly awaking, he rubbed his eyes, and looked at Plume, who stood before him. "Respected sir," Plume began, "I love your daughter." — "So do I," said the old man, chuckling. — "I would marry her," continued the lover. — "Very well," said the father, "that 's right; you shall have her." — "But," said Plume, "it is nothing but right that you should know my affairs; I 'm rich, you know." — "I know it; at least, I suppose so." — "But," continued Plume, "my money is invested in a queer way. It is all in copper stocks and railroad bonds, that have n't paid a cent of dividend for ten years; and, though it probably will all come out well enough, I can't see exactly when." The old gentleman started up. "Stocks!" cried he in a tone of voice that would have done credit to Elder Kean, the eminent tragedian; "ruinous risks — ruinous risks, sir — my daughter cannot marry mortgage-bonds and copper certificates! Sell your stocks, wait a year, and then we'll see." Plume ran for comfort to Julia. "Dearest," said he, "I am in despair. Can you marry Pewabic? Will you annex your fortunes to Ogdensburg?" She had listened at the door, and knew all. — "I think," said she, in a voice tender with emotion, "we'd better wait a year." He thought so, too, and left. The next day's inquiry revealed that Plume did not own a dollar's worth of any stock he had named, and the old man found he had put his foot in it. Plume never went again, and when, in a warm letter, reminded of his former intimacy, he was requested to renew it, he simply said he was very busy selling his stocks, and could n't possibly come. He never believed in human professions after that, and always very unjustly reckoned women among the copper stocks, and the bonds of matrimony as mortgage-bonds much reduced. That was the reason he gave for never getting married.

THE WORLD.

This is a funny old world, — a queer mosaic of combinations, as multihued as the good dame's patch-work quilt that was exhibited in the Fair; everybody sees this, and in a spleeny spirit asks, "What 's the use?" Everything seems to jump by opposites of feeling and impulse, and clanging and jarring the big world goes round, inharmonious and discordant, we think. We are right among it, and it is through our want of faith that it is discordant. It is a grand orchestra, the world, and all of us are engaged in playing in it, and we cannot tell, as each sounds his note, its effect. It seems discordant to us, but the Great Leader who notes its time sees the harmony in it, sees the effect of the great notes sounded by the maestros, and that of the tiny efforts of the least, and recognizes in all the elements of a perfect harmony. There is encouragement in this faith, that, where in self-pride the performer takes upon himself airs, his performance is no more valued in the grand whole than the humblest second fiddle of them all, who sleeps in a garret at night, poorly paid and poorly fed. We find it hard to reconcile the difference in compensation for performance, but leave that for the great day of adjustment. A large balance may then be due those who are less favored. What is the use? In this view the use becomes apparent, and the world spins down the "ringing grooves of time," adding its song to that of the spheres, which gave the first concert in the grand academy of the universe.

NIAGARA FALLS.

O, SHEET of standard melody sublime!
  My ravished ears drink in thy liquid notes,
A cherished anthem of the ancient time,
  That, still unchanging, to far ages floats;
An "old folks' concert" of undoubted age,
  That fears no check of innovation's bars,
So perfect that no Vandal dare engage
  To mend the song coëval with the stars! —
In hearing of thy solemn monotone,
  The universe with pulseless awe might list,
Whilst I, struck dumb, hark to its strains alone,
  And feel my wandering soul among the mist,
That, like an echo of the chorus grand,
Quavers responsive to the thrilling land.

BALLAD ABOUT BUNKER.

'T was dreadful hot on Bunker's height, —
  The patriots in their trenches lay, —
While, bellowing with a bitter spite,
  The British cannon blazed away;

When Parson Martin wiped his brow,
  And, turning round, to Prescott spoke:
"I guess I 'll go, if you 'll allow,
  A while among the Charlestown folk.

"I feel there 's danger to the town,
  I see the clouds there gathering thick;
And ere the storm comes rattling down,
  I think I 'll tell them cut their stick"

And then he took a glass, — good man! —
  And through the village made his way
A glass, I mean, with which to scan
  The hostile vessels in the Bay.

He saw the British barges fill
  With arméd soldiers fierce and strong,
And told the folk it boded ill,
  And that they 'd better push along.

But no, not they; a dogged trait
  Impelled them to incur the pinch.
And so they thought they 'd better wait,
  And vowed they would n't budge an inch.

Again good Parson Martin went
  Down to the village all alone;
From digging hard his strength was spent,
  From watching he was weary grown.

"Now rest ye," goodman Cary said;
  "Your tottering limbs pray here bestow,"
And pointed to a bounteous bed,
  A solace meet for weary woe.

And on the bed the parson fell,
  But scarcely had his eyelids closed,
When, crashing through the roof, a shell
  Disturbed the dream in which he dozed.

"I think," quoth he, upstarting straight,
  "'T will be here somewhat warm to-day,
And that, if you should hap to wait,
  You 'll find the deuce and all to pay."

And then from out the fated bound
  The people sadly made their tracks,
But Parson Martin he was found
  Where fell the most determined whacks.

His heart to heaven went up in prayer
  That it would aid each mother's son;
And heaven made vocal answer there,
  In every deadly patriot gun.

ATTENDING THE ANNIVERSARIES.

Ike came home, soaking with the wet, and threw himself in a chair, and his cap at a nail on the opposite wall. "Well, Isaac," said Mrs. Partington, with a slight cloud on her brow, "where have you been?" — "Been to the anniversaries," replied he, with a smile playing all round his mouth. — "Glad of it," said she, brightening up; "glad of it, and I hope it did you good. What anniversaries have you been 'tending?" — "I 've been to training, and to the circus," replied the young hopeful, looking down at his wet shoes. The old lady sighed deeply, as she went about her household affairs, thinking what would become of that boy, if he went on so.

THE COUNTRY RIDE.

BEING A VERACIOUS HISTORY, REVEALING A NEW EXPEDIENT BY WHICH A BOSTONIAN STOPPED A RUNAWAY HORSE.

'T IS a capital thing to ride, they say,
O'er a country road in a one-horse shay,
With a country cousin or two in;
To crack one's whip in a sporting way,
And kiss the cousins in mode au fait,
Which means as often as ever you may,
With none but the horses to cry out "Nay,"
Or to see what you are doing;
It is capital, too, when the skies are blue,
To drive the shady old forest through,
And kiss the maids
'Neath the ambient shades,—
That is, if such you fancy to do;
For myself, I 've long renounced such vanities,
As being among the lesser insanities,
Tending, Heaven knows,
To mar the repose
Of sensitive folk, and such as those
Who belong to the finer humanities.

'T was on a day
Not long away,
That one, abroad on vacation
(Somewhere up in New Hampshire State,
Famous for raising men of weight,
And hills that stump creation,
And beautiful streams, and famous trout,
That fishers skilfully tickle out
For gastronomication),
Took it into his head to ride,
With a beautiful coz on either side—
Position most delectable!—
The horse he chose was a quiet beast,
Not disposed to shy in the least,
Whose speed, 't was true, had some decreased
But still he was not rejectable;
Not 2.40 nor 40.2,
But over the road he 'd "put her through"
In time deemed quite respectable.

His mane was combed and greased anew,
He wore his tail done up in a queue,
And he hung his head as if lots he knew,
In manner very reflectable!

Now off they go —
Gee up, gee whoa!
There 's fun on a country road, we know,
And so knows the knight of Hanover —
(Hanover-street is the one I mean,
A knight of the yard-stick he, I ween,
A capital fellow as ever was seen) —
Who often in youth one ran over.
He held the reins as a Jehu might,
Till by and by the horse took fright,
At something offensive to his sight,
Or smell, as some have pretended,
And well knew the driver that in his way
A terrible granite boulder lay,
Just where the road descended!

Now, what to do
He scarcely knew,
But, heeding the old "*in media tu-*
tissimus ibis," on he flew,
Keeping the road in the middle,
The while the pony straightened the rein
So hard it gave his fingers pain,
And hummed like the string of a fiddle.
On they sped with jolt and bolt,
The old horse wild as a yearling colt,
As maddened and as frisky
As a toper on a sennight spree,
Just on the edge of delirium tre',
Quenched in him each sane idee,
By villanous rifle whiskey.
Out from the doors the people ran,
Every woman, every man, —
O, they 'll be killed for certain!
And certain it seemed that the hand of Fate
Only a moment more did wait
To drop their mortal curtain.

* * * * * * *

Old Squire Lee was taking his tea, —
    Perhaps it was something stronger, —
'T was a very hot day, and he sipped away
    Than usual a little longer,
    When dash and crash
    There came a smash
Like a bolt of vengeful thunder
    When the head of a horse
        And half of a chaise,
    With an earthquake's force
        Broke in on his gaze,
Filling him full of wonder!

Right through the side of the house they ran,
Horse and chaise, and woman and man —
    A most insane intrusion; —
That is, they would have done so, but —
They did n't — the chaise-shafts only cut
A hole where one his arm might put —
    The rest was an illusion;
But there upon the cold, cold ground
The three excursionists sat around,
    In most sublime confusion.
Sure such a sight was never seen,
Such fearful destruction of crinoline,
    And there sat the fallen hero;
A moment he thought of his cruel fate,
And then he placed his hand on his pate
His wig was gone! and, bald as a slate,
    He sat there stiff as Zero.
    And Squire Lee, quite jolly was he,
Well pleased the thing was no sadder;
    Says he, "My lad, I'm heartily glad
    You 're not disposed for this to die mad,
Like those who sometimes dye madder."
    Then Squire Lee
    Gave them some tea,
    And everything ended right merrily
And, homeward soon returning,
    The horse behaved like a sensible beast,
    And did n't bolt or shy in the least,
    His wisdom very much increased
By the lesson he'd been learning

ECONOMY.

We were delighted with Blifkins' account of his saving, by an economical expedient, and give it in nearly his own words. "Mr. Blifkins," says my wife, "our kitchen needs painting." — "Does it, my dear? Well, then, need it must; for I assure you, Mrs. Blifkins, that the accruing dimes do not warrant the outlay, at present." I saw that she was unhappy, and knew that she would not relinquish her point. "Mr. Blifkins," said she, a few days thereafter, "I have thought of an expedient by which we can have our kitchen painted." Her face was lighted up with an expression that it too seldom wears, as she spoke. She is a great woman for expedients, is Mrs. Blifkins. "You can do it yourself!" continued she, touching me with the point of her forefinger in the region of my fourth vest-button. "A dollar saved," said she, still further, "is as good as a dollar earned, you know." I looked with admiration on that wonderful specimen of her sex, as she said this, and "allowed" (as the western people say), to myself that, as an economist, she had no peer. And well I might allow it; for, at the very moment were her shoulders covered by a sort of monkey-jacket made of one of my worn-out coats, and a pair of galligaskins had assumed the form of a basque, that was worn by a juvenile Blifkins. "Your suggestion," says I, to my wife, "is a good one, and to-morrow shall develop a new phase in my character. I will turn artist, and give the world evidence of a talent that needed but the Promethean spark of necessity to draw it out. I will procure pots and brushes, and Michael Angelo, Raphael, Salvator Rosa, and Claude Lorraine, shall yield the palm to Blifkins."

Mrs. B. was delighted. "Mr. Blifkins," said my wife in the night, as I was about settling into my solid nap, "you 'd better make it pale-green." — "Do what?" said I, starting up, forgetting all about the painting. — "The paint," replied she. I am afraid that I used some expression of spleen that was unworthy of me. I turned over to try to sleep again. "Mr. Blifkins," said my wife, "don't you think the window-sills would look better some other color?" — "Any color you please, my dear," said I; "but let us dismiss the subject from present discussion, as this is no place for a brush." I carried my point, as she had her paint, and I was allowed to sleep. But I was all night dreaming of my undertaking. No roseate hues mingled with my sleeping fancies, fraught with the odors of celestial bowers; but paint-pots were piled in pyramids about me, brush-handles, like boarding-pikes, I encountered everywhere, and a villanous smell of raw paint almost suffocated me.

I was up with the lark, and, after breakfast, went down to Bristle, the painter's, to procure my paint. That eminent professor of art mixed me two pots of the right article, of hues that were of a satisfactory shade, and I went home with anticipations of the most exalted character. "Mr. Blifkins," said my wife, "you have dreadfully daubed your pants with the paint — strange that you should be so careless." Sure enough, on both sides I had bestowed impartial donations of the adhering color. The pants were new, and I had congratulated myself on their being a wonderful fit. This was a discouragement. "Mr. Blifkins," said my wife, "you 'd better put on an old pair." I have always boasted of my ability to compete with anybody in the particular property known as old clothes. I knew that the decayed fashion of many years hung by their allotted pegs in the closet, which had been facetiously denominated the "wardrobe," and hastened to procure the garment desired. In the name of all of the tribes of Israel, where were the bifurcated teguments that for years had met my view? The pegs were bare, and my first impression was that they had taken to their own legs, and walked away. "Mrs. Blifkins," said I, to my wife, on the top of the stairs, and at the top of my lungs, "where are the — the — garments?" I heard her say something about "sold," and concluded that she was trying some little trick upon me, as wives sometimes will, and was adopting the formula so much in vogue for expressing it. She came up stairs. "Mr. Blifkins," said she, "I declare, I sold all of your old clothes, only yesterday, for a beautiful pair of vases, and some tin ware." I looked at her earnestly; but the evident calmness that prevailed in her own breast softened and subdued the violence in mine. "You'd better put on this," said she, holding up an article of female apparel, the name of which I disremember, but which, when secured to my waist, as I recollect, fell to my feet. She smiled as she placed it in my hand, and I put it on. "Mrs. Blifkins," said I to my wife, "why am I, thus accoutred, liable to be more extravagant than ever?" She said she did n't know. "Because," said I, triumphantly, "I am bound to waist!" She pretended not to see the reason, and I did not explain, but went to work. "Now shall you see, wife of my soul," said I, "such work as you can find alone in the Vatican at Rome, or the Louvre at Paris, should you feel inclined to seek it. Here, before this door, I take my stand, and here I commence. You shall see." — "Mr. Blifkins," said my wife, "don't drip it over on the floor." — "Never fear," said I, dipping in the brush, and sopping it up against the side in the most approved form.

My first aim was at the upper part of the door, — a panelled door, — and I applied the brush vigorously. "Mrs. Blifkins," said I, to my wife, "as the morning is rather cold, should n't you think it well to put on two coats?" She took the pleasantry as an unkind reflection on the disposition made of the old clothes, and didn't say anything. I worked away on that door, severely; but I found, before I had half done it, a weariness in the wrist; and a cold sensation up my sleeve, attracting my attention, revealed the fact that a stream of paint was stealing along the handle of the brush up my arm. I laid down the implement, and went to procure something with which to wipe the paint off. "Mr. Blifkins," screamed my wife, "look at the baby!" I looked, as she held that young prodigy up to view, and was much shocked. The baby had crawled to the paint-pot, and had immersed his two hands to the elbows. Not content with this, he had laid hands on the brush, and, when Mrs. Blifkins saw him, he was engaged in an insane effort to get it into his mouth. The precocity of that child is most wonderful! The paint was washed off, and I commenced again. "Mr. Blifkins," said my wife, when I had been working about two hours, with my hands cramped, my wrist and back aching, my eyes full of paint, and my face tattooed by the same, like a New Zealander, "are you most done?" The "*No*" that I returned I fear was not pleasant. All that forenoon I worked at that terrible task, and at about dinner-time I saw it accomplished. "Mrs. Blifkins," said I, "the work is completed; come and look, and admire." She came at my request, and I noticed a mischievous twinkle in her eye as she looked. "Why, Mr. Blifkins," said my wife, "you've put more paint on the paper and the carpet than you have anywhere else." Her criticism seemed unkind; but I looked where she had directed, and round the doors and window-frames were rays of paint, like the surroundings of islands on a map, and below were large blotches of paint upon the carpet, that had assumed geometrical forms enough to have puzzled the judgment of a professor. "I confess, my dear, that in this particular I have been a little slovenly; but look at that work." — "Mr. Blifkins," said my wife, "if there's no better painting in the what's-its-name at Rome, I don't care about seeing it." The door-bell here rang, and, "accoutred as I was," without thinking of it, I rushed to see who had come, and met a whole bevy of ladies, and suffered the mortification of a sensitive nature under such circumstances. I here sum up the whole:

J. Blifkins in account with Domestic Economy.

1858.	Dr.	1858.	Cr.
To painting one room,	$5.00	Time and labor spent in painting,	$3.50
		Pants spoilt in ditto,	8.00
		Paint,	1.00
		Spoiling carpet,	3.00
		Daubing wall,	5.00
To Balance,	$25.50	Mortification,	10.00
	$30.50		$30.50

I throw in the dangerous experiment of the baby and the injury to health, both of which, could they be estimated by numbers, would swell the amount to an alarming figure. I came solemnly to the conclusion that it would have been better to have hired it done.

Such was Mr. Blifkins' story about his economy. It is a case not much over-stated.

LIFE'S MASQUERADE.

Put on your mask, O living soul! and hide
  Your features from the world's obtrusive eye,
As, launched upon the turbid earthy tide,
  We float unheeded on its current by.

For there be rich emotions quick in thee,
  Imprisoned gems, and thoughts of import sweet,
That might, whate'er their priceless rarity,
  Fall sacrifice beneath unworthy feet.

I would not have the coarse and careless look
  Profane the spot where my hushed step has trod,
Where conscience keeps its daily record-book
  In just accordance 'twixt itself and God.

The vulgar glance would seem like baleful light,
  And to my shuddering sense a thrill impart,
Like that the touch of vagrant fingers might,
  Feeling in darkness round my slumbering heart

Put on the mask, and let it haply wear
  A smile, to feign it were but lightly donned,
Gayly as though you had no real share
  In aught the present sly deceit beyond.

So shall you, O my soul, the meed obtain
  Frivolity to folly ever brings;
But not one tassel of the golden grain
  Worthy to shrine among your treasured things.

But, though thus hidden, there be those for whom,
  When the world sees not, you may drop the mask;
Twin with yourself in feeling, give them room,
  And in a warm reciprocation bask.

And let such incidents of transient joy,
  Through memory's aid, delightedness impart;—
The world cannot joy's secret seeds destroy,
  Sown by God's husbandmen within the heart.

O, haste the time when, masking disallowed,
The soul stands up in grandeur unconcealed,
Of its own new-found birthright duly proud,—
The right to live in truthfulness revealed.

MRS. PARTINGTON PHILOSOPHIZING.

"I 'VE always noticed," said Mrs. Partington, dropping her voice to the key that people adopt when they are disposed to be philosophical or moral—"I 've always noticed that every year added to a man's life has a tenderness to make him older, just as a man who goes a journey finds, as he jogs on, that every mile-stone brings him nearer to the place where he is going, and further from where he started. I have n't got the exorbitance of feeling that I had once, and I don't believe I shall ever have it again, if I live to the age of Methusaleh, which, heaven knows, I don't want to. And, speaking of long life, I have n't any desire to live any longer than the breath remains in my body, if it is n't any more than eighty years. I would n't wish to be a centurion, and the idea of one surviving her factories, and becoming idiomatic, always gives me a disagreeable sensoriousness. But whatever is to be will be, and there is no knowing how a thing will turn out till it takes place. Gracious goodness!" she exclaimed, as a torpedo snapped on the floor by her feet; "you might as well kill a body as frightem 'em to death. Isaac!" Ike did n't respond; but, Mrs. P., hadst thou but glanced through the window, thou mightst have seen a little face, hid just below the window-sill, beaming with mirth and jollity, and it is more than probable that a portion of the coppers thou gavest the boy hath returned to plague the investor.

LUCK.

Luck is a sort of semi-Providence, or substitute for Providence, which some believe in as a controlling power in human destiny; deeming that it begins with man's existence, and goes all the way through with him, administering on this hand the choicest tit-bits that fall to human enjoyment, and, on the other, hard fare, comprising the whole catalogue of ills. Some, through the magic of superseeing Luck, turn everything to gold that they look upon; while others, so strange is Luck, have all that which is gold turn to ashes in their hands. To be lucky is the grand desideratum, — the cardinal point in human fortune, — though the proportion of lucky ones to the unlucky is very small. It is curious to trace the operations of Luck in its results. Lord Timothy Dexter affords us an excellent example. But examples everywhere occur. A dozen boys start on the road of life, with equal advantages, equally endowed with capacity, equally ambitious, and equally hopeful. One of them alone will be lucky, the rest will fail signally; the one will never lose a dollar, the rest will never save a cent. In every transaction Luck is evident. Two men may embark in the same business, in which double the amount of exertion on the one part is expended that there is on the other, and he who makes the least will win. *Why*, no one knows. It is Luck, and that is all that can be said about it. Hood's unlucky man in Tylney Hall, to whom all manner of adverses happened, was a melancholy instance of the victim to unrelenting Luck. He, it is remembered, at some crowning calamity, asked that a handful of sudden deaths might be thrown down, for one of which he said he would scramble, as heartily as ever a beggar scrambled for a sixpence. This feeling often takes possession of one, when badgered and cornered of Fate; but it is wrong to feel so. When the great and true light breaks upon us, by which we shall see the real meaning of things, we may find that ill-luck, with its experience of sorrow and aggravation, is not so ill, after all; and that Fate, so inconsiderably spoken about, may be Providence in disguise, working for good through the medium of dark circumstance, to be shown in future realization, while in that light the specious show of good luck may prove but the tinsel decoration that belongs merely to time, and flashes no ray beyond. It may not always be lucky to be in luck.

ON SUCH A NIGHT AS THIS.

The angry rain is cold without,
  The wind is bleak and high,
And as we sit the hearth about,
  And hear the storm go by,
We glance out through the spreading gloom,
  While pain invades our bliss,
And sigh and say, God help the poor,
  On such a night as this!

And then our thought far o'er the main
  On ready pinion speeds, —
Thought needs no shelter from the rain,
  As the poor body needs; —
We see the white-capped waves uprear,
  Below, the dark abyss;
Heaven guard the sailor! is our prayer,
  On such a night as this.

The ruddy fire sends forth its glow,
  And cheerful faces meet,
Where conversation's charms outflow
  In loving cadence sweet;

The raging winds our ears assail,
And by the casement hiss,
Our haven shields us from the gale,
On such a night as this.

And thoughts of distant friends awake,
And thoughts of bygone hours,
When their fond offices of love
Bestrewed our path with flowers.
Where are they now, the loved, the lost,
Whose forms we ever miss?
Turn they a passing thought for us
On such a night as this?

And one sweet child, our joy and pride,
Has wandered from our sight,
We miss her prattle by our side,
We miss her eyes so bright;
We know she dwells where storms ne'er come
To mar her perfect bliss;
O! does her tender thought come home,
On such a night as this?

The social game or books beguile
The hours as they flee;
The pleasant word awakes the smile
The genial love to see;
The surging of the angry rain
Cannot disturb, I wis,
The goodly cheer that clusters here,
On such a night as this.

With grateful thrill the heart outpours,
Though winds and rains assail;
We have no fear within our doors,
Where love and peace prevail;
The rattling rain may dash amain,
It hinders not our kiss—
That household charm the heart doth warm,
On such a night as this.

THE REASON.

A PLEASANT story is told about a minister of *our* denomination, who obtained much notoriety in this vicinity, a few years since, for his good-nature and keen wit, and whose sayings are treasured still as choice things to while away an hour withal, and make it pass pleasantly. He now officiates acceptably a short distance in the interior, and, from the following specimen, we should deem that he had not departed from the geniality of faith that erewhile distinguished him. A widow lady of his acquaintance, who had sighed in her loneliness for some years, had received a proposition to marry again, and had made up her mind to accept; yet she thought she would go through the form of asking the advice of her friend the parson. He came in, one day, and she broached the subject very delicately, by intimating that she thought of improving her condition. "My dear madam," said he, looking admiringly at her healthy form, "that, I think, would be impossible, as I never saw you in finer condition in my life." — "I mean," said she, blushing, "that I thought of changing my situation." — "Very injudicious," said he, looking out of the window; "your situation here is very fine, and it would be hard to find a better." — "You do not divine my meaning, sir," persisted she; "my little Edward is now of an age when a father's authority is essential for his control, and, having an advantageous offer, I thought I should get married again." This was said so timidly, and the eyes were cast down so sensitively, that it was very touching in the widow. "Ah!" said he, "that is it, then; and so you are going to get married to raise Ned, are you?" The crimson deepened a little in the widow's cheek, and the light quickened in her eye; but she knew the kind heart of the man that spoke the pleasantry, and she was not angry. His congratulations and advice were given, and she was happy.

THE BANKER'S DREAM.

THE long, long day had wearily flown,
  And now 'neath his own roof-tree
The banker sat by his hearth alone,
  And an anxious man was he, —
No cheerful light from his eyes outshone,
  As he sighed right heavily.

He had felt the fever and fearful strife, —
  That gnawing at the heart,
Which, with trouble and sorrow rife,
  Had swept above the mart;
And he thought of the joys of a humble life,
  From cares like his apart.

His aching eyelids drooped to a close,
  His head sank on his breast;
Forgot was the world, its ills and woes,
  In the moment of peaceful rest,
And the wave of sorrow that round him rose
  A joyful hope expressed.

No notes to pay mixed with his dreams, —
  He moved as free as the air, —
No speculation's subtle schemes
  In his present thoughts had share,
But plenty around him shed its beams,
  And followed him everywhere.

Domestic joy upon him smiled,
  And he felt its blissful power;
The precious presence of wife and child
  Illumed his peaceful bower;
And the sweets of home the ill beguiled
  Of every passing hour.

All faces were lit with glad content:
The day of banks had flown;
By joy men reckoned their rate per cent.,
And owned this rule alone;
And the sharpers who by usury lent
Had all to Tophet gone.

And growing love 'twixt man and man
Assumed the selfish place,
And a happy brotherhood began
Again to unite the race,
And man ne'er from his brother ran,
With shame on his bankrupt face.

The busy wheels of a thousand mills
Made music grandly sweet,
And the cattle upon a thousand hills
Looked comely, sleek, and *neat*,
While Labor smiled by the mountain rills,
With plenty and peace replete.

And calmly he slept in his ample chair,
His breathing was soft and low;
No darkened shapes obtruded there,
With their burthen of pressing woe;
Forgot was the gloomy weight of care
That had checked his spirit's flow.

He started and woke. "Sweet vision, stay!
O, can it be all in vain?
Must the beauteous and angelic ray
Be lost in the clouds of pain?
I'd give all my hopes of wealth to-day,
To dream that dream again."

SEA-SICKNESS

Among the disagreeables that chance to fall upon humanity, there is nothing more painful than sea-sickness. Those who go down on the sea for fun, after reading romances glowing with eulogies of the ocean, or poetry liquid with its praises, think they are going to have a nice time. They laugh, and sing, and joke, and affect sea-talk, and look after the small stores, and indulge in thoughts of chowder, and even a broad hint of fat pork fails to awaken any other feeling but one of mirth. Thus they start. The breeze is fair, the water is smooth, and far off is the deep sea, that "likeness of heaven" they have read about, and which they will now become acquainted with. By and by a motion in the vessel is perceptible. Rising and falling with the sea, she pitches in, right and left. A glance over the side reveals the yeasty waves dancing in a mad game of touch and run, here, there, and everywhere, up and down. Here is a hill to climb, and here a vale to cross. Now right in her teeth the vessel meets the sea, and trembles from stem to stern. Anon she receives a blow on one side, and then, without turning the other also, she gets one on the opposite side. Mr. Verigreen, who was so gay a moment ago, is now very ill. He smiles, however, as he is addressed, and swears it is the tobacco. The smile is a base counterfeit, — a lie, — for there is no joy in his heart. He cannot define the feeling that fills him. There is an utter goneness about him. It is dreadful. There is a grateful smell of chowder from the galley. To Verigreen it is execrable. He thinks of the beautiful shore and its substantial rocks, and wonders why anybody ever wants to go to sea. The sea, as if angry at his uncomplimentary reflection, growls and hisses all around him. His head aches, and his heart aches. Comfort with him has long since fled. He still thinks, if it had n't been for the cigars, he should have done very well. There never was a vessel before, he knows, that pitched so much, and he asks the man at the helm if he can't hold her a little more steady. Will he be just so polite as to try? He is a stern man, — he is always astern man, — and laughs at poor Verigreen. Everybody laughs at him. They call upon him for small stores, and he answers with a groan; they try him with cigars, and he puts them by; they hint at pork and molasses, and he collapses. He begs them to throw him overboard, as an act of personal kindness. He condemns the cigars. He sits next the rail, because the prospect is better. There is lead on his stomach, and he throws it. He knows he should not have been sick but for the cigars. Poor Verigreen! there is no mercy or compassion for him. His experience ended, hear him, as his foot presses terra firma, record his opinion of the sea: "Great is thy majesty, O Ocean! Thy waves are high, and thy waters brackish. Powerful are they, besides, and very tumultuous. Poetry has sung thy praises, and eloquence spouted thy glorification. And I have believed them, — have yielded myself to the fascination of the delusive song, that, like the chant of the siren, has brought me to sorrow and misery. Henceforth, O Ocean! when thy beauties I would contemplate, I will hie me to a high hill and feast my eyes, nor trust thy unstable waters more."

HOW CURIOUS IT IS!

When the life of Daniel Webster — that grand drama — was about drawing to a close, he is represented to have said, "Life — Life — how curious it is!" The word curious was deemed a strange one, but it expressed the very thing. How curious life is, from the cradle to the grave! The forming mind of childhood, busy with the present, and unable to guess the secret of its own existence, is curious. The hopes of youth are curious, reaching forward into the future, and building castles in the perspective for those who entertain them, that will fade away in the sunlight of an older experience. How curious is the first dawning of love, when the young heart surrenders itself to its dreams of bliss, illumined with — moonshine! How curious it is, when marriage crowns the wishes, to find the cares of life but begun, and the path all strewn with anxieties, that romance had depicted as a road of flowers! How curious it is, says the young mother, as she spreads upon her own the tiny hand of her child, and endeavors to read, in its dim lines, the fortune there hidden! Curious, indeed, would such revealing be. How curious is the greed for gain that controls too much the life of man, leading him away after strange gods, forgetting all the object and good of life in a chase for a phantom light, that ends at last in threefold Egyptian darkness! How curious is the love of life that clings to the old, and draws them back imploringly to earth, begging for a longer look at time and its frivolities, with eternity and all its joys within their reach! How curious it is, when at length the great end draws nigh, — the glazing eye, the struggle, the groan, proclaiming dissolution, and the still clay — so still! — that lately stood by our side in the pride of health and happiness! How curious it is that the realities of the immortal world should be based upon the crumbling vanities of this, and that the path to infinite life should be through the dark shadow of the grave! How curious it is, in its business and its pleasures, its joys and its sorrows, its hopes and its fears, its temptations and its triumphs; and, as we contemplate life in all its manifestations, we needs must exclaim, "How curious it is!"

EARTH SPEAKETH TO EARTH.

A GRAVE LYRIC.

I LEANED me over a grave-yard wall,
Where the grass before me grew rank and tall,
And bowed in the wind its heavy head,
As if in reverence for the dead;
The acacia-tree rustled its mournful leaves,
Like the rustle of silk when the widow grieves:
As I listened, a still voice met my ear —
Come over here! come over here!

Come over here! come over here!
Said the old calm grave-yard dark and drear;
I will hold you clasped in a fond embrace,
And watch o'er your silent resting-place.
The grand old trees o'er your bed shall swing,
And the birds in the waving branches sing;
Naught shall disturb your slumbering ear —
Come over here! come over here!

Come over here! come over here!
Leave the world with its tumult, its strife and fear.
Here is peace that speaks from the deep green grass
In whispers, as o'er it the breezes pass;
Here is quiet and rest to the weary heart,
That long has suffered 'neath sorrow's smart;
O, leave the heart-ache anguish drear —
Come over here! come over here!

Come over here ! come over here !
This is the garner of many a year ;
This is the bourn where the weary rest,
The high and lowly, the bad and best ;
Their voice is stilled and their heart is cold,
In the chilly damp of the grave-yard mould,
But from their forms bright things uprear —
Come over here ! come over here !

Come over here ! come over here !
The child, and the youth, and the old man sere,
Have lent their strength and lent their charms
To grace the grave-yard's folding arms !
I will deck your couch with the vernal flowers,
And tears shall fall in the summer showers,
The smiling sun your bed shall cheer —
Come over here ! come over here !

Come over here ! come over here !
O, gaze not on me with looks of fear.
I will clasp you close to my motherly heart
Till you grow of my very self a part ;
My teeming breast shall yield anew
With the strength of its motherly love so true ;
For the mother earth loves her children dear —
Come over here ! come over here !

WITHOUT A SPECK.

Mrs. Partington, in speaking of one who had enjoyed the blessing of good sight up to a late period of her life, said "she never had a speck on in her life." What a consolation it would be for us, when we get into the vale of years, if, in "looking back o'er the scene of our errors," we could say the same in a moral sense, with never a speck on our escutcheon to reproach us ! Alas ! the best of us, in such position, would see many dark specks, and our life, like a pear over-ripe, prove to be infected with many unsound spots. The best of men have so little to be proud of ! — even those who are laboring so hard in behalf of fallen man now-a-days may be found to have the blemish that all possess, in common. This is comforting to sinners who are crowded down by disadvantageous circumstances, who see the shaky tendency of those better than they, and take courage. The suspicion of a speck redeems the humanity of the very perfect man. We do not love what the world calls perfection. It has no heart beneath its jacket; the throb of sympathy is not there; it has no recognition of kindred weaknesses; it forgets old ties and old obligations. We like to think of the worthies who have lived of yore in this light of imperfection— to think of men with a speck or so on them, be it never so small. To think of Washington, and Paul, and Peter, as men, makes us love them better than though they were myths. St. Peter's impetuosity and Paul's temper endear them to us; and after reading the denial scene, we say, "Peter, you acted like a man;" and his penitence was more manly still.

FORCED OBEDIENCE.

I SAW a damsel holding by a string
  A little puppy, who, disposed to stray,
Choked at restraint, and made a frequent spring
  In effort vain to tear himself away.
But yet, the more he strove, the more he choked,
  Until he deemed his conduct would n't pay,
And moved along as though he were provoked,
  And held his head down in a sullen way.
My soul was touched the emblem thus to see
  Of life's too frequent scenes, where day by day
Strings clog the spirit's elasticity,
  And kill the willingness that would obey,—
Men, like the puppy, follow at a word,
But, try to drag them, and their dander 's stirred.

A LIFE'S FORTUNES.

It is a simple story, possessing moderate interest, of an every-day life. Things of a stranger character than these described are happening all the time, and a writer need scarcely draw on fancy for his incidents, when there are realities enough about him, made to his hand. The chief character is no "Don" or "Lord;" but a plain man, born of plain parents, and destined for the same plain duties and struggles that await all who are born outside the pale of luxurious plenty. James Trevor was a quick-witted and ready youth, indifferently honest, very ambitious, and passably good-looking; a fair average character, as a boy, — prone to trade and boyish speculation, in which he always came off best, — selfish as boys almost always are, and enjoyed the reputation of being "dreadful smart," which old Jacob Trevor, his father, was very proud to hear, seeing in the promise of the title-page a richly-wrought book, as full of good things as a Thanksgiving-day is of blessings.

Mr. Trevor was an old farmer in a back town in Massachusetts — Sweetfern, I will call it, though there is not a sprig of that fragrant herb within many miles of it. He was well to do, as everybody said, though not rich. His farm had come to him from his father, one of the earliest settlers of Sweetfern, and was the most fertile of any in the section where it was located. The land was watered by a beautiful stream that flowed among the hills, which now serves as a power to turn the wheels of thriving manufactories, but, at the time of which I write, was deemed simply a manifestation of the good-will of Providence towards the Trevors. The Trevors were out in the Revolution, and James could point to Bennington and Saratoga, in which his grandfather and father both figured, or go away back into the French war, where his grandfather was wounded in the ambuscade at Fort Edward, at the time Colonel Williams was killed.

When James Trevor was about sixteen years old, his father informed him that he had procured him a position in a store, in a town some miles away from Sweetfern; which announcement he received with great pleasure, as he had become weary of the monotony of farm-life. The store was a new field for the development of his budding genius, and he accepted the position without any hesitation. The next week saw him installed in the coveted situation. It was a large country store, occupied by Edes & Co., the name of which firm was blazoned on a wide, white sign, extending along the whole front of the largest building in the place; and, by the side of the door, on long strips of black board, were painted the names of the various articles sold there — molasses and muslin, tobacco and tongues-and-sounds, crockery and crackers, Indian-meal and indigo, hats and hay, calcined magnesia and calico, and "other articles too numerous to mention,' as the advertisement of the firm in the local paper expressed it. It was said of Edes' plug-tobacco, by the farmers, that he soaked it in a little brandy and a little molasses, and it was as good as any they ever wanted to see. Contented souls! they had not yet dreamed of the bliss of silver-leaf.

Thus, at sixteen, James Trevor found himself in business, indentured, as was the custom in those days, to learn the trade of a country storekeeper, with a quick fortune and a life of dignified ease in perspective. He dashed into the performance of his duties with all the enthusiasm of a boy, and became very soon convinced that on his individual efforts alone the existence of the firm of Edes & Co. particularly depended. Mr. Edes was an aristocrat, by nature, — a village aristocrat, one of the meanest and most contemptible of that class, who by a shrewd venture in early life had made a large sum, with which he had embarked in trade, and been very successful. Fortune, however, rather than sagacity, had favored him. He had small intelligence, and less feeling, and was most distinguished for the tenacity with which he would hold on to a dollar when he got it. He never lost a cent in his life, and never gave away one until he had ciphered out its return through some other channel. He was a strict attendant upon church, and his whole household — consisting of an only daughter, a half-sister, Mr. Merrow, the Co. of his firm, who boarded with him, and James Trevor — were expected to accompany him; which meant that they must go — and they did.

Julia Edes, the daughter, was a delicate and pensive child. Her mother had died when she was quite young, and her father's half-sister, a maiden lady of forty, had been installed mistress of the household, assuming to herself the entire charge of the young heiress, a charge which the unsympathetic father never interfered with. The child's outward wants were all attended to, as was her education; but it was a frosty atmosphere that her shrinking nature had to develop itself in. The aunt, though a kind woman, had no feeling in common with her own. Propriety of conduct was her only ideal of human excellence, and work the ultimate of human endeavor. She conceived every kind of pleasure to be sin; and hence all of the promptings of the young nature of her charge were checked by the hydrostatic influences that weighed her down. The bounds of her association with other children were meted out to her, beyond which she dare not go; and constant surveillance was held upon her conduct, that she might not be led into any insubordinate mirth, that would trench on the province of propriety. One ghastly skeleton stood forever in her young path — the fear of offending; and, though she loved her aunt, it was a love that was begloomed by that estimable woman, who, like a good many other estimable persons, placed herself between her and the light of joy. She was named for her aunt, and felt grateful for many attentions; but often, in the midst of her tenderest reflections regarding her, the thought would steal in and mar all, that she was a slave, and that the poorest child that sported on the village-green, or roamed in unrestrained freedom in the fields and woods, was an enviable object.

At the time James Trevor came to reside with her father, she was about fifteen years old. She was not handsome, and there was a shyness and reserve about her that rendered her anything but prepossessing. Her pale, wan face was surmounted by very dark hair, that hung in careless masses around her forehead. Her eyes were black, and were almost all the time bent upon the ground, except at moments when the utterance of a fine sentiment, or a note of music, or a strange voice, would attract her attention. One quick glance would then betray her pleasure or her curiosity, instantly to subside again into seeming indifference. Such she appeared to him when she first fell beneath his eye, and he made up his mind that a union with his master's daughter at least would form no part in his programme of prospective greatness. Beyond merely looking at her once or twice his interest did not extend; for an introduction was not deemed essential. He was a proper, smart-looking lad, of which it is presumed the young lady took notice; for, after she had retired to her chamber with her aunt, she remained for some time very thoughtful, and then said,

"Aunt, don't you think the young man, down stairs, very good-looking?"

"Child!" replied the aunt, with a tone of sternness that turned the maiden's heart to stone, and her lips to iron rigidity, "your question is highly improper."

That was the end of the first lesson, so far as propriety had anything to say about it; but, dashing madly through her brain, came troops of bewildering thoughts, that made her downy pillow a scene of wild fancies. Love reared an idol before her, crowned with beauty and grace. It smiled upon her, and pointed to a vacant pedestal by its side, which, when she strove to ascend it, crumbled to pieces; and, as she gazed, the idol also faded away, the roses turned to thorns, and a mocking laugh greeted her ears as she awoke. She was glad the vision had passed, and felt provoked that it had obcruded itself, unsolicited, especially because it had not ended happily, as all dreams of love should, agreeably to the rule of romance. James Trevor slept soundly enough all night; for his was a mind not yet capable of dreaming of anybody or anything but himself.

First meetings are always tender turning-points in a story, wherein mutual love springs into life with the glance of the eye or the pressure of the hand. But, from the very material fact that neither the glance of the eye nor the pressure of the hand were exchanged, I am denied the delightful task of describing any such phenomenon. They met for some time as strangers, never speaking a word, although glances were accidentally exchanged by them at times, throwing both into inexplicable confusion, as though they had done some guilty thing in looking at each other.

It was on the second Sunday of James Trevor at the Edes's, while on their way to meeting, that Mr. Edes, who walked behind with Mr. Merrow, called his sister to his side to speak to her upon some matter then uppermost in his mind, leaving Julia, with whom she had been walking, alone. By one of those strange accidents, that happen with great opportuneness to draw people together, as though there were some invisible master of ceremonies engaged in an eccentric, though sensible, mode of introduction, Julia's handkerchief was swept out of her hand by a gust of wind that, with sportive violence, rolled it over and over in the dirt, and bore it along with great rudeness, depositing it at the feet of James Trevor, who was walking along ahead of the party, unmindful of anything that was transpiring. He came near stepping upon the delicate fabric, but did not; and, as it rolled over again, as if to take another start, he reached down and seized it, somewhat as though he were afraid of it, and, turning back, placed it, with a low bow, in the young lady's hand. She received it with a pleasant smile, and a "Thank you," that by its sweetness gave him a thrill of pleasure he had never before experienced. He walked along by her side, occasionally glancing at her through the corner of his eye, and began to think she was very pretty; her form, too, taking new grace in his fancy. He couldn't say anything, however, though he made twenty attempts to speak. He had ideas enough, but he couldn't think of them. At last, he mustered resolution to say, "Miss Edes, I hope we shall be friends." It was an immense speech, and its tone was tender and manly, too; and she replied, with charming frankness, "I hope so, with all my heart; for I have very few friends." Her voice trembled as she said this, the tone of which set him to thinking how fine it would be if she were shut up in a castle, and were to wave her handkerchief from some loophole, and he should see it, and should rush in and kill a dragon or two, and the entire garrison of men-at-arms, and set her free, and she should accept him as her lover! The train of his thought here ran off the track, as the aunt took her place by the side of her niece, freezing James Trevor into his old position, though he turned the sweet little sentence over in his mind that had echoed his hope, and dwelt upon the unhappiness conveyed in the remark that she had very few friends.

This first day was the beginning of a more intimate relation between the two. They met now as friends, whenever they did meet, though the occasions were rare. The keen eye of the aunt saw the impropriety of their meeting alone, and she always was in the way at such meetings. The restraint thus placed upon them was a continued invitation to break through it; and the catastrophe feared and guarded against transpired through the excess of vigilance used for its prevention. The boy and girl — now older, as two years had elapsed since they had first met, and he had grown in manly grace, and she in womanly development — had actually fallen over ears in love. They had stolen many a march on the old aunt, by letter, and by such blissful snatches of time as chance had favored them withal; and they had found many. A low balcony that ran by her chamber window admitted of many a meeting in the summer nights, for your lover has ever been as spry as a cat. All noticed the change in the fair Julia's manner, for she had wonderfully improved. From the dull and moping girl, she became lively and vivacious, and even "Old Propriety," as James Trevor profanely termed the aunt, admitted that she had never known so wonderful a change.

Alas! that I must dash this beautiful scene to pieces, and strew salt upon its ground, so that nothing shall grow there more! But I am truthful in my narration, and a reputation achieved by a long life of veracity must not be endangered by any wrong statement. A letter — O, that lovers should ever know how to write! O, that they knew enough to avoid ink! O, that they would write their tender missives in paregoric or water! — directed to "Julia Edes," appointing a meeting on the balcony, fell into the hands of the aunt, instead of the daughter. The night was dark, and the youth, full of love and impatience, climbed upon the balcony, where Julia awaited him. It was the wrong Julia, though, and, as he clasped her in his arms, unaware of the difference, in his impetuosity, and imprinted a dozen kisses upon her lips, she brought him a box upon his ear that almost knocked him down, saying, at the same time,

"There, you sauce-box, take that!"

He had already taken it, and her remark seemed superfluous, considering that fact. He mumbled out some apology, and at that instant the window opened, and Mr. Edes stepped out, having been attracted by his sister's sharp voice.

"What's the matter?" was his question. "Thieves?"

"The matter!" said she, tartly. "O, nothing, nothing. This youngster has presumed to make an appointment to meet Julia here on the balcony, that's all; and, as I chose to take her place, I came very nigh being smothered with kisses."

"Young man," said Mr. Edes, drawing himself up from five feet eight to five feet eight and a half, "have you presumed to take such liberties with my child and sister?"

"I have, sir," said James, boldly; "and all that I regret about it is that I made this mistake. I certainly never should have taken such liberties with your sister, had I seen who it was."

"And have you no regrets to express at your men dacious — mendacious — impropriety in presuming to make an appointment with my daughter, sir?" said the old man, sternly.

"No, sir," he replied, frankly; "I could not help loving her, as she loves me. We have told each other so, whenever we could; and I have hoped that some day, when I was a man, she would be my wife, with your consent."

"How improper!" said Miss Edes, holding up both her hands.

"Well, young man," continued Mr. Edes, "you can be no longer a resident of my house; this presumption divides us. I have a higher aim for my daughter, and with the morning you will depart for your home."

James clambered down from the balcony as heavily as though two fifty-sixes had been thrust into his coat-pockets; but it was really because his heart was so heavy. He crawled away to his chamber, mortified and chagrined, and then sat down and wrote Julia a letter, vowing constancy, and swearing, in the approved style, that he would come back and marry her, when he had won fortune, which he was sure to do. He sealed his letter, and, stealing out, placed it beneath her door; then, putting a few things together, he stepped lightly down the stairs, and passed out of the house forever. His path led by the store, the key of which he had in his pocket. Recollecting some trifle that he wished to take with him, he opened the door and went in. The old store-dog growled fiercely as he entered, but, perceiving who it was, he licked the hand held out to him, and took his place upon the mat, where he had been sleeping, satisfied that all was right.

A wicked spirit was near James Trevor as he stood there, and whispered in his ear many tempting and insidious words. "There is money in the safe, as you know," it said, "which you must have, in order to get away. You have earned it," the voice continued; "you have not been half paid: take it. Revenge is sweet, James Trevor, and you cannot touch the old hunks so keenly as through his pocket." Alas, for poor human weakness and dull conscientiousness! the tempter won; and, though a good spirit whispered "Julia," the rustling of the bank-notes he was handling drowned the sound, and, pocketing a considerable sum of the money, he passed out into the world, appeasing the little conscience that troubled him with the assurance that he would pay the amount, with interest, when he came back rich. He threw the key of the store into a pond, and struck across the fields in an opposite direction from his home, to where a stage-road led to the seaboard. He thought that they would not miss the money for several days, and then, as he had left no traces of his being in the store, that they would have no proof that he had stolen it; and he reckoned rightly.

The amount taken was part of a large sum reserved to pay for an invoice of goods expected to arrive by the slow wagons that plied between Campton and the seaboard and it was not missed until the package was removed from the safe for conveyance, by the stage-driver, to its destination. Confusion instantly prevailed when the loss was discovered. Mr. Edes raved in a manner very severe, accusing everybody of a disposition to swindle him; when some one, in order to vindicate himself from so general a charge, asked if James Trevor might not have taken it, as he had so very mysteriously disappeared from the store, which disappearance he and the other associate had vainly tried to account for. The suggestion was made to Mr. Merrow, who gladly received it, as he had latterly taken a repugnance to the young man, on account of the interest manifested in him by Julia, which his jealous instincts had perceived, whose good graces he wished to secure to himself. He immediately mentioned the suggestion to Mr. Edes, who, admitting its reasonableness, became more frantic, and at once sent a messenger to Sweetfern to bring the fugitive back, as he conceived he had taken that direction.

Great was the astonishment of old Mr. Trevor at the tale the messenger told him of the disappearance of his son, and his imputed dishonesty. It was a severe blow to him, as his hope of his son's greatness had grown with time Now dishonor and shame were about to descend upon a name that had long been respectable. He went back to Campton with the messenger, and was informed by Mr. Edes, in private, of the boy's presumption. — he would not for many dollars have the fact public, — and of the probability of his dishonesty. There was, it is true, no positive proof that he had committed the crime, but he would advertise him through the country, and have him brought back for trial. The father saw all this through his fears, and compromised the matter by supplying the missing amount. He sorrowfully returned, with the reluctantly-admitted belief that his son, for whom he had indulged such hope, was a villain. He was a wanderer, he knew not where, and there was no possibility of communicating with him, in order to make an effort to save him, if he had not fallen irremediably.

The letter that her departed lover had written to Julia had not reached its destination, and the poor girl knew not what had befallen him. His absence alarmed her, and, in reply to the timid question she asked her aunt regarding him, she was told that he had stolen money from her father and run away. What a blow was this for young love! But her faith in her lover's honesty was strong, even though appearances might be against him. Yet why should he have gone, at all? and why should he not have told her that he was going? The questions were very perplexing, and the attempt to solve them wrought a fever of anxiety in her mind, that brought with it the illness of body that follows despair. It was long before she recovered, and when restored to health her step had lost its elasticity, and her eye the joyous fire that had characterized it when reflecting the sunlight of requited love. (I have submitted the close of the preceding sentence to the criticism of those who have for twenty years been accustomed to read love-stories, and they say that the "sunlight of requited love" is good. Poor Julia!)

We left James Trevor on the road, waiting for the stage-coach, with determination in his heart, and stolen money in his pocket. Tender thoughts of Julia flitted through his mind, amid the whirl of conflicting emotions, like the gleam of an angel's wing in the dun and smoke of battle. For a moment he would feel like a scoundrel; and then the tempter, who had never left him, would whisper "Chicken-hearted milksop" in his ear, and suggest that it was "only a loan." About the time the stage came along, he felt quieted, and mounted to the top with something like cheerfulness in his manner. It was a delightful morning in summer; the birds sang from every bush, and universal nature seemed glowingly alive with melody and bloom. A grateful coolness filled the air, which flung incense abroad from myriad censers, and the human soul, rightly attuned, arose with the spirit of the morning in responsive praise.

There was on the outside of the stage, with James Trevor, a rough and poor-looking man, whose cheerful and pleasant face denoted a happy heart within. He seemed fully alive to the beauty of the scene, and his lips were constantly expressing the joy that filled him.

"How good men should strive to be," he said, "in view of the blessings the good Father sends!" He looked at James, as he spoke, who, with a half-consciousness that he could read his secret, faltered out a timid "Yes."

"But, for all this blessing," the rough man continued, "which should bring us to our knees, we return nothing but wrong-doing and baseness."

James tried to look attentive and interested, while he felt his heart beating very fast, and his conscience sorely troubled.

"Man is the only thing in the universe," the rough man went on, "that is false to God. The flowers bloom, the winds blow, the stars shine, the glorious sun warms and invigorates, and all are 'good,' as when pronounced thus in Eden; but *man* —— strange perversity!"

The poor runaway could not resist the feeling that had been coming upon him, and here bowed his head with the deepest contrition. His companion observed it, and, thinking James some boy grieved at leaving home, strove to comfort him, by telling him that with honesty and probity he might secure wealth and fame, and return again to honor those from whom he had sprung. But the counsel only added fuel to the fire. That was a miserable day for him on the top of the coach, and he was very glad when he arrived at his destination, and pleased to be rid of one who, it seemed, had either been especially sent to torment him, or as an angel to warn him against future danger. He accepted the latter signification, and, sitting down, wrote his father the whole story of his love, and his indiscretion, and his dishonesty, with the tale of his strange conversion, returning the money, and begging forgiveness, stating his determination to leave the country, and never come back until he had made fortune enough to claim his bride, and give her the position she was fitted to grace. From this time he became a wanderer in search of fortune.

There is a description of special Providence in the affairs of men, termed *Good-luck;* and those favored with it have but to will, and the slaves of good-luck, and all the other slaves, instantly obey, as readily as did the slaves of the lamp in the hands of Aladdin. Their touch seems, Midas-like, to turn everything to gold. They speak, and their words coin into guineas, or take the form of bank-notes. They step, and whole territories of real estate, never known before, spring into being. They wave their hands, and mighty factories stand beside the subservient streams. The converse has too many disagreeable associations of a personal character to induce me to dwell upon it. James Trevor was lucky. He had changed his name, and had found his way to Hayti, where, in a few years, he acquired a sufficient amount to justify his return to claim his bride, from whom he had not heard since he left his country. It was at the time when the fever of the revolution had spread to the outer limit of the French jurisdiction, and Hayti was in a great state of fermentation. The antagonism of the blacks and whites was every day growing more and more bitter. The whites, from an overweening sense of their own superiority, did not deign to conciliate, and James Trevor, who had become a prominent man, less than any; for one who has only the idea of achieving gain in his heart has small room for humane considerations. The storm so long gathering at last burst, and, just upon the eve of Trevor's embarking for home, and when he had adjusted everything for his departure, those violent scenes began, which ended in the establishment of the Haytien republic, and the subjugation of the whites. Every dollar of his money was swept away, and, barely escaping with his life, by the aid of a faithful slave, he was again cast upon the world.

The sweet Julia of his boyish dreams still held place in his affections; but he had taught himself to see her only through a worldly mist of money and establishment, and doubt of womanly constancy, that had grown up within him in an atmosphere of intrigue and licentiousness, caused him at times to entertain the possibility that she had forgotten him; and these feelings, in his hour of ruin, came upon him with a force to dispel the half-formed resolution to return, while pride, that unsafe counsellor, recalled the promise he had made not to return until he was rich. "I will keep my promise," he said to himself, and he did. There was no chance of hearing from his native place, it being remote from the seaboard, and, though he had at several times sent letters to Julia and his father, by transient ships, to be dropped into remote post-offices, those letters were never received by those to whom they were sent

Ten years more had passed over his head, and once more fortune had smiled upon him. He had located himself in Marseilles, and — O, treachery to love! — he was about to marry. The gentle Julia, though not all forgotten, had become the memory of a vision, seen in the air some bright morning, that the sudden cloud had obscured, or of an angel that appeared in some distant reverie, impalpable and unsubstantial. The fascinating glitter of a fashionable woman had captivated his senses rather than won his heart, and he was about to marry her—as thousands marry, most happy reader, who bind that knot with their tongue that their teeth cannot untie, to hold them in irredeemable wretchedness, as must be the case where love sheds not its benediction — seeing nothing beyond present aggrandizement or convenience. He married, and the white image of Julia floated out of his mind, as the angel of Peace flees the scene where the demon of Discord asserts his claim for supremacy. And thus we leave him, selfish, false, ungrateful — to find his reward, perhaps!

The gentle Julia, in all these years, had proved true to her first love, treasuring his memory with commendable persistency, which must have been very refreshing to witness. We know nothing like it in these latter seasons, when constancy to a first lover depends oftener upon the accident of never knowing a second one than upon a principle. The venerable aunt had died and been buried according to the gravest and most approved propriety, and mourned up to the expected shade. On her death-bed she confessed to Julia the great wrong she had done her, and produced the very letter James Trevor had written the night of his departure, which she had adroitly purloined, having suspected, from a shrewd knowledge of human nature, that he would write such a letter, and seen him from her own door deposit it beneath her niece's. That letter breathed the most ardent promises of constancy, and vows that he would return to marry her in spite of "Old Propriety," and begging her to be true to him. The same old story!

She had been besieged by Merrow as soon as his rival was out of the way, but was obdurate to all his entreaties, and had uniformly refused to listen to the addresses of any. Time found her an heiress of her father's property, the old gentleman having paid the debt of nature without a discount, which was considered a strange departure from his usual mode of operations. The business passed into the hands of Mr. Merrow, who had married, and who became purchaser of the Edes mansion, the daughter desiring to remove from a scene to her so full of painful recollections. This she did, and, with the strange and unaccountable caprice of woman's character, chose to locate in the very city from which her lover had taken his departure in quest of fortune. She bought a residence there, and, with a single female companion, spent her time in benevolent actions.

It is not a very pleasant part of a writer's duty to kill off all the characters of his story before the dénouement, though that plan is adopted sometimes by fictionists when they wish to get troublesome people out of the way. This veracious story, however, is that of a life, with a lapse of time that operates with subtle and certain force upon human years, as most people know; therefore they, at least, will not be surprised when we gather old Jacob Trevor to his fathers, or mention that he died at a good old age, the farm having been sold to a cotton manufacturing company, and the money therefor distributed among the heirs-at-law.

Few were living that could have recognized, in the rich Mr. Merton, merchant, of Marseilles, the humble boy, James Trevor, who had left the American hills forty years before. He scarcely knew himself, and scarcely wished to, for life to him had become identified with foreign scenes and foreign circumstances, and the money was all there for which he had sold himself. He had, through correspondents in New York, learned of his father's death, and he had also, by the same means, learned of the departure of the Edes family from Campton. His domestic life had been a stormy one. He had no children, his wife was wildly extravagant, and addicted to the prominent vices incident to some phases of fashionable life, — gambling and wine-drinking, — and the wealth that had come to him, under the domination of good-luck, was in constant danger of being swept from him by her excesses. Did he not have his reward? At length, in a time of panic, the crash came, and, ruined in health, commercial credit, and personal reputation, James Trevor found himself a bankrupt. His wife left him, and his wreck was complete.

But he was richer in ruin than when in his highest state of opulence. It led him to think, and with thought came repentance, and with repentance resolution. And, as his feelings softened in the atmosphere of trial, the good spirit came into his heart again, and, though years of time and a further distance of estrangement had separated them, he thought of Julia Edes, and wept — that ruined old man — like a child. He never was so rich in his life as at that moment. His soul was coining ingots of golden treasure, and laying it up in a heaven of returning tenderness. To talk of earthly riches, in comparison to this!

The ship-fever was raging among emigrants arrived at the city where the "good Miss Edes," as the poor called her, resided, and early and late was she busy in ministering to the wants of the sick and dying. The hospitals were full, and nurses were hard to be procured; so she herself went from ward to ward, alleviating, as far as possible, the pain of the sufferers. Blessings followed her wherever she went. One morning she was told that a poor old man had been brought in during the night, and there was no place for him. Every bed was full, and room could not be found for more.

"Send him to my house," said she; "he must not suffer for this care;" and he was accordingly sent there on a litter.

As soon as she had gone the round of her duty, she returned to her home, and there, upon a comfortable bed, she found the stranger. The fever had taken a fearful hold upon his feeble system, and upon its paroxysms delirium attended. She merely glanced at him as he lay in his unconsciousness, his features disfigured by the disease, and gave directions to the physician who had accompanied her home to bestow on him all needed attentions, and to procure a nurse for him, whose duty she would for the present perform. He went away, and left her alone with the sick man. The sufferer muttered incoherently, as he lay with his eyes shut. At length every faculty in her was absorbed by a word he uttered. She did not breathe, but leaned over him, with all her senses acutely alive, to catch a repetition of the sound.

"Julia!" he murmured, "dearest Julia, why will you not come to me?"

She looked in the face so fearful with distemper, and around the lips she saw the same smile that had beamed upon her in the long years ago, never once forgotten; and, kneeling down by the bedside, she bowed her head upon her hands, while the tears — tears of pity and love — flowed copiously, and cried aloud, from the fulness of her heart, "Thank God! thank God!" The doctor, on his return, found her thus. She had swooned from excitement and exhaustion.

The life of the stranger was spared, and through the long watches of his illness she never left his bedside. Slowly he recovered, and his first inquiry was as to the place where he found himself. He was told that he was in the house of a friend, who would see that all his wants were answered.

"Thanks — many thanks," he said; "but I can make no return for your kindness. I am a poor, ruined man, and, though I recently could command everything, I am now dependent upon charity for my very life."

He lay still, but his proud spirit seemed to struggle with the ignominy of dependence, and with a deep sigh he fell asleep, — into one of those half-conscious sleeps wherein the soul involuntarily reveals itself, and during which she often heard her name taken upon the dreamer's lips. But now a fearful storm was raging in his mind, in which she heard more than she should have heard of reënacted strife, of recrimination and retort, and bitter taunt, and severe invective, and through it she knew that James Trevor had proved false to his early vows. But there came no anger with the thought.

Her love for him was too pure for that; it sought his good and happiness alone, irrespective of conditions As she listened to him, the storm in his mind subsided, and, in the sweet tones of the olden time, again came the beloved name —

"Julia!"

She bent over him, and, taking his thin hand in hers, looked down into his eyes as he awoke, and breathed the name he had not for years heard —

"James Trevor!"

The tenderness and singularity of this scene surpass all my powers of description. I could, having been young myself, describe a meeting of young people under such circumstances; but these were venerable lovers, and it is not to be supposed that the rhapsody of youth could have any part in the meeting. There were doubtless a few kisses exchanged under the first impulse, and then came the explanation of mutual fortunes, tender reminiscences, and future prospects, which were not very bright conjugally, provided they had been still young, with an ugly French wife in the way. But the heyday of their blood had grown tame, and a mellowed and subdued affection had taken the place of that fiercer passion which marked their early years. It was no longer passion, and in the calmness of its sacred glow they both found a healthy happiness. They lived in the same house together for many years, agreeably to a propriety that would have delighted Julia's aunt; but his arm was her support, and her affectionate counsel his encouragement in his new effort to be a better man. And thus the Fortunes of a Life turned out.

MOUNT WASHINGTON.

WRITTEN AT THE GLEN HOUSE.

THE Queen of Sheba said of Israel's glory,
When Solomon his wisdom did unfold her,
That far inadequate was every story,
And not one half the truth had e'er been told her.

And here, Mount Washington above me rising,
I feel myself in that same situation,
For not a tithe of all its wealth surprising
Hath pen or tongue made fitting revelation.

O, beautiful and grand the gross amount
Of mountain scene, from which there 's no discounting;
Where Nature figures in a wild account, —
Like compound interest, evermore a "mounting."

I watch the flitting shadows yonder dancing
Like sportive elves among the granite boulders;
Anon I see the cheerful sunshine glancing
Like epaulets on Washington's broad shoulders.

Around the awful peak now vapors gather,
And darkly-lowering clouds the valleys threaten
There 's no postponement on account of weather,
Or compromising to defer the wettin'.

The lavish rain outpours, — I hear it rushing
Far o'er the forest, on its work baptismal;
A holy wet from primal fountains gushing,
That gives the heart no contemplation dismal.

'T is past, — the birds, their cheerful song renewing,
Pour forth their lays in grateful adoration;
The rivulet, its pleasant way pursuing,
Joins its glad note in musical oblation.

The self-same song comes from yon sylvan bowers,
In notes as wild, as sweet, and as sonorous,
As when, in Nature's first awakening hours,
The glad creation sang Time's opening chorus.

How green and bright the garniture appears
Which Nature throws about those kingly bases!
Its fashion changeless in the lapse of years,
Perfection found in its primeval graces.

But here to stand and view it I 'm contented,—
Though others soar, it is not my ambition,
I am not sad that I have been prevented,
For those who 've soared are sorer in condition.

ALBUMINOUS.

APROPOS of Albums. Some regard them as bores and even use a harsher term in speaking of them, and shudder when one is placed in their hands, as some sensitive people do when asked to hold a baby. The voice asking the favor of a line in an album sounds harsh and unpleasant in the ears of such, though flute-like in its intonation, and the request to climb a greased pole, or turn a back somerset in the street, seems easy in comparison. My boarding-house experience embraced an endless round of albums,—the boarding-house numbering three or four young women among its occupants, forming a sort of intellectual exchange of such, —and it was the practice of the fair owners to make a direct assault upon all new-comers, as soon as the ceremony of introduction had been gone through with, so that the albuminous was largely predominant in our circle, and, like mucilage, made us stick together. Those albums exhibited very fine displays of rhetoric, representing every phase of intellectual calibre, ranging, as may be imagined, through the whole field of profession, with very doubtful evidences of sincerity in any of them. Juliana! O, how well is she remembered, even at the distance of ever-so-many years, with her flaxen hair in papers, and her blue eyes beaming upon the boy who gazed upon them with a feeling of admiration, that it took a long time to prove the folly of! Juliana's album was the most favored. Her album was made the altar of as many beautiful fancies as there were leaves contained in it. Herein glowed the thoughts that breathed and the words that burned with different degrees of intensity. Here a page of pink gleamed with *couleur de rose* imaginings, and there the yellow bore the bilious lucubrations of diseased fancy; here the green betrayed the verdancy of young heart-burn, and there the blue glistened with fervent words like the firmament with its wealth of stars. Above and through and in all, the sugar of flattery prevailed, to catch the credulous fly, Vanity; and succeeded but too well, as was apparent in the fact that one page, which contained the only honest sentiment that had ever been written in it, was torn out, on the pretence that it was so stupid! There were many vows and many protestations, and much honey about the leaves; but, before we divided, the falsity of half the two former had been seen, and an infusion of gall in the latter that rendered its sweet slightly acrid. The boarders married off, or changed their boarding-places, and hatred, or, what is worse, indifference, took the place of the intense sentiment that lied still upon the centre-table. Poor Juliana! She will pardon this allusion to herself, if she can stop from her manifold duties long enough to read it; for she is now a woman of many cares, and the flaxen curls, no more in papers, have a tinge of gray pervading them; but her album was a model. I recollect a tall, sentimental young man who wrote in it, — who wore his collar turned over, and encouraged a slight beard on his chin, who eschewed meat, and chewed

Graham bread and raisins, to induce right conditions for intellectual emanations. His muse was prolific, and we remember well the pride Juliana displayed when she pointed out the following:

"TO JULIANA.

"The harp once struck to that dear theme,
My Juliana's prays,
Should never sound again, I deem,
With no ignoble lays.

"My harp, a loan, her prays shall sing;
No other theme shall clame
To hold dominion o'er a string
Yet thrilling with her name.

"The wild discordancy of life
Around may roar and rave, —
Her name I 'll sound amid the strife,
And still the trubled wave.

"And though we part to meat no more,
And such stern fate must be,
I still shall look towards the shoar
Where first her smiles I *see*."

The inspiration was apparent in the bad spelling, and the sincerity in the fact that he ran away without paying his board, leaving the "shoar" and Juliana's smiles behind him. A few pages further, another muse blazed with the following:

"TO MISS JULIANA.

"When upon these lines you gaze,
Think of him who 's gone his ways;
Think of him that once you knew,
Who will evermore prove true;
Think of him who on life's sea
You may never again more see;

Think of him who with a sigh
Bid you and your mother and all good-by,
Then in the depths of his misery
He took his trunk and went and shipped to go to sea."

These two specimens are sufficient. Juliana still keeps the book, and marks are discoverable in it of tear-drops, or of greasy fingers, and it is an object of great interest with her grown-up daughter. But albums are really desirable things, discreetly used. They embalm the friendship of to-day, and may be made the mediums of pleasant and affectionate thought. Dedicated to high-toned sentiment and sincerity, they become invaluable for reference in after time, when the heart is sad with stings and slights the world inflicts. Unworthy names may mar their pages, but they may be easily expunged, or retained as mementoes of the fact that we are all weak creatures, and liable to fall.

PARTED TIES.

The hand still warm with the imparted touch
  Of friendly farewell, and the ears still hearing
The sounds of kindness that we 've prizéd much,
  That long our varied pathway have been cheering,
We scarce can deem that touch has been the last,
  Or that the words which friendship's tongue has spoken
Will be but tender memories of the past —
  Strains of a lute whose strings are rudely broken

'T is hard to feel that smiles we know to-day,
  Blessing our pathway with their radiance cheering,
May ere the sunset fade in gloom away,
  In death's dark shade forever disappearing;
That the warm heart which, throbbing with our own,
  Has felt with us, e'en now, each joy and sorrow,
May cease its sweet and sympathetic tone,
  And leave us sad and lonely on the morrow.

But such is fate, and the entwining ties
  By which the lives of men are here united
May break like threads of wax before our eyes,
  And all our fondest schemes of love be blighted!
Vicissitudes o'er every moment lower,
  And life's full cup, with pleasure's cordial brimming,
May be o'erturned by some mysterious power,
  Or its fair surface with hot tears be dimming.

But for a day — and fairer scenes await
  The passage of the loved across the river,
And what we know as Death is but the gate
  To scenes beyond of joy and peace forever.
And we take heart in faith sublime as this,
  And see a loving hand to us extended,
To help us on the road that leads to bliss
  When earth's dull pilgrimage with us is ended.

We joy to think that friends thus gone before
  May still be mingling their fond hearts with ours,
That love enkindled on time's shifting shore
  May live anew with more exalted powers;
That by our side they now as then may stand,
  And smile upon us with benigner feeling,
Shedding the influence of the better land,
  And newer promise of its state revealing.

UNCONDITIONAL CHEERFULNESS.

The snow upon a morn was falling fast,
  Borne on the cold and driving wind along,
When, mid the whirl of snow-flakes and the blast,
  Rose the sweet cadence of a robin's song.
Upon a leafless bough he sat, and trilled
  His matin-hymn in tone as glad and high
As if the air with blossomy breath were filled,
  And golden sunshine sparkled in the sky.
I thought how like was this to that true soul
  Which upward soars and sings mid earthly strife,
That yields no moment to adverse control,
  But makes the best of good and bad in life;
That feels as jolly with a scolding wife
As when the day with fortune's gifts is rife.

MRS. PARTINGTON GROWS DESULTORY.

"THERE'S many a slip 'twixt the cup and the lip," said Mrs. Partington, with a philosophical upraising of the index-finger, putting her specs up on her head, "and it's no use to be particular about the portion which Providence sends us; for, however much we may say we'd rather have this and we'd rather have that, we can't any of us have the druthers that we want. It has been said that doubtful things is very uncertain, and that we can't tell who's to be mayor till after election; and that reminds me to say that them that buys the most of cheap goods has to pay the most for 'em, and heaven knows when the costiveness of the times will be any better." She ran down here, like an eight-day clock, and those who heard her wondered at the wisdom of her remarks, which, though they could n't make out what it all meant, glistened in the light of affectionate partiality, like a piece of glass beneath the rays of the moon.

EMBLEMATIC.

WHILE in my wanderings, lately, I descried,
Close by an ancient hut dilapidated,
An apple-tree in guise of blooming pride,
Scarcely in prouder precincts to be mated.
Its graceful branches o'er the old hut threw
An air of bloom that seemed rejuvenating;
I quite forgot the hovel was not new,
Among the odors that were round it waiting.
And here methought an emblem I had found
Of age with brightest virtues round it resting;
Though life's dark night steals on to fold it round,
The bloom of cheerfulness is still investing
The crazy fabric, bowed by Time's rude storms,
And waves above it in divinest forms.

A NIGHT OF IT.

We were out in the country — Jarvis and I — on a little bit of a "tower," as the landlord of Hardscrabble "guessed," as we stopped there for the night. Hardscrabble is a queer little place, away up in New Hampshire. It is so far away from railroads and the bigger sort of civilization, that the wonder is, among those who forget that it was built up before the railroads, how it came there. But it is on what was once the great stage-road to the shire town, and in old times the "tavern" — there were taverns in those days — was a bustling place, and abounded with stable-boys and loafers, and men more respectable, who dropped in, upon the arrival of the stages, to get the last news from Boston, then some days old, but still new. Then the great pine-knot-lighted bar-room was hung all around with stage-drivers' great coats, with more capes than a continent, and formidable whips, with lashes long enough to tickle the ears of the lagging leaders of the team. The walls, too, were all hung with advertisements of horses, and "vendues," and cattle-fairs, and up by the ceiling hung rows of "Canada crooknecks" to "keep" in the mild atmosphere. The bar meant something then; and the decanters, with lemons dotted in between, filled with Santa Cruz, and Jamaica, and Old Medford, and other fluids, furnished the essential oil that lubricated the tongues of travellers to a degree that rendered the cold nights of winter perfectly jolly with social hilarity, and made the name of stranger an entire misnomer. Then, broad-shouldered and thick-booted men sat before the big fireplace, their ruddy faces glowing in the light, and their tongues jubilant with joke or song, or grave with the weightier matters of court-business or of umpireship, and wise with speculations about crops, or the weight of pork or cattle. Anon some new one came in from the cold with a remark that it was "master cold out," when the current of conversation changed a little for reminiscences of some "cold Friday," away back years before, when the oldest inhabitant froze his ears as he went a-courting. All this while the logs in the big fireplace sent a cheerful blaze up the chimney, and the handles of one or two iron loggerheads were seen projecting from the flame, denoting that flip could be had for the asking, — a fluid which men of the ancient regime indulged in, — and the landlord, up to the full standard of the host in good nature and inches, leaned over his bar-room door, benevolently contemplating the scene, ready to answer summonses, then legal, for the commodities within his bar, to welcome new comers, or to book the names of passengers by the morning stage. Then, there was the "sitting-room," as it was called, with its sanded floor, where the lady-guests in unsocial frigidity awaited the return of their male companions, who had a long story to tell, on their return, about the difficulty there was in "these country taverns" about getting things comfortable.

Such was the old Hardscrabble tavern, as I remember it, with its queer picture of a face, surrounded by rays of best chrome-yellow, called the *Sun*, which swung in chains out in front of the house, and creaked in dismal discontent in the wintry wind; and such was not the old Sun tavern, as I saw it on my return to it, last winter, after an absence of twenty-five years. Long before, its glory had departed, and so had the former landlord.

We were out at the close of one of the very coldest of cold days, going towards Hardscrabble, in an open sleigh. It had never seemed in such an impracticable place before. The scene, as we approached the town, with which I had formerly been very familiar, was now all new to me; for the bushes that I had left had grown up to be trees, and a small brook, that had formerly crossed the road, had been dammed in an effort to save the place by building a little one-horse saw-mill, which made a lake that we crossed on the ice. All seemed odd enough; and Jarvis, as far as he ventured to speak, said that he fully appreciated, now, the remark of the old lady who wondered how any one could live so far off. It was too cold to question the relevancy of the remark.

Says I, Jarvis, miboy, there 's comfort awaiting us. I do remember me a country tavern, and hereabouts it was; and, if we don't find there roaring cheer, and good entertainment for man and beast, — that is, you and I, — set me down as an arrant cheat and deceiver. He settled back into his rigidity with some remark, the only part of which that I could distinguish was, "suthin hot!" It was only about ten o'clock; but, early as it was, every sign of life had ceased about the place. Not a soul was stirring, not a light beamed from a window, and the dead solitude of the north-pole could be scarcely more drear than the utter deadness that just then rested upon Hardscrabble. We drove on towards the "tavern," whose windows, illuminated with the old watch-fire, seemed to the traveller a veritable smile of welcome, and a promise of good cheer; but no such welcome met us—"darkness there, and nothing more!"

I could not be mistaken in the house; for there was the old sign-post, with the crane projecting, that had once sustained the Sun, now set forever.

I knew that Jarvis was alive, because I had heard him a few moments before uncork a little flask that he carried, containing some aromatic drops, but I did not know how long he would hold out; so, emergency warranting, I got out of the sleigh, went to the door, and gave a volley of raps with the handle of my whip, such as a man might be supposed to make who was in a severe strait, but who had wherewithal to back his demand. No response to the sound came, when I repeated the summons, and this time with better success; for a window over the door opened, a head looked cautiously out, and a voice, tremulous with fear or cold, demanded,

"What the plague 's the matter?—what d' ye want?"

"Want to come in," said I. "Here are two travellers, hungry and cold,—one of them now in an insensible condition in the sleigh, yonder,—and we want you to open your doors to them, and take them in, as you, undoubtedly, are disposed to do."

"O, shet up!" said the voice, which I supposed was addressed to me; but, from its subdued tone, I afterwards concluded that it was intended as a reply to some one in the house, which proved to be the fact, as I heard a female voice, in a moment, say,

"S'pos'in' 't should be thieves?"

"Say!" said the voice from the window, "who are ye, any way?"

"Two belated travellers," I replied, "from Boston, the metropolis of Massachusetts, who have business in the town of Hardscrabble, where they will remain to-morrow, and are desirous of resting and refreshing themselves beneath your roof."

"Wal, I'll be down in a minnit. Thunderin' cold, is n't it?"

He disappeared from the window, and, from the sounds that I heard, I judged there had arisen an disagreeable domestic discussion concerning the propriety of letting us in, which created a little unpleasant reflection as to what could be done in such a contingency as being shut out, relieved, however, by the clattering of feet upon the floor inside, the withdrawal of a bolt, and the swinging of the door upon its hinges, disclosing a tall, cadaverous-looking man, half-dressed, holding a tallow candle in his hand, and a woman, as thick as she was short, at his elbow. Says I, "Friends, I am very sorry to disturb you; but we are in distress. It *is* thunderin' cold, as you very truly remarked, just now, and I have a friend there under that pile of buffalo-robes who may even now be frozen as stiff as Mount Washington."

The buffalo-robes, however, collapsed, and Jarvis stepped from the vehicle. He walked towards the house, and entered with me, after I had embraced him and congratulated him on his escape from petrifaction.

"Is n't this a tavern?" I asked.

"Yas, I s'pose some 'd call it so; we call it the Pavilion Hotel."

"The —— you do!" said Jarvis, thawing out with a warmth of expression, that the landlord, had he not been a little oblivious just then, must have heard.

"Much business here?" I further asked.

"Wal," said he, "in summer it's tip-top — lots of people come here to get the prospective scenery —

but 'n winter 't an't much. It 's a mighty pretty place when the trees is out."

"Please hurry things up, now, and give us something comfortable soon, there 's a good fellow," I broke in. —"Ah, madam," said I, turning to the lady, who looked as cool as the season, "it is rare that one meets with so happy a face. The twenty-five years of your life must have been a season of continued cheerfulness." (She looked forty, to say the least.) "Blessing and blest,— that 's the way. A cup of tea, some hot toast, and your pleasant company, will make our adventure very happy." She went off smiling in reality, while the husband— Mottle was his name—continued dismally trying to infuse heat into a parlor wood-stove,—an innovation on the old fireplace.

I looked round the room, and recognized many things as they had once existed. We were really in the old bar-room. What a flood of ghostly fancies ran through my brain! I seemed surrounded by departed spirits, so full the scene was of remembrances. But the decanters had all fled, the whips and great coats had all vanished, the fireplace had been bricked up, and —— "Where is the old landlord?" I asked, as the memory of him obtruded itself at this point in marked contrast with the cadaverous man on his knees, blowing away at the old stove.

"Gone to Kansis," said he, betwixt the puffs; "took to drink arter the custom gin aout, and sold the consarn."

The fire was a success; it sent out a glowing heat, the blaze roared up the funnel, the astonished iron cracked and snapped as it expanded, and Jarvis and I sat before the warm flame in magnificent content, all the while hearing the sound of preparation going on in the room beyond, a promise that did n't disappoint us.

"Landlord," said I, with a wink, "where are the little fellows that once stood along the shelves yonder, with labels around their necks? Any of 'em left?"

"Nary one," said he; "this is a temp'rance house. You see Hardscrabble is nat'rally an onlicensed place, and so we gin it up. Been here before, I guess?"

I assured him I had.

"Been a mighty cold day," he said; "Jo Chesman says 't is the coldest day we 've had sence the cold Friday, forty year ago; but I don't know, for that was before I moved into the caounty. But I must go aout 'n see to your horse."

A supper was soon set before us, more extensive as regarded quantity and quality than variety. It was good substantial fare, such as one meets with all through our country towns; and the landlady waited upon us with delightful urbanity of manner, sitting at the table and pouring out our tea for us in the most social way.

"Are you related to Squire Mooney, of Greenborough?" I asked the landlady; "the one that invented the India-rubber knitting-needles, and made an immense fortune out of them?"

She assured me that she was not.

"Well, I declare," said I, "I never saw such a likeness! Did you, Jarvis?"

Jarvis averred that if she were to be dressed like the 'Squire he should n't know them apart, except from the superior good looks of the lady; and this remark finished what was wanting to counteract the effect of rising from a warm bed to perform a disagreeable duty.

She was all good humor, of which we had many proofs while we remained in the house.

We sat down before the fire again after supper, and the landlord told us stories about the old house and the old people of the neighborhood, while Jarvis took out his cigar-case, and smoked in drowsy indifference to what we were saying. It was getting near midnight, when there came a rap at the door, that started us all to our feet. It was not very loud, but it was peculiar, — a sort of half emphatic and half timorous affair, — and we all three proceeded to the door. I was curious to see the intruder, as I felt he was; and, upon opening, the most singular object that I had ever seen presented himself. He was an oldish sort of a man, short and thick-set, with a dress that, for incongruity, would compare favorably with that of Madge Wildfire. An old fur cap was on his head, that fitted closely to it, and it was tied down in some inexplicable way below the chin. He was belted round the waist, like a brigand, and carried in his hand a staff, of formidable dimensions, that had, apparently, been wrenched from a tree.

"Can I come in?" he asked, in a hollow voice. Permission being granted, he came in before the fire. I am a man of some considerable nerve, have been in scenes where pluck was required to carry a matter through, have faced men that I would not care to see again; but the first glance at that face, as it appeared before the blaze of the fire, was so revolting that I felt my courage giving way. The eyes were sunk in the head, the features were shrivelled and thin, and around the mouth a smile was constantly playing that appeared fiendish to my shocked fancy. But, I said to myself, 'T is only a man; you are not going to fear clay that is, perhaps, not much more ugly than yourself in the eyes of superior perfection! So I sat still and watched him.

He took a seat in front of the fire, into which he gazed with an abstracted air. The muscles of his face seemed entirely beyond his control, and the fiendish laugh assumed another phase. I could not make him out, as he sat there, his face twisting into all manner of most villanous contortions. Whether he was insane, or idiotic, or diseased, I could not divine. Jarvis took the seat he had occupied, which was very near the strange comer, and had resumed his cigar, when, looking round into the stranger's face, he became aware of the fearful seeming of the new guest. His lips refused to draw at the cigar, which dropped from between his teeth; his hand trembled, which reached for his handkerchief; his eyes dilated, and terror took complete possession. The man — if it was a man — sat looking into the fire, not one word being spoken, when, with a half-start, he felt in his pocket and took out a very large and savage knife, which he opened with a jerk. Poor Jarvis was apparently powerless from terror. The man's fingers clutched convulsively about the knife, until he held it in a position suited to his intent, when he raised his arm, leaned a little forward, and ——

Jarvis started to his feet, with a yell that might have been heard a mile, swinging his chair back to the wall, and placing himself on it, in entire prostration.

The man reached forward, and, taking a splinter of wood from the floor, proceeded to whittle.

The landlord and myself rushed to Jarvis.

"Don't be skeered," whispered mine host; "he won't hurt ye. He 's only old Bob Haize, who 's been half dead more 'n a hundred times of delirium trimmins, and now it 's settled into his sistim. There 's nothing harmonious about him."

Jarvis swore stoutly that he was n't afraid, and quarrelled with me for saying that he was; but the landlord will support what I say. We went to bed about one o'clock, and a better bed I never slept in than that in the Pavilion Hotel at Hardscrabble, where we had the night of it.

THE PREACHER AND THE CHILDREN.

He spake unto the little ones
  In childhood's simplest, tenderest word,
While warm love trembled in his tones,
  And eyes were moist and hearts were stirred.
The quivering lip and eager glance
  Bespoke the young soul's answering thrill;
Yet 't was of simple utterance,
  As gentle as a summer rill.

And older ears, too, drank the sound,
  And loved the music of its strain,
As thirsty plants and thirsty ground
  Hark to the drip of falling rain!
It was as dew to sturdy trees,
  That wakes their half-unconscious powers,
The note of distant melodies,
  That breaks the gloom of dreary-hours.

The mightiest words that men can speak
  May not be those that touch the heart,
May never pale the ruddy cheek,
  Or cause the willing tear to start.
The fierce tornado's bitter blast
  Or thunder's crash assail in vain;
The still small voice sweeps gently past,
  And God, confest, is in the strain.

OUT WEST.

"Ann Arbor!" cried the conductor, looking in at the door. Mrs. Partington looked round, and, seeing nobody move, she resumed her knitting. "Ann Arbor," said another voice, at the door of the rear end of the car. "Well, I declare," said the old lady, "I hope he will find her. — Can you tell me, sir," said she, reaching over the back of the seat, and speaking to a gentleman with a plush cap on, and a ticket sticking in the front of it, "who Miss Ann Arbor is?" — "Nein ferstan," replied he. — "Well," she continued, "I did n't mean nothing contemptible, and it would n't have cost you anything to have given a civil answer." The man looked persistently out of the window, and the cars moved on, Mrs. Partington consoling herself with the reflection that Ann Arbor must be in the other car.

CONSCIENCE.

Sharper than whip of scorpions is the sting,
  As conscience turns its searching eyes within,
Where broods the spirit with its sullied wing,
  Each pinion drooping in the damps of sin.
The face may bear the evidence of joys,
  And mirth ring out in the exultant laugh, —
The silent monitor the cheat destroys,
  The shout is hollow as an epitaph!
Outlooking through the gloom, the conscious soul
  Shudders in silence with its secret pain,
Till life and its allurements gain control,
  And dulled, not cured, it onward moves again, —
A woodlawn garniture of joy concealing
Beneath its bloom the graves of joyous feeling.

BABIES.

Babies, we believe, have never been considered as being in any way connected with the fine arts, and perhaps "judicious criticism" might have little benefit in improving, in the estimation of the possessors, the cherubs chiselled by the hand of nature. The style of babies is illimitable, and each family that is the delighted possessor of one deems, of course, its own the most in accordance with classic taste. Therefore it is impossible to fix any standard, beyond mere opinion, by which to establish the fact of beauty in a baby; and we are obliged to leave it with the possessor to fix the degree, and say whether pug-nosed or aquiline-nosed, big-eyed or little-eyed, dumpy babies or more extended babies, are most worthy of the claim to beauty. And this brings out the fact that the Great Artist who made the work gives also the faculty of appreciating the excellence of each particular production to the ones most interested. There is great wisdom in this; for, if the same general idea of beauty prevailed, nobody's baby would be safe. There would be endless envying, and strife, and bickering, and more rivalry to obtain the handsomest baby than now prevails at an auction to secure some choice article of vertu. [The printer will please not put this *virtue*, as that is an article which is rarely sought with such avidity.] Now all are secure, and each one is happy in the possession of the handsomest. There is not a more interesting study in the world than a baby as a work of art — aside from its humanity, the grandeur of its destiny, and all that. The tiny hand, so delicately modelled, is a lesson of beauty. The transparent nails, the dimpled knuckles, the delicate tracery of the palm-lines, all are so admirably executed, that it seems a pity to mar so sweet a work by manly growth. Some one has said that infants are always graceful in their motions. This is a mechan ical view of the baby, but it is true. From rolling over on the carpet to pulling Bub's hair or papa's whiskers, the baby's motions are beautiful. The chiselled marble never can attain the exquisite finish of the rounded cheek, the delicate eyelash, the beautiful mouth, the funny nose, the dimpled chin. Ask the happy mother or the proud father if they ever saw any one half as beautiful as their own little laughing, crowing, cooing, drooling, rollicking, rolling, tumbling, fretting little doll of a baby, that sits there on the floor, or wherever it may be, sucking its little fist, and the answer will be a most decided negative.

AGRICULTURAL.

MRS. PARTINGTON was out, one morning, scratching about the roots like a hen or a lexicographer, with a black bonnet on her head, when her neighbor, Mr. Vintner, who deals largely in wines, reached his long neck over the gate. "Good crop of grapes, ma'am?" said he.—"'T will be pretty burdensome," she replied, looking up to where the seven bunches hung which had been left after Ike made himself sick by eating the eighth green.—"Any ordium upon the vine?" he asked. —"I don't know as regards the odium upon my vine," replied she, "but I am not going to make any wine that will be likely to have the odium that some wine has that is sold for good, that never saw a grape in its life." She wondered why he turned away so suddenly, but supposed he had an errand round the corner. The black bonnet hovered again over the yellow flowers, as a maternal biddy might over a flock of young ducks, and the old case-knife was plied vigorously among the roots. "Ah, there is health in it," said Mrs. Partington, "depend upon it; for since I 've been soiling I 've moved a structure from my chest, and feel like somebody else." Bless her, what an example hers is to follow!

MRS. PARTINGTON AND PATENT MEDICINES.

"I 'M shore's he 's very kind," said Mrs. Partington, as she took out of its wrapper a box of "Hallelujah Pills," accompanied with the request that she should take them for the sake of old friendship — the agent being an early acquaintance of hers. "He 's very kind, but taking them is another thing, though they are good for all the ails that are impertinent to the flesh, double X inclusible. O, what malefactors these medicine men are to the human family, to be sure! I remember a pictorial expectant once that brought up a whole family of children, and entirely cured a gentleman who had been troubled for a great while with a periodical depot. Depend upon it, sir," continued she, addressing old Roger, "there 's so much virtue in 'em that everybody will be made virtuous, and everybody be made over again new, and there 'll be no excuse for dying at all." The old lady put the box of pills up on the top shelf, out of Ike's way, lest he should take them by mistake, as he often did the preserved damsons. "They 're doubtless purgatory," said she, getting down out of the chair in which she had stood. — "Worse than that, I dare say," said Roger, buttoning up his coat; "for I smelt sulphur in them." He went out, and she wondered what he meant.

SONG OF CHELSEA FERRY.

WHICH WILL ANSWER FOR ANY LOCALITY WHERE A FERRY IS EMPLOYED

Hear our Song of Chelsea Ferry—
Of its bustle, mirth, and rattle,
Where the social and the merry
Ever actively are shown;
Where the charm of friendship's prattle
Gives the heart a faith more cheery,
That in life's perplexing battle
It would scarce have known!
Chelsea Ferry! Chelsea Ferry!
Hark the chorus: Ding, dong, bell!
Chelsea Ferry! Chelsea Ferry!
Hear the cheerful Ferry Bell!

Sparkling bright is Chelsea Ferry,
With its blue and flashing water,
With its voices rich and merry,
In the morning blush of day;
When around, on every quarter,
Foamy waves in tumult hurry,
And the sun, an ardent sporter,
Dances 'mid the spray.
Chelsea Ferry! Chelsea Ferry!
Join the chorus: Ding, dong, bell.
Chelsea Ferry! Chelsea Ferry!
Hear the warning Ferry Bell!

Calm and fair is Chelsea Ferry,
When the warm sun, sinking slowly,
Backward smiles with radiance cheery
On the toilers homeward bound;
When the moon, with aspect holy,
Drives the shadows dark and dreary,
By her splendors melancholy
Lighting all around.
Chelsea Ferry! Chelsea Ferry!
Join the chorus: Ding, dong, bell!
Chelsea Ferry! Chelsea Ferry!
Hear the evening Ferry Bell!

Wider waves than Chelsea Ferry
  Men may sail to grander places,
Where the tropic's ruddy berry
  Gleams the glossy foliage through;
But we own no higher graces
  Than where heart and tongue are merry
Where the "old familiar faces"
  Beam with aspect true.
Chelsea Ferry! Chelsea Ferry!
  Join the chorus: Ding, dong, bell!
Chelsea Ferry! Chelsea Ferry!
  Hear the jolly Ferry Bell!

MR. BLIFKINS' BABY.

THAT first baby was a great institution. As soon as he came into this "breathing world," he took command in our house. Everything was subservient to him. The baby was the balance-wheel that regulated everything. He regulated the temperature, he regulated the food, he regulated the servants, he regulated me. For the first six months of that precious existence, he had me up, on an average, six times a night. "Mr. Blifkins," says my wife, "bring that light here, do; the baby looks strangely; I 'm so afraid it will have a fit!" Of course the lamp was brought, and of course the baby lay sucking his fist like a little white bear, as he was. "Mr. Blifkins," said my wife, "I think I feel a draught of air; I wish you would get up and see if the window is not open a little, because baby might get sick." Nothing was the matter with the window, as I knew very well. "Mr. Blifkins," says my wife, just as I was going to sleep again, "that lamp, as you have placed it, shines directly in baby's eyes,— strange that you have no more consideration!" I arranged the light and went to bed again. Just as I was dropping to sleep again. "Mr. Blifkins," said my wife, "did you think to buy that broma to-day for the baby?"—"My dear,' said I, "will you do me the injustice to believe that I could overlook a matter so essential to the comfort of that inestimable child?" She apologized very handsomely, but made her anxiety the scape-goat. I forgave her, and, without saying a word more to her, I addressed myself to sleep. "Mr. Blifkins," said my wife, shaking me, "you must not snore so; you will wake the baby." —"Jest so—jest so," said I, half asleep, thinking I was Solon Shingle.—"Mr. Blifkins," said my wife, "will you get up and hand me the warm gruel from the nurse-lamp for baby?—The dear child! if it was n't for his mother, I don't know what he would do. How can you sleep so, Mr. Blifkins?"—"I suspect, my dear," said I, "that it is because I am tired."—"O, it 's very well for you men to talk about being tired," said my wife; "I don't know what you 'd say if you had to toil and drudge like a poor woman with a baby." I tried to soothe her by telling her she had no patience at all, and got up for the posset. Having aided in answering the baby's requirements, I stepped into bed again, with the hope of sleeping. "Mr. Blifkins," said my wife.—I made no answer.—"Mr. Blifkins," said she, in a louder key.—I said nothing.—"O dear!" said that estimable woman, in great apparent anguish, "how can a man who has arrived at the honor of a live baby of his own sleep, when he don't know that the dear creature will live till morning?" I remained silent, and, after a while, deeming that Mrs. Blifkins had gone to sleep, I stretched my limbs for repose. How long I slept I don't know, but I was awakened by a furious jab in the forehead by some sharp instrument. I started up, and Mrs. Blifkins was sitting up in the bed adjusting some portion of the baby's dress. She had, in a state of semi-somnolence, mistaken my head for the pillow, which she customarily used for a nocturnal pincushion. I protested against such treatment in somewhat round terms, pointing to several perforations in my forehead. She told me I should willingly bear such trifling things for the sake of the baby. I insisted upon it that I did n't think my duty as a parent to that young immortal required the surrender of my forehead for a pincushion. This was one of many nights passed in this way. The truth was, that baby was what every other man's first baby is, an autocrat, absolute and unlimited. Such was the story of Blifkins, as herelated it. It is but a little exaggerated picture of almost every man's experience

---

PATIENCE.

Patience !—great virtue !—I thy praise would sing—
Sublimest of the virtues Heaven sent—
(I once admired a maid named Patience King,
But she is not the Patience herein meant)—
Patience, that, catlike, by persistence wins ;
Which sees the corn submitted to the earth,
And waits until it 's gathered into bins,
Or smokes in Johnny-cakes upon the hearth ;
Patience, that brooks a note's maturing pace ;
Patience, that tracks a ship across the deep ;
Patience, that weaves the complicated lace ;
Patience, that sings a crying child to sleep ;
Patience—grand culmination of my strains—
That, when allied with baize, cures rheumatiz and sprains.

IKE'S COMPOSITIONS IN SCHOOL.

IKE is well advanced in his class. He is, in some things, beyond the teacher's art, and could, in fact, give that functionary some lessons in arts wherein he is perfect. Ike dislikes composition where a theme is given out to be written upon by the scholars, and his credits are not very great for his efforts in that direction generally; but one day he astonished the master and every one by an elaborate article on the Horse. He was called upon to read it aloud to the scholars; and, getting upon the platform, he made a bow, and began:

THE HORSE.

THE horse is a quadruped, with four legs — two behind, and two before. He has a tail that grows on to the hind part of his body, that nature has furnished him, with which to drive the flies away. His head is situated on the other end, opposite his tail, and is used prin cipally to fasten a bridle to to drive him by, and to put into a basket to eat oats with. Horses are very useful animals, and people could n't get along very well without them — especially truckmen and omnibus-drivers, who don't seem to be half grateful enough because they 've got 'em. They are very convenient animals in the country in vacation time, and go very fast over the country roads when boys sticks pins into 'em, a specie of cruelty that I would n't encourage. Horses generally are covered with red hair, though some are white, and others are gray and black. Nobody ever saw a blue horse, which is considered very strange by eminent naturals. The horse is quite an intelligent animal, and can sleep standing up, which is a very convenient gift, especially where there is a crowd and it is difficult to get a chance to lay.

There is a great variety of horses — fast horses and slow horses, clothes-horses, horse-mackerel, saw-horses, and horse-flies, horse-chestnuts, and horse-radish. The clothes-horse is a very quiet animal to have round a house, and is never known to kick, though very apt to raise a row when it gets capsized. The same may be said of the saw-horse, which will stand without tieing. Horse-flies is a very vicious beast, and very annoying in the summer, when a fellow is in swimming. Horse-mackerel I don't know anything about, only that they swim in the water, and are a specie of fish. Horse-chestnuts is prime to pelt Mickeys with, and horse-radish is a mighty smart horse, but bad to have standing round where there 's small children.

The horse is found in all countries, principally in lively-stables, where they may be hired to run by the mile, considered by them as can get money a great luxury, especially in the sleighing season. In South America they grow wild, and the Indians catch them with nooses that they throw over the horses' heads, which must be thought, by the horses, a great noosance.

He received so much credit for this, that he continued his efforts, and the following succeeded :

TOBACCO.

This is a great article of commerce, and forms one of our greatest social institutions. It enters into the do mestic circle, and drives away care; because the one who smokes in the domestic circle does n't care a snap who likes it or not. It comes in different shapes — silver-leaf, fine-cut, cavendish, and nigger-head. This last has its name from the negroes in Virginia, who get it up for the market. Tobacco was first introduced into England in the year 1600, and some say by Sir Walter Raleigh; and the people did n't object to being introduced to it, though King James wrote something about it, intending to give it fits; but it became in everybody's mouth, and soon more "old soldiers" of tobacco were to be seen than there was in the army of England. Sir Walter Raleigh's appetite for the weed was afterwards impaired by having his head cut off. His memory has been puffed as a great benefactory to the human race that smokes. Tobacco, when rolled up into cigars, is a very agreeable preparation, and the mildest form in which it is used. Some people take it in snuff, by holding the snuff between the thumb and finger, and drawing it up into the nose. This is an exciting operation with elderly females, and it is interesting to watch its effects when the nose is fully charged and primed, before it sneezes off. Chewing and smoking belong only to men, and such boys as do it on the sly, when the old folks is n't round. The essential oil of tobacco is said to be very dilatorious to human life. I don't know why it is essential that there should be any oil about it; but the apothecaries will have it so. Tobacco is called a great leveller, especially when a fellow gets sick in trying to learn. Then it levels men flat enough. But it is called a leveller because a rich man does n't feel above asking a poor chap for a light when his cigar is gone out — a beautiful and sublime instance of magnificent condescension!

Tobacco may be, from this, put among the incentives to virtuous action, and a box of short-sixes become a missionary in the cause of civilization. It is estimated that over ten millions of cigars are smoked in Boston in a year, and that, if they were stretched, one behind another, they would reach round the world three times! It is also said that, if all the old chaws of tobacco should be put together at the end of a year, that they would make a pile bigger 'n Mount Washington. The great invention of spittoons, which has done so much to fulfil human expectoration, is the offspring of tobacco, and gives a new claim of that delightful plant to our gratitude. It is a great help in agriculture, and its smoke is used to kill bugs on flowers, when boys can do a useful turn, and have fine fun in smoking, and nothing be said about it. Much more might be writ about tobacco, but I will conclude by just saying that it is a great pickpocket, and takes the money away from a fellow like sixty.

The following, of a similar character with the above, also excited considerable remark among the scholars:

THE AMERICAN EAGLE.

This is the greatest bird that has ever spread his wings over this great and glorious country. The place where he builds his nest is called an eyrie, away up on the precipices where the foot of man can't come, though perhaps a boy's might. The eagle is a ferocious fellow, and sits on the top of the cliffs and looks sharp for plunder. He gets tired of waiting, and then he starts out in the blue expensive heavens, and soars all around, on his opinions, over the land and the water, to see what he can pounce down upon. But, though he is called a very cruel bird, he always preys before eating, just like any good moral man at the head of his family. He eats his victuals raw, which is an unfavorable habit, but it is supposed that he eats it so because he likes to. He is a very courageous bird, and will fight like blazes for his young, and steals chickens wherever he can see them. He has been known to carry off a young baby to his nest, which seems to show that eagles love little children. He is a bird of great talons, and is much respected by birds of the feathered tribe that are afraid of him.

This bird is a great study for artists, but appears to best advantage on the ten-dollar gold pieces, and fifty-cent pieces, and pretty well on the dimes, as he sits gathering up his thunderbolts under him, as if he was in a great hurry to be off. He has lately broke out on the new cent, and seems as if, in his hurry, he had dropped all his thunder. The American eagle is the patriot's hope, and the inspiration of Fourth of July. He soars through the realms of the poet's fancy, and whets his beak on the highest peak of the orator's imagination. He is in the mouth of every politician, so to speak. He is said by them to stand on the Rocky Mountains, and to dip his bill into the Atlantic, while his tail casts a shadow on the Pacific coast. This is all gammon. There never was one more than eight feet long from the tip of one wing to the tip of tother. His angry scream is heard ever so far, and he don't care a feather for anybody. Take him every way, he is an immense fowl, and his march is over the mounting wave, with the star-spangled banner in his hand, whistling Yankee Doodle.

Ike's composition upon the Dog has obtained a world wide celebrity, and has already been installed as a classic:

THE DOG.

THE dog is a very useful animal, and very intelligent. He knows lots and noses more, and runs after sticks and goes overboard after stones delightfully. He is a fine companion in the fields, and chases grasshoppers and ground sparrows beautifully. He is a loving animal, and licks your hand when you lick him. He don't never smile, but has a ridiculous way of wagging his tail when he is glad, as if by his tail he would tell the story of his joy. Dogs is very apt to quarrel, especially when they are set on by bad boys, and growl and bark at nights, and howl under windows where folks are sick, and scare timid folks to death for fear they are going to die. A dog's nose is a prime thing to pinch, and seems to be put where it is on purpose. Some say that it is made of India-rubber, but that 's all nonsense.

A great many things are told about dogs and their intelligence. Some of 'em are true, and some of 'em is n't. They can carry bundles, and know when it is time to go to dinner, and love to tease cats, and make a terrible fuss when any one puts turpentine on 'em or ties kettles to their tails. There is a great many different kinds of dogs, and no one kind alike. There are pointers, and setters, and tarriers, and bull-dogs, and lap-dogs, and spaniels, and water-dogs, and Newfoundland dogs, and St. Bernard's dogs, and watch-dogs, and dog-watches, and Lion. Pointers and setters are used by hunters in finding game, and are liable to get shot by near-sighted people who can't tell a dog from a rabbit. Newfoundland dogs were sent by Providence on purpose to pull little children from the water, and the St. Bernard's to keep folks from freezing to death in the Rocky Mountains. They take little boys on their backs, and carry them to some safe place, and then go back after more. Bull-dogs are vicious beasts, and don't like to have boys meddle with 'em, and the boys, being very considerate, does n't meddle with 'em. They let 'em alone ever so much, and don't tackle 'em into wagons, as they do some others. Lap-dogs an't of no use to nobody but for women to play with who an't got no children, and it is a pity they had n't. They are made on purpose, and have long, white, silky hair, and blue ribbons round their necks. All the lap-dogs are named Fiddle. The faithful watch-dog is an unwholesome chap for burglars. "I love to hear the watch-dog's honest bark," and it is prime to strike on to the shutters of a store in the evening, and hear what a muss the watch-dog makes about it. They don't like to be disturbed, I guess, from their cat-naps. Lion is a great dog.

> **He is gentle, he is kind,**
> **And his tail sticks out behind,**

and you can't find a better dog anywhere than he. He is black all over, only he is white on his stomach, and on the end of his tail. He loves fun, and goes into the dirt with perfect impurity. He knows when it is dinner-time, and is very useful in clearing up stray bits of meat that might be wasted. He 's a great friend to the Metropolitan Railroad, for it is over two years since he first attempted to bark the omnibuses out of Washington-street, and if he has one failing stronger than another, it is a love for the butcher on Shawmut-avenue, whom he never fails to call upon when passing. I could tell you more about dogs, and dog-vanes, and doggerel, and sad dogs, and merry dogs ; but you might think me dogmatical, and I guess I 've said enough.

Ike's ideas of Politics are very profound, showing a remarkable astuteness in the mind of Young America :

POLITICS.

POLITICS is a name derived from two Greek words, *poll* and *tick*. Polls is the place where people exercises their free sufferings, after they have paid nine shillings for 'em into the city treasury; and tick is trust, that all the parties want the people to have in 'em before election ; and both together make Politics, an institution of our country next to the house of correction in importance. Politics is a business that has to be followed pretty close to make anything by it, and is made up of hurras, torch-light processions, music, mass meetings, and humbug. Politics is an interesting element in families where the people all think differently, and go in strong for discussion ; it keeps things lively, and is excellent for weak lungs. Torch-light processions are great for lightening the minds of the people, and the pockets of them that gets 'em up. These, with American flags and Hail Columbia, makes the people take fire with enthusiasm, and take cold in the night air, as they go round making Judies of themselves and everybody that looks at 'em. Politics is very apt to bring about broken heads among them that indulges in 'em too freely, like whiskey, and it is always best to see that you get the right article. There 's a number of kinds of politics, and every politician believes his kind is best. The Democrats think theirs is best, and the Whigs, and the Republicans, and the Americans, theirs. They can't be all best. Those are the best that are the strongest, and elections always result in favor of them that has the most votes. Politics is capital exercise for the ingenuity of women who have n't anything else to do at home, whose babies can take care of themselves, and won't tumble into the fire if they leave 'em to go to political meetings, or to see torch-light processions. Politics is the meat that the American eagle feeds on when he soars to heaven, and then comes down again as hungry as a meeting-house. Politics should be sustained among our most cherished institutions, and next to fun, clam-chowder, and going smelting, they are the best thing round.

> "The star-spangled banner, O, long may it wave
> O'er the land of the free and the home of the brave!"

The following, relating to a famous locality, will be read with deep interest, for its truthfulness to history, and for other reasons:

PLYMOUTH ROCK.

THIS rock was brought to this country in the May Flower, in the year 1492. by the Pilgrims, under directions of Elder Brewster, who afterwards moved to Boston, and became an alderman of that city. Plymouth Rock was put on a wharf, where part of it remains to the present day, as people may see, if they will take the trouble to scratch the dirt away. No reason is given for putting the rock up so far from the water, except it was to keep it out of the wet. It was on this rock that Governor Carver shook hands with Samoset, who said, "Welcome, Englishmen." It is recorded that when Samoset came up Governor Carver asked him if he was a real Ingine, or only a member of an Ingine company. The rock has long been regarded as a very famous place, and a great many things have been written about it. Strangers coming on the coast always climb to the mast-heads with a spy-glass to see Plymouth Rock. The American Eagle for a great many years used to come and whet his beak on it; but in 1653, Miles Standish, in order to keep it from getting stolen, took all there was of it above ground under his arm, and carried it up and put it in front of Pilgrim Hall, where it remains at the present time, invested with great interest and an iron fence. The fence bears the names of all the Pilgrims in cast-iron letters that can't be rubbed out. The other part of the rock the descendants of the Pilgrims have covered up with land, probably to save it from being worn out by the allusions touching it, that are thrown off by Fourth of July orators and other patriots. Plymouth Rock is the corner-stone in the cellar wall of our republican structure, paregorically speaking, and the spirit of Liberty sits upon it with a drawn sword in one hand and the torch of freedom in the other. The monument to the Pilgrim Fathers, upon Plymouth Rock, will be three thousand feet above the level of the sea, and can be easily seen from New Haven, the place the Pilgrims came from, with the naked eye. It was concerning this rock that Pierpont wrote his celebrated ode, commencing,

"We 've found the rock, the travellers cried,"

supposed to allude to the Cushman procession that visited the spot, at the time of the great famine. Peregrine White, the first white child born in Massachusetts was born on Plymouth Rock, and Miles Standish, when John Alden swindled him out of Priscilla, in 1803, sharpened his sword on Plymouth Rock, swearing revenge. In short, Plymouth Rock is one of the palladiums of our liberty; and if foes invade the shores of Plymouth at high water, — for they can never get in at low tide, — the people will throw this rock in their teeth. It is a precious legacy from the Past to the Present, and from it may be reckoned the Pilgrim's Progress.

MRS. SLED PUT OUT.

"I 'VE just come from seeing old Mr. Sprat," said Mrs. Sled, dropping in upon Mrs. Partington, suddenly, and sinking into a seat as she spoke. "Poor creatur, he does look miser'ble; he 's got one foot in the grave, you may depend." — "Has he, indeed?" said the sympathetic dame. "Well, I noticed, the other day, he walked rather limpid, as he went along." Mrs. Partington sniffed as if she smelt something. "It seems to be cotton a burning," said she, drawing a long breath; "don't you smell anything?" Mrs. Sled informed her that she had a bad cold in her head, and could n't be exactly said to possess any of her five senses. Mrs. Partington sniffed again. "I declare," said the lady whose five senses were blunted by the cold, "I declare I feel something," which showed that the sense of feeling was not wanting, and, jumping to her feet, disclosed her dress on fire behind. "Get off my match-rope!" said Ike, dashing in with half a bunch of crackers in his hand. The intimation was unnecessary, and, as Mrs. Sled extinguished herself in the sink, she breathed an inward prayer for the hope of the house of Partington.

TALE OF A HORSE

When Topple was in the horse-trade, he had his eyes constantly about him for a speculation, and one day, in Vermont, he fell in, among other specimens, with a horse whose principal points were the points of bone projecting through his skin, — a long, lean, lank, white animal, that had got some way beyond his teens, whose qualities as a good horse were vouched for by a neighbor, who said he had knowed him for twenty-four year, and a kinder critter never led oxen in a plough than he.

The horse was bought at a discount, and shipped, with three others, on a car for Boston, where he arrived safe, but scarcely sound. Topple thought it a hard investment, and felt somewhat anxious as to how he should get his money back again, concluding at last that he would undoubtedly make enough on the other three to cover the loss which he must, he conceived, sustain on this one. He had him stabled, and then the idea occurred to Topple that he would attempt a little factitious excellence for the poor beast, and endeavor to put him off respectably. A horse of some celebrity had died just before, and Topple borrowed a large cover that was wont to envelop the animal after running, and covered up his own Rosinante therewith.

Immediately afterwards appeared an advertisement in the *Post* and other papers, that the famous trotter White-Foot was on exhibition at Bailey's, and would be sold on a certain day, inviting people to call and see him. The usual formula was gone through with, of "sound," "kind," "stand without tieing," &c., concluding with the statement that he had gone his mile in less than three minutes. The advertisement brought many horse fanciers to the stable, where White-Foot stood in a bed of straw, covered by the robe that had been borrowed.

Topple thought that boldness was the best policy and called the attention of his visitors to the fact of the horse being so poor, making the statement gratuitously that he had fairly run the flesh off his bones; and it seemed probable, as the flesh was not there.

As the day of sale arrived, Topple visited his racer at regular periods, and with a lath, rigorously applied, endeavored to excite in him a disposition to appear vigorous on inspection before the public; and succeeded so far that, before the time arrived, the sound of Topple's feet on the stable-floor wrought the poor beast up to a perfect frenzy. He stamped and struggled in a manner extravagant enough to establish a large reputation for mettle, and Topple was satisfied. "Perhaps," whispered he to the auctioneer, "we may get fifty dollars for him."

The horse was brought to the block, and at the sight of Topple he manifested every sign of spirit. His nostrils were distended, his eye brightened, and he stepped round nervously, as though he were impatient to have somebody buy him, that he might be going, inside of three minutes, over the road.

"How much am I offered for the horse?" said Bailey; "how much for White-Foot? Shall I have a bid?"

"Seventy-five dollars," said a voice.

"Seventy-five — thank you — seventy-five — shall I hear any more?"

"One hundred," another voice.

"Twenty-five," first bidder.

"Fifty," second.

"Go on, gentlemen," said Bailey, letting the bidding proceed, seeing the competition; "any more than one hundred and fifty for a horse that has been his mile in less than three minutes?"

"One hundred and sixty," another bidder.

"Sixty-five," first bidder.

"Seventy," a new voice.

"Seventy-five!" first and second together.

"Any more than one hundred and seventy-five? All done at one — seventy — five? Sold! Dr. Small, of Cape Cod, takes him at one hundred and seventy-five."

"The bid was mine," said the second bidder; "and I insist upon it."

The contestant was a man living in town, and the auctioneer thought that, for prudential reasons, it would be better to let the beast go out of town, if he had strength to get out; so he gravely decided that Dr. Small's bid was the one he had heard, and to him he had knocked off the bargain.

So anxious was the disappointed man to procure the horse that he offered the doctor fifteen dollars for his bargain, who informed him that he could not trade. The price, he said, was not much to him; he wanted a horse that would go quickly, and, as he had got a good one, he should hold on to him.

The money was paid over, and the animal delivered to the purchaser, who procured a wagon and harness and started for home, in the hope of reaching Cape Cod in about two hours. About that length of time after he left, a horse was heard moderately approaching the stable, and the face of old White-Foot was seen once more in the precinct.

"Well," said the doctor, as he got out of the wagon, "I want to do now, what I should have done before, ask about this horse. Who knows anything about him? This advertisement says" — holding up a copy of the

Post and reading the description — "that he has been his mile inside of three minutes. Now, I should like to know when."

"Not more than three weeks ago he did it," replied Topple; "I saw him myself."

"Where, for goodness' sake?" said the doctor.

"On the down grade of the Rutland Railroad, in a freight-car," replied the imperturbable Topple.

MRS. PARTINGTON ON THE CURRENCY.

"It 's always so," said Mrs. Partington, turning over in her hand a Spanish quarter of a dollar; and Ike, who was tackling Lion to the clothes-basket, lifted up his eyes inquiringly to her face. "It 's always so," she continued, "that the muscular gender is put before the ephemeral. No matter what it 's about. If a baby is born into a family, it is *Mr.* So-and-so's baby — the mother has n't anything to do about it. She is n't anywheres in courts of law or iniquity, and her rights is thought no more of than the wind, which goes where it listeth. She has n't nothing to say about the disposition of her property, or that of her children, though heaven knows *their* disposition would be bad enough unless she did have something to do with it. And everything bad is laid against her. Now, here is this occurrency business, as soon as its value is deprecated the women is blamed for it." Ike got up and looked at the coin, and thought how many marbles, and how many peanuts, and how many oranges, and how many sticks of molasses candy, it would buy, and asked her if it was n't a good one. "Yes," replied she; "it is good as far as it goes, and this is the mischief of it —

when it was worth twenty-five cents it was said to be *par* value, and now that it is cut down it is *mar* value. It 's always so about everything. There an't nothing like justice ever done to the women." She dropped the coin into her pocket, and it jingled merrily among the keys; and the seven copper cents, and the old silver thimble, and the scissors, and the knitting-sheath, and the steel spectacle-case, as if it were not a poor, depreciated thing at all, but were yet a full quarter. And Ike thought out this moral from it, with the help of Lion: That, though the world depreciate *us* twenty per cent., we should feel just as happy with a self-consciousness of par value at heart, and jingle on merrily among the old copper or brass that may be around us.

A FOURTH OF JULY INCIDENT.

PHIZ! snap! bang! and a half-bunch of red crackers cut up mad capers in Mrs. Partington's little kitchen, while the old lady mounted in a chair, with terror on her face and blue yarn stockings on her feet, to get out of the way of the concussion. The crackers were thrown into the windows, and the smoke of the villanous saltpetre scaled the newly whitewashed ceiling, and rolled up in volume before the profile of the old corporal that hung upon the wall, a fitting offering to the military hero thus preserved. "Gracious goodness!" said Mrs. Partington, with a voice of alarm, looking amid the smoke like the sun in a foggy morning. "What upon airth is coming now? who throwed them snap-dragons in here to frighten me into my grave before my time comes?" Snap! went another cracker, directly beneath the chair on which she was standing. "Bless me! who 's a-doing of it? I see you, you inflammable scamp!" said she, looking hard at the window; but it was a pleasant fiction, an expedient of her fancy that the exigency suggested. She waited a moment and got down from the chair, when, bouncing in through the window, came another cracker, exploding close to Mrs. Partington's ear. Incensed at this, she looked from the window to see the perpetrator of the outrage, but could see nothing. Could she but have looked around the corner of the house, she would have detected Ike's red face wrinkled with mirth, and a piece of port-fire about an inch long between that promising young gentleman's fingers. "Something certainly must be afire," said she, shortly afterwards, searching round, under the table, in the clothes-basket, in the reticule upon the chair; but not a spark of fire could she find. "It must be cotton a burning," continued she, feeling anxious. — "Your cap 's blazing," said Ike, looking in innocently; and the old lady tore the burning muslin from her head and threw it on the floor. As she told the story to Ike about the crackers, how he wished he had been at home that he might have defended her! and the dame gave him a bright dime for his earnest devotion.

SCRATCHED GNEISS AND BEAR SKIN.

"WHAT is the meaning of 'scratched gneiss'?" said Ike, stopping in the perusal of Dr. Kane's work, as his eye was attracted by a picture of a rock thus indicated. The old lady had listened to some passages of the book, which he had read to her, with tearful interest. "It must be," said she, after a few moments' reflection, "where they scratched 'em in climbing up over the rocks." --"Scratched what?" cried Ike, interrupting her.—"Their knees," replied she.—"Who said knees?" responded he, saucily; "I said gneiss — g-n-e-i-s-s — what 's that?"—"I guess it means knees," said she; "the printer has spelt it wrong. It is strange what queer arrows they do make in printing. They were in their bare skins, you know, and got their knees scratched. How cold they must have been, to be sure!" Ike turned to the picture of Accomodah, and asked her if he was in his bare skin, emphasizing the word "bare;" and asked her, too, if she had lived so long in the world and did n't know the difference between a bare skin and a bear skin. What knowledge the youngster evinced *He* could show *his* grandmother how to suck eggs! Mrs. Partington looked gravely at him. "I could know very easily what a bare skin was," said she, "if I was to treat you as you deserve, for your misrespect." Ike seemed penitent, and she gave him a three-cent piece to save till he got enough to put into the Five-Cent Savings Bank.

WATERING-PLACES.

"ARE you going to any watering-place, this summer?" asked a young friend of Mrs. Partington, on one of the rainy days, the present week. She had just put up the window to keep out the damp and disagreeable air, and pulled her handkerchief more up over her shoulder to keep off the chill. "Watering-places," said she, with a gentle tap on the cover of her box, at the same time looking at Ike, who was engaged in making a kite out of the last *Puritan Recorder*, that the dame had lain by for her Sunday reading,—"watering-places I don't think much of, now-a-days. There an't no need of em since the lucky-motives have run off with the stages; but once, as the old pumps stood by the waysides, under the ambiguous trees, with a hollow log for the cattle to drink out of, it seemed like a horses in the desert, as some of 'em used to say." — "My dear madam," said her young friend, "I mean the fashionable watering-places, where people go to spend the summer." — "O," she replied, "that 's it, is it? Well, we need n't go away from home to find a watering-place to-day; and, them that do, depend upon it." — and here she laid her mouth close to his ear, and spoke in a whisper, — "they go for something else besides the water!" She gave him a queer look as she said this, and pointed significantly to the little buffet in the corner, where an old-fashioned cut-glass decanter stood, surrounded by half a dozen little glasses, as if they were young decanters just hatched out; but what she meant we dare not attempt to explain. Ike just then finished his kite by burning the holes for the "belly-band" with the small point of Mrs. Partington's scissors, that had been heated red-hot for the purpose.

HEZEKIAH AND RUTH.

A STORY WITH A MORAL.

'T was in the summer season of the year,
  In some town somewhere near to Lebanon,
One Sabbath afternoon serene and clear,
  The Shaking Quaker meeting being done,

That Hezekiah Drab and Ruth his sister
  Left the conventicle and homeward went;
The service had been a tremendous "twister" —
  Three mortal hours of sleep and silence blent.

And Hez., to make the distance somewhat shorter,
  Proposed to Ruth to cut across the field,
And she, as an obedient sister ought to,
  Said but " Yea, verily," and round they wheeled.

They wandered on in silence, Hezekiah
  With his broad brim substantially put on,
Whilst Ruth, straight down, in simplest of attire,
  Looked like a chest of drawers, the brasses gone

And on they went across the fields of fern,
  And on through meadows drest in greenest guise
Not to the right or left did either turn,
  But kept right on, just as the wild bee flies.

At last they neared a brook of wide expanse,
  No bridge or ford to cross its turbid flood.
" Verily," quoth Hezekiah, in advance,
  " It seemeth me we 're stopped, as clear as mud.

" But yet the distance is but small, forsooth,
  And when a boy I 've jumped far more than that."—
" Yea, but, my brother," said the prudent Ruth,
  " Now thou art older grown, and round, and fat.' —

" Thou talkest like a very foolish woman,
  And thou shalt see my speediness of limb;
So stand aside and give me ample room in
  Which to run, and o'er the pool to skim!"

" Thee cannot, Hezekiah," urged the maid;
  But Hezekiah's pluck, 't was vain to stump it!
He looked broad at her, saying, " Who 's afraid?
  I tell thee, Ruth, assuredly I 'll jump it."

He threw his broad brim on the turfy ground,
  Then walked away a distance from the brook,
Then started onward with a mighty bound,
  The while his fat form like a jelly shook.

He leaped — O, cruel Fate, that thus will dash
  The finest hopes that ever yet did spring! —
Down went the Quaker in the pool, " ker-splash,'
  Just like a brick, or such ignoble thing.

And Ruth's clear voice rang out right merrily;
 O, laughed she with unquaker freedom stout!
"Thou well hast proved thy great agility—
 Come hither, brother, and I 'll help thee out!

Then Hezekiah, with a doleful look,
 Cooled the ambitious fever of his blood,
Crawled from the bottom of the turbid brook,
 And from his face wiped the obscuring mud.

"Now, sister Ruth," cried he, "this brook is wide;
 And though my foot is firm and fleet my bound,
I must confess that I am satisfied
 'T is best not jump upon uncertain ground."

MORAL.

All ye who, like the Quaker, choose to leap,
 Be sure at first that you can clear the flood,
Lest, like the Quaker, you may come off cheap,
 And find your fortunes floundering in the mud.

BURGLARS IN THE PARTINGTON MANSION.

THE conversation turned upon various burglaries that had been committed in the town, and Mrs. Partington gave it as her opinion that any one who would bulgariously break into a house would be mean enough to steal, particularly if he took anything. This opinion was given without any hesitation, and the listeners admitted that they thought so too. The old dame was standing with her snuff-box in her left hand, and her right fore-finger raised, preparatory to making some new remark, when a door was heard to slam violently in the attic. "What can that be?" said one, listening attentively, with ears and eyes wide open.—"It must be the cat," replied Mrs. Partington, calmly. "I am not infected with fear of bunglers. Blessed is he that has nothing, for it can't be taken away from him." A noise as of a stealthy step on the attic stairs was heard a moment after. "What 's that?" was asked by one of the most timid. — "Don't be decomposed," said Mrs. Partington; "it may be a breath of air, but we will go and see what it is." She was always very resolute, and never heard a sound in the house that she did not ascertain at once what caused it. The dame and her guests opened the door, and proceeded to the attic; but there was no evidence of disarrangement there. They then proceeded through all the rooms to the cellar, with the same result. They stopped a moment to listen, when they heard the door of a closet in the room above gently closed. There were numerous garments hung in this closet; and, among the rest, the black bombazine dress that had mourned for forty years the loss of Paul. Cautiously moving towards the spot, they opened the door. Everything hung in its position. There were the dress and sundry flannel garments, that we forget the name of, and Ike's Sunday jacket, and lots of other things. They were just about turning their attention to a search in other quarters, when the timid one cried out, "There is the bugler!" And sure enough, there, from beneath the bombazine dress, protruded a pair of legs encased in blue woollen stockings, and terminating with a pair of thick brogans. "Who are you, and what do you want?" said Mrs. Partington, in a tone denoting great strength of mind, and some lungs. There was no answer to the question, though a spasmodic movement in one of the blue stockings denoted consciousness. "What do you want here?" she repeated, a little tremulous, as if she were slightly "infected." "Do you come here to rob us in our beds, and murder our propriety?" She probably meant "murder us in our beds and rob us of our property," but she evidently was confused. The blue yarn stockings still maintained their position. "If you don't come out, I 'll call in a policeman and have you shut up in solitary confinement." The stockings moved; and now a chink opened among the pendent garments, through which protruded a face glowing with mirth and mischief, and a laugh, rich and unctuous with boyish glee, broke the silence. "Why, Isaac!" said the good dame, "how could you do so? I have a great mind to punish you severally for your naughty conduct." But Ike and the blue stockings passed out of the door, and anger passed from the memory of Mrs. Partington. But Miss Prew, who had reached the period when chance for matrimony had become a sort of dead reckoning, said to Mrs. Spry, another of the party, that if that boy was her'n, she guessed he 'd have to take some.

A TEXT APPLIED.

LOVE one another, says the sacred word, —
  A good authority, by all admitted;
And every heart by human feeling stirred
  Has owned the high command as for it fitted.
Without this love the world were worse than — well,
  I 'm not particular the place to mention,
And yet, howe'er with it the bosom swell,
  We must restrict its general extension.
Our brothers we may love, but ne'er a sis
  Beyond the limit of a nice convention,
And we should never entertain a kiss
  E'en in our most remote wish or intention.
Woe be to him who loves some little sister,
And woer still should he by chance have kissed her.

JUSTLY CRITICAL.

"WELL, I am so glad it all came out right!" said Mrs. Partington, wiping her eyes at the closing scene in Sonnambula. "I confess," continued she, "that it did look agin the young woman to be found in the bed of the strange gentleman; but she had her shoes and clothes on, and, if the young man had really loved her, he would n't have believed her to be guilty so soon, — indeed, he would n't; for, depend upon it, if a young man really loves a young woman, he will be the last to believe anything to her decrepitude, and be the last to cast her off. And them pheasants, too, — only think of the sneaking way in which they come in to detect her, as if it was their business, anyhow. I dare say none of 'em was any better than they ought to be; and what a to-do they made, to be sure, because they thought she was guilty! O, I despise sich pretensiveness! And as for the girl that made all the trouble, I could see that she was enviable, and wanted the young man herself, and did n't care any more about the virtoo of the thing than the fifth wheel of a coach." She here stopped, and thrust the lorgnette that she had borrowed into its case, and drew her shawl up about her neck; while Ike stood with the blue umbrella at "present," waiting for her to come out of her seat.

STARRY.

MRS. PARTINGTON opened her eyes wide, as Ike read in the paper that there would be an "occultation of Jupiter with the moon." — "Occultation!" what a word for Mrs. Partington, who had not quite all of Worcester's unabridged dictionary by heart. "Occultation?" queried she, with an air of doubt, as if but half sure that she had heard rightly, and looking earnestly at the boy, to unravel her doubt.—"Occultation," replied Ike, putting his finger on the word with an emphasis that made a hole right through the paper, entirely ruining the story of the "Seven Champions, or the Bloody Wreath," on the other side of the sheet; "it is so here."—"Well," said she, "get the directory and see what is oc—oc—"—"Occultation," prompted Ike, as he passed out to find his school-books, hid during vacation time.—"That is a queer word," meditated she, like Harvey among the tombs; "and what occupation Jupiter can have with the moon, I don't see. I declare I am all in the dark about it; and these explanatory matters, and consternations and things, I believe are all moonshine. Let me have all the stars to look at, and other folks may see what else they can in the corncave on high." Ike came back without the "directory," and there was a strange dark mark about the corners of his mouth, that looked like the raspberry-jam the old lady kept up stairs for sickness.

BIRTH-DAY OF LAFAYETTE.

Bright memory of the past! thy lofty name
  Is woven with our land's exalted story,
And on the tablet of her lasting fame
  Is wrought in fire the record of thy glory.
Entwined with Washington's in one grand line,
  'T will live undimmed while Freedom's sons inherit
The love of priceless Liberty, divine,
  Secured to them by his chivalric spirit.
While generous deeds are held in just esteem,
  While Virtue claims the meed of approbation,
While Valor weaves the warm enthusiast's dream
  While Right within the land upholds its station,
Will grateful memories, like to-day's, return,
To wreathe anew the garland round his urn.

CROAKING.

Commencing about frog-time, which leads to a half belief that there is an affinity between the croakers of the human family and those of the marshes, the croakers begin to open their throats, and find abundant scope for their fancy in all sorts of directions. The weather is an immensely prolific theme. "How confounded cold it is!" says one croaker; "'t seems to me we never shall have any warm weather again."—"Well, did ever anybody see such infernal weather as this is?" says another croaker; "'t is nothing but rain, rain, all the time."—"This abominable dust," says another croaker, "is enough to blind one. It is a thundering nuisance."—"Here 's this east wind been here for a fortnight," says the mercantile croaker, who has a ship just ready to go to sea. The wind has, in fact, been "out" but two days, but the growler's imagination extends the time. "Will this mud *ever* dry up?" asks the votary of fashion, as she looks out upon the sloppy street with the remembrance of a dress sent home three days before, with the probability of the fashion changing before she has a chance to wear it out. The splenetic croak as they watch the vane for a change of wind, and others croak because it does change. The world is full of croakers.

We have wondered if there is anything else in the animal kingdom, but men and frogs, that croaks. The croak of the latter, however, is his song. He can't help it. He feels jolly in his drink, and utters himself — not very pleasantly, it is true — for the fun of the thing. The frog does n't inveigh against Providence for sending bad weather; he never growls at the east wind, never complains at the heat — he sings the same song at all seasons. Proving this, leaves man the undivided honor of being the only croaker. The horse goes on uncomplaining in his course, not croaking a bit about his fate; Lion, though compelled to wait for his dinner till five o'clock, never croaks about it, but wags his tail and waits; the robin sings the same joyous song in an east wind that he does in a westerly one; all with an instinctive content at the dealings of Providence. The flowers bloom happily, and never fire off their pistils in petulance or anger; the trees heed not the fair or the foul, but keep on, weather or no; and the humble grass, though universally regarded as green, keeps right on growing, true to the allegiance it owes the sun, irrespective of little outside influences.

What's the use of croaking? Does it make one hair black or white? Is an east wind shorn of a single shiver by it? Does the rain cease to chill because of it? Does the sun relax his melting beams because we don't like it? No. Then, why should we croak? Ah, why?

HEATHEN SYMPATHY.

THE Brahmin, with his eyes all wet with tears,
  Stood still to hear a Christian damn his horse, —
I mean by "Christian" only what one hears
  In heathen lands applied to ours, of course! —
He saw the trembling creature cringe to feel
  The thong applied with venom to his flank,
The while those curses poured with blistering peal,
  And marvelled which it was wherefrom he shrank.
The blows continued, and the storm of words
  Rained round the quadruped with equal might;
It moved the Brahmin's sympathetic chords,
  Who stretched his hand to stay the cruel fight.
"Look here," quoth he, "you cursed, cursing file,
Your conduct, let me say, is cursed vile!"

WHITEWASHING.

SPRING is the season of cleanliness, — the sanatory sabbath, where people whitewash up into respectability of appearance, and try to look decent for a year. Whitewashing is a great institution, and it comes to a brush with other domestic institutions about the season when the flowers open, and housewives and tulips blow at the same time. It is well to own a brush yourself, and mix your own whitewash; then, with the pale fluid by you, you can get up mornings and apply it at your leisure, or spend the evening in beautifying and purifying your premises. This is the way you will be likely to do, if you are an economist. Buy your brush, procure your lime, slack the mysterious mass to a creamy fluid, and then attempt the purification of your wall overhead. "Don't spatter!" will be the injunction of the prudent house-wife, of course; but heed it not, — women are proverbial for their caution, — lather away, with might and main, and she will leave the field. The wall is dark with smoky accumulations, but, thanks to the science of the brush, it will soon be made spotless. You dip boldly into the wash, and the first dash at the wall brings a drop into your eye. It may be that some petulant expression escapes you — may-be not. A second attempt is better. You mind your eye, and go along, this way and that way. There is a struggle going on overhead between light and darkness, as there was when Lucifer, the Dark Angel, struggled with Michael on the plains of heaven, and the light is bound to succeed. You feel encouraged, as you see the wall wet with the application, knowing that the warm air will render it very pure and white. You feel dizzy with looking up, and your neck aches, and your sinews are sore with your efforts; but persevere, and the crown is yours. And now leave the wall to dry, with the reflection that you have saved at least a quarter of a dollar by the operation, and a fancy of the satisfaction youself and wife will feel at the pleasant change in the appearance of the premises wrought by your exertions. A few hours afterwards, you return to your room. There is a cloud on your wife's brow as dark as the wall before it was whitewashed. You are minded of the cause by a significant pointing to the wall overhead, and the carpet below, and the furniture around. The former looks like an enlarged map of the United States, including Kansas and California, with very dark prospects for Kansas; the carpet is flecked with white stars, like a chart demonstrative of mundane astronomy; the furniture is dotted with endless blotches of white, as if it had been struck with a sudden snow-squall. You begin to get it through your hair what it is that has caused your head to itch so confoundedly all day. You have been limed. But you are in for whitewashing, and, as in the case of the late amiable Gen. Macbeth, it is about as well to go ahead as to go back; so you vigorously seize the brush again, with less heart, however, than at first. But with less confidence come more pains, and fewer drops spangle the floor, and the map disappears from the wall. When it is dry, it takes a new guise. It is white, with here and there a shallow pool, with a dark bottom. The brush is again applied. Better and better. At last, after a week's application, a good deal of fretting, and labor enough to raise a two-story barn, the wall is completed, and the brush is laid aside, for some other time; but whether that time will ever come or not, depends upon the scarcity of whitewashers. But it *is* a triumph, after all, to look at the milky firmament that spans your home, and feel that your "neat and cunning hand" laid on the purity, even though discolored dresses and soiled carpets mark your course, as the traces of violence follow the sanguinary brush of war.

PROSPECTIVE SUMMER

PASSED the boundary dividing spring from the domain of summer, and, upon our senses gliding, steals the breath of the new comer — gentle Deity of Flowers, in whose genial warmth outspringing, from a myriad chosen bowers, floral sweets abroad are winging. Where the crystal brook is brawling through the summer woodland shadow, and the bob-o'-link is calling from his home within the meadow; where the dark ravines are dimly, coolly with our memory pleading, and remembered shadows grimly through our heated minds are speeding; where the tall pines, dark and solemn, murmur constantly their story, and the crag, in mighty column, stands in monumental glory; where the sweet birds' songs are gushing from the bushes by the river, and the little waves are rushing, and the leaves with music quiver; where the trout in cool, still places wait the tempting bait to swallow; where the winding path one traces, with delighted foot to follow; where the cascade white and foaming o'er the rocks in glee is leaping, and the lake where perch are roaming, or big pickerel are sleeping; where kind hearts and pleasant voices all combine to mark the hour, where the gentle heart rejoices in the summer's sovereign power; — all stand beckoning to us, beckoning, coaxing us to leave the town, leave our books and money reckoning, led 'mid rurals "up and down." But there comes a memory speedy of fierce flies and fierce mosquitos, for our sacrifice most greedy, putting on our comfort vetos; of long walks uncompensated, thunder-showers in the mountains, of long hours with ennui freighted, of foul bugs in pleasant fountains. Thus our dreams in summer weathers draw us from the city torrid, and the leaves which memory gathers with their freshness cool our forehead.

LIST OF NEW PUBLICATIONS.

MAILING NOTICE.—Single copies of any of these Books will be sent to any address, post-paid, on receipt of price. This very convenient mode may be adopted where your neighboring bookseller is not supplied with the work. Address,

JOHN E. POTTER & CO., Publishers,

No. 617 Sansom Street, Philadelphia.

LIFE AND PUBLIC SERVICES OF ABRAHAM LINCOLN. **Containing his early History and Political Career. By Frank Crosby, of the Philadelphia Bar. With Portrait on steel. 12mo., cloth. Price $1 75.**

THE SAME TRANSLATED INTO THE GERMAN LANGUAGE. **By Professor Carl Theodor Eben. 12mo., cloth. Price $1 75.**

LIFE AND PUBLIC SERVICES OF STEPHEN A. DOUGLAS. **To which are added his Speeches and Reports. By H. M. Flint. With Portrait on steel. 12mo., cloth. Price $1 75.**

LIFE OF DANIEL BOONE, the Great Western Hunter and **Pioneer. By Cecil B. Hartley. With illustrations. 12mo., cloth. Price $1 75.**

LIFE OF KIT CARSON, the Great Western Hunter and **Guide. By Charles Burdett. With illustrations. 12mo., cloth. Price $1 75.**

LIFE OF DAVID CROCKETT, the Original Humorist **and Irrepressible Backwoodsman. With illustrations. 12mo., cloth. Price $1 75.**

LIFE AND ADVENTURES OF MISS MAJOR PAULINE CUSHMAN, **the Celebrated Union Spy and Scout. By F. L. Sarmiento, Esq., of the Philadelphia Bar. With Portrait and illustrations. 12mo., cloth. Price $1 75.**

THRILLING STORIES OF THE GREAT REBELLION. Including an Account of the Death of President Lincoln, and Capture of the Assassins. By Lieutenant-Colonel Charles S. Greene, late of the United States Army. With illustrations. 12mo., cloth. Price $1 75.

THRILLING ADVENTURES AMONG THE EARLY SETTLERS. Embracing Desperate Encounters with Indians, Refugees, Gamblers, Desperadoes, etc. etc. By Warren Wildwood, Esq. Illustrated by 200 engravings. 12mo., cloth. Price $1 75.

THRILLING INCIDENTS IN THE WARS OF THE UNITED STATES. Embracing all the Wars previous to the Rebellion. With 300 engravings. 12mo., cloth. Price $1 75.

OUR BOYS. The rich and racy scenes of Army and Camp Life, as seen and participated in by one of the Rank and File. By A. F. Hill, of the Eighth Pa. Reserves. With illustrations. 12mo., cloth. Price $1 75.

OUR CAMPAIGNS; or, a Three Years' Term of Service in the War. By E. M. Woodward, Adjutant Second Pennsylvania Reserves. 12mo., cloth. Price $1 75.

THE BEAUTIFUL SPY. An exciting story of Army and High Life in New York in 1776. By Charles Burdett. 12mo., cloth. Price $1 75.

THE ROYALIST'S DAUGHTER AND THE REBELS. A tale of the Revolution of unusual power and interest. By Rev. David Murdoch, D. D. 12mo., cloth. Price $1 75.

THE HERO GIRL, and how she became a Captain in the Army. By Thrace Talmon. With illustrations. 12mo., cloth. Price $1 75.

HUNTING ADVENTURES IN THE NORTHERN WILDS. By S. H. Hammond. Illustrated. Cloth. Price $1 75.

WILD NORTHERN SCENES. By S. H. Hammond, author of "Hunting Adventures in the Northern Wilds." Illustrated. Cloth. Price $1 75.

FANNY HUNTER'S WESTERN ADVENTURES. Illustrated. 12mo., cloth. Price $1 75.

WONDERFUL ADVENTURES BY LAND AND SEA of the Seven Queer Travellers who met at an Inn. By Josiah Barnes. 12mo., cloth. Price $1 75.

THE EARLY DAYS OF CALIFORNIA. By Col. J. T. Farnham. 12mo., illustrated, cloth. Price $1 75.

NICARAGUA, PAST, PRESENT, AND FUTURE. By Peter F. Stout, Esq., late United States Vice-Consul. With a Map. 12mo., cloth. Price $1 75.

FEMALE LIFE AMONG THE MORMONS. By Maria Ward, the Wife of a Mormon Elder. Illustrated. 12mo., cloth. Price $1 75.

MALE LIFE AMONG THE MORMONS. By Austin N Ward. Illustrated. 12mo., cloth. Price $1 75.

THE WHITE ROCKS; or, the Robber's Den. A Tragedy of the Mountains of thrilling interest. By A. F. Hill, author of "Our Boys," etc. 12mo., cloth. Price $1 75.

TUPPER'S COMPLETE POETICAL WORKS. With Portrait on steel. 12mo., cloth. Price $1 75.

THE YOUNG LADY'S OWN BOOK. An offering of Love and Sympathy. By Emily Thornwell. 12mo., cloth. Price $1 75.

SUNLIGHT AND SHADOW; or, the Poetry of Home. By Harry Penciller. 12mo., cloth. Price $1 75.

GREAT EXPECTATIONS. By Charles Dickens. With steel engravings. 12mo., cloth. Price $1 75.

THE SOLDIER AND THE SORCERESS; or, the Adventures of Jane Seton. 12mo., cloth. Price $1 75.

THE ORPHAN BOY; or, Lights and Shadows of Humble Life. By Jeremy Loud. 12mo., cloth. Price $1 75.

THE ORPHAN GIRLS. A Tale of Southern Life. By James S. Peacocke, M. D., of Mississippi. 12mo., cloth. Price $1 75

BOOK OF ANECDOTES AND JOKER'S KNAPSACK. Including Witticisms of the late President Lincoln, and Humors, Incidents, and Absurdities of the War. 12mo., cloth. Price $1 75.

WAY DOWN EAST; or, Portraitures of Yankee Life. By Seba Smith, the original Major Jack Downing. Illustrated. 12mo., cloth. Price $1 75.

THE LADIES' MEDICAL GUIDE AND MARRIAGE FRIEND. By S. Pancoast, M. D., Professor of Physiology in Penn Medical University, Philadelphia. With upwards of 100 illustrations. 12mo., cloth. Price $1 75.

BOYHOOD'S PERILS AND MANHOOD'S CURSE. An earnest appeal to the young men of America. By S. Pancoast, M. D. With numerous illustrations. 12mo., cloth. Price $1 75.

THE CURABILITY OF CONSUMPTION by Medicated Inhalation and Adjunct Remedies. By S. Pancoast, M. D. With illustrations. Cloth. Price $1 50.

THE AMERICAN TEXT-BOOK. Containing the Constitution of the United States, the Declaration of Independence, and Washington's Farewell Address. 24mo., cloth. Price 25 cents.

HORSE TRAINING MADE EASY. A New and Practical System of Teaching and Educating the Horse. By Robert Jennings, V. S. of the Veterinary College of Philadelphia, author of "The Horse and his Diseases," etc. etc. With illustrations. 16mo., cloth. Price $1 25.

THE HORSE AND HIS DISEASES. By Robert Jennings, V. S., author of "Horse Training Made Easy," etc. etc. With numerous illustrations. 12mo., cloth. Price $1 75.

CATTLE AND THEIR DISEASES. By Robert Jennings, V. S. With numerous illustrations. 12mo., cloth. Price $1 75. (Uniform with the above.)

SHEEP, SWINE, AND POULTRY. By Robert Jennings, V. S. With numerous illustrations. 12mo., cloth. Price $1 75. (Uniform with the above.)

EVERYBODY'S LAWYER AND COUNSELLOR IN BUSINESS. By Frank Crosby, Esq., of the Philadelphia Bar. 12mo. Price $1 75.

THE FAMILY DOCTOR; containing, in Plain Language, free from Medical Terms, the Causes, Symptoms, and Cure of Disease in all forms. By Henry S. Taylor, M. D. With illustrations. Cloth. Price $1 50.

MODERN COOKERY in all its Branches. By Miss Eliza Acton. Carefully revised by Mrs. S. J. Hale. With numerous illustrations. 12mo., cloth. Price $1 75.

THE EARLY MORN. An Address to the Young on the Importance of Religion. By John Foster. 24mo., cloth. Price 25 cts.

FAMILY PRAYERS. Adapted to every day in the week. By the late Rev. William Wilberforce. Cloth. Price 37 cents.

THE HISTORY OF PALESTINE from the Patriarchal Ages to the Present Time. By John Kitto. With illustrations. Cloth. Price $1 50.

THE WREATH OF GEMS. A gift book for the young of both sexes. By Emily Percival. Cloth. Price $1 50.

THE RAINBOW AROUND THE TOMB; or, Rays of Hope for those who Mourn. By Emily Thornwell. Cloth. Price $1 50.

THE LIFE OF OUR LORD AND SAVIOUR JESUS CHRIST, from his Incarnation to his Ascension into Heaven. By Rev. John Fleetwood, D. D. With steel and colored plates. Crown 8vo., library style. Price $4.

THE RELIGIOUS DENOMINATIONS IN THE UNITED STATES. Their History, Doctrine, Government, and Statistics. By Rev. Joseph Belcher, D. D., author of "William Carey, a Biography," and editor of the "Complete Works of Andrew Fuller," "Works of Robert Hall," etc. With nearly 200 engravings. Crown 8vo., library style. Price $4 50.

THE GOOD CHILD'S ILLUSTRATED INSTRUCTION BOOK. With more than sixty illustrations. Quarto, bound in cloth. Plain pictures, $1. Illuminated, $1 25.

THE LITTLE FOLKS' OWN BOOK. With sixty illustrations. Quarto, cloth. Plain pictures, $1. Illuminated, $1 25.

UNCLE JOHN'S OWN BOOK OF MORAL AND INSTRUCTIVE STORIES. With more than fifty illustrations. Crown quarto, cloth. Plain pictures, $1 50. Illuminated, $2.

GRANDFATHER'S STORIES. With sixty illustrations. Crown quarto. Plain pictures, $1 50. Illuminated, $2.

NATIONAL NURSERY TALES. With sixty illustrations. Folio, bound in cloth. Plain pictures, $1 50. Illuminated, $2.

NATIONAL FAIRY TALES. With more than seventy illustrations. Folio, cloth. Plain pictures, $1 50. Illuminated, $2.

THE LITTLE KITTEN STORIES. With fifty beautiful illustrations. Folio, cloth. Plain pictures, $1 50. Illuminated, $2.

THE FUNNY ANIMALS. With more than sixty illustrations. Folio, cloth. Plain pictures, $1 50. Illuminated, $2.

OUR NINA'S PET STORIES. With fifty beautiful illustrations. Folio, cloth. Plain pictures, $1 50. Illuminated, $2.

FAMILY AND PULPIT BIBLES. Nearly sixty different styles; with Family Record and with and without Photograph Record. With clasps or otherwise, and ranging in price from $5 to $30.

JUVENILE AND TOY BOOKS. Embracing 150 varieties, beautifully illustrated and adapted to the tastes of the little ones everywhere; at prices ranging from 10 cents to $2.

PHOTOGRAPH ALBUMS in every size and variety, holding from twelve to two hundred pictures, and ranging in price from 75 cents to $20.

Persons wishing a full catalogue of all our Books, Albums, and Bibles, will please send two red stamps to pay return postage.

The trade everywhere supplied on favorable terms.

Address, **JOHN E. POTTER & CO., Publishers,**
617 Sansom Street, Philadelphia.

www.ingramcontent.com/pod-product-compliance
Lightning Source LLC
LaVergne TN
LVHW021148110826
845150LV00005B/1160

* 9 7 8 1 4 2 5 5 4 6 9 8 4 *